Gideon Lincecum's Sword

Dr. Gideon Lincecum—photo made on his eightieth birthday at a studio in Austin (courtesy Center for American History, University of Texas, Austin)

Gideon Lincecum's SWORD

Civil War Letters from the Texas Home Front

Edited by

Jerry Bryan Lincecum

Edward Hake Phillips

Peggy A. Redshaw

University of North Texas Press · Denton, Texas

Printed in the United States of America.

10 9 8 7 6 5 4 3 2 1

Permissions:
University of North Texas Press
P.O. Box 311336
Denton, TX 76203-1336

The paper used in this book meets the minimum requirements of the American National Standard for Permanence of Paper for Printed Library Materials, z39.48.1984. Binding materials have been chosen for durability.

Library of Congress Cataloging-in-Publication Data

Lincecum, Gideon, 1793–1874.
Gideon Lincecum's sword : Civil War letters from the Texas home front / edited by Jerry Bryan Lincecum, Edward Hake Phillips, Peggy A. Redshaw.
p. cm.
Includes bibliographical references and index.
ISBN 1-57441-125-X (alk. paper)
1. Lincecum, Gideon, 1793–1874—Correspondence. 2. United States—History—Civil War, 1861–1865—Personal narratives, Confederate. 3. Texas—History—Civil War, 1861–1865—Personal narratives. 4. United States—History—Civil War, 1861–1865—Social aspects. 5. Texas—History—Civil War, 1861–1865—Social aspects. 6. Physicians—Texas—Washington County—Correspondence. 7. Scientists—Texas—Washington County—Correspondence. 8. Washington County (Tex.)—Biography. I. Lincecum, Jerry Bryan, 1942– II. Phillips, Edward Hake. III. Redshaw, Peggy A. IV. Title.

E605.L75 2001
973.7'09'2764--dc21 00-064907

Design by Angela Schmitt
Cover art by Betsy Warren

DEDICATION AND EPIGRAPH

In memory of Francis B. (Chick) Redshaw,
a son of the North
(1918–1995)
and Mildred Jones Lincecum,
a daughter of the South
(1916–1998)

Long Point. Texas. 20th March 1859

I have this day opened and commenced blotting this fine, large new letter book. At this moment its pages are without stain or blemish, and it is worth six dollars.

REFLECTION

Shall I, by filling it up with my unpolished thoughts, be able to induce him, into whose hands it may chance to fall, to feel that its worth is as great as when it was a blank?

Time will decide that question.

But if a sincere desire for the development of true principles from a natural basis will make it worth more, I promise myself that that desire shall not be departed from, and that I shall, with all my mental strength, strive to avoid two sins which, from time immemorial, has almost universally obtained with that type of our species who have deemed it proper to place their thoughts on paper: viz.,

Diminution and Exaggeration.

Gideon Lincecum

Contents

Acknowledgments

The editors are grateful that Gideon Lincecum did fill several letterpress volumes with his "unpolished thoughts" and that his youngest daughter Sarah and her sons saved the letter books and gave them to the University of Texas. We are also thankful for the anonymous copyists, employed by a New Deal program in the 1930s, who transcribed the letter books. Additional financial support for that project was provided by the Texas Medical Association. Although we found numerous errors in the typewritten transcriptions when we compared them with the original letter books, our work in selecting and copying Gideon's letters from the Civil War era would have been much harder without access to the typescripts.

In making our own copies, we had the ready assistance of the staff at the Center for American History at the University of Texas at Austin, headed by Dr. Don E. Carleton, with special courtesy rendered to us by Ralph Elder and Janis Olsen. At Austin College, special assistance came from College Support Services, directed by Cynthia Holloway and staffed by Mary Cole, Sharon Bennett, and Vicki Mansfield, who were unfailing in their willingness to help. We received financial support from Austin College's Richardson Endowment for many of our research expenses. Without sabbatical leaves, Professors Lincecum and Redshaw would not have been able to devote the time for concentrated research necessary to complete this project in a timely fashion. Members of the staff of the Abell Library at Austin College, most especially associate librarian John R. West and Carolyn Vickrey, coordinator of public services, rendered valuable aid in tracking elusive sources and arranging vital interlibrary loans as well as contacts at other libraries.

Ronald B. Roache II, head of book service at the Library of Congress, located rare periodicals for us and placed them on reserve to expedite our research. Linda Rima, head of acquisitions/serials at Texas Woman's University Library, enabled us to examine microfilm of early Texas newspapers. Two staff members at the Boston Public Library, Dorothy Keller in the interlibrary loan office and Henry Scannel in microtext, sent us microfilm.

Jerry Bryan Lincecum wishes to thank his father, Jack Lincecum, for passing on some of Gideon's traits of persistence, curiosity, and optimism to the sixth generation of Texas Lincecums. Edward Hake Phillips owes much to his wife, Patricia, for her forbearance and sacrifice during this project. Peggy A. Redshaw wishes to thank her mother, Margaret Lee Redshaw, for her unfailing support.

Jerry Bryan Lincecum
Edward Hake Phillips
Peggy A. Redshaw

Gideon Lincecum's Sword

Gideon wrote his letters in this small building constructed of red cedar which served him as a combination office and laboratory. It was recently moved from the old Lincecum place at Long Point in Washington County, Texas, to a nearby location to insure its preservation. (photo by Keith Carter)

Introduction

What effects did the Civil War have on the daily lives of noncombatants in Texas? According to Alwyn Barr, whose "Essay on Texas Civil War Historiography" is considered both comprehensive and definitive, civilian life in Texas during the war is a topic that needs more exploration.[1] From the correspondence of Dr. Gideon Lincecum (1793–1874), who had moved to Texas in 1848 with his family of ten, mostly grown, children, and settled on eighteen hundred acres in Washington County, we can learn a great deal about the effects of the war. Consider this letter he wrote in the late summer of 1863 to his sister and brother-in-law in south Texas:

Long Point. Texas. 5 Augst. 1863

D. Boone Moore[2]
Hondo Valley
Castroville, Texas
Dear Brother & Sister.

Your kind letter of 12th July did not reach me until yesterday. We were all truly glad to hear from you all, for it had been so long since we had received a letter from or heard from you in any other way, that we began to conclude that the Indians had got you sure enough. We are all proud, however, to hear that you are all safe and prospects pretty good.

You desire me to give you the war news. For a long time—ever since the fall of Vicksburg—we have had no dispatches from East of the Mississippi River. Madam rumour has been very busy since that disastrous event, but there is so much and such flagrant contradictions in those reports and rumours that we place no reliance in any of them. By these rumours and slack twisted reports, Washington City has been captured half a dozen times. As also Baltimore and Philadelphia. There is no truth in any of it.

Our forces this side of the great river are doing very well. They are fighting more or less every day. We get letters from Jo and Cash [grandsons] almost every week; they say the fighting is fine—good as could be desired; but the privations and hardships are heavy and fatiguing. They have so far, though they have participated in many battle[s], come out without a scratch, and are all the time healthy. We heard from them by a returned soldier today. They are both enjoying vigorous health, and in good spirits.

Leonidas and Leander [sons] are both over 40 years of age, but they are too in the service. Lon is War tax collector for this county, and Leander was detailed to attend to the sick in the absent soldiers' families. Lucullus [son] was detailed for the same service in another settlement. Lachaon [son] is beef contractor, buying up beef cattle and driving them to the army. The last drove, he took across the river at Natches, but a few days previous to the fall of Vicksburg. He crossed 956, swam them over. Lysander [son] has tried the camps three or four times, but the diseased condition of his lungs incapacitates him for the life and duty of a soldier, and he was twice [r]ejected.

George Campbell [son-in-law], after returning from the Arizona campaign, drank himself to death. He dropped dead in a dogery [saloon] at Brenham, leaving his wife [daughter Leonora] and seven children poorly provided for. Matson [son-in-law], Mary's husband, is here, fat and doing well. He has been superintending the negroes on his own and his brothers farms. His brother has been in the army all the time since the war. Durham [son-in-law] is War tax collector for the state.

Cassandra [daughter] lost her two pretty little girls last year; they died of putrid sore throat, and she grieved herself half to death about it. Mary and Leonora have all their children, alive and healthy. The connection at this time are all healthy, and was it not for this infernal war, are all well to do.

My family has increased considerably since I saw you. When we are all together, counting the old lady and myself, there is 61 of us, with a prospect for considerable increase. There has been no change in our household since I saw you. Sarah [daughter] and Lysander constitute our white family, and from appearances now our family will be apt to remain at that number.

The old lady and I were enjoying the evening of life in good stile and should have past off the life stage quite pleasantly, but for the interruption provided by the damned yankee invasion. We were spending our summers in the mountains and a portion of our winters on the delightful sea coasts. In both situations the sources of enjoyment was very great and we appreciated it finely. We can't go now, our horses have all been used up in the army as well as our money and other appliances. And so we shall be compelled to rust and rot where we are, which to me is by no means an agreable reflection. However, when I get through the rotting process, it is likely that I shall not care what the yankees does then. But until I do rot, they must keep out of my way.

. . . Remember me to all the family and receive for yourselves my best wishes and affectionate prayer

Gideon Lincecum

Having retired from an extensive botanical medical practice that in Mississippi had earned him a fortune (allowing him to pay cash for the land he bought in Texas), Gideon devoted much of his time in Texas before the Civil War to studying the natural sciences and carrying on an extensive correspondence with various scientists, including some from the

North and even Charles Darwin.[3] Moreover, he used a letterpress to make copies of almost all of his letters, and these letterpress volumes (totaling more than a thousand pages) were preserved by one of his daughters and given to the University of Texas at Austin, where they are available for study at the Center for American History.[4] Gideon's letters provide a rich and detailed account of how, on a day-to-day basis, one individual and his large extended family, all of whom were strongly committed to the Confederacy, kept up with the progress of the conflict and coped with the multitude of problems it presented.

Another thing these letters do is provide insight into the psyche of the patriarch of the Lincecum family, who celebrated his seventieth birthday in 1863. Despite his age, Gideon still possessed fiery emotions, abundant energy, and a remarkable ability to express himself—remarkable indeed, considering his lack of formal education.[5] Secondly, insofar as Gideon was, in part at least, representative of the heart and mind of Texas and even the South, his outlook takes on a much larger significance. For example, Gideon's letters help to answer the question of how Texans on the home front coped with the wartime shortages of commodities that ranged from luxuries, such as imported ink and stationery, to such necessities as clothing and shoes.[6]

By the time the war ended, the lives of Gideon and the other Lincecums had changed drastically. On 24 December 1865 he wrote as follows to a friend: "When the war broke up, and I had time to look around, I found I had lost everything but the homestead. It is the truth, that I did not have a blanket, nor horse nor mule nor jackass left to my name, nor one single dollar."[7] His lack of funds in 1865 appears more striking when contrasted with the fact that in 1860 he did not hesitate to spend more than five thousand dollars on a futile effort to drill an artesian well on his farm.

At different times during the war all of the able-bodied men of the Lincecum family served in the Confederate army. By mid-April 1864, when Gideon wrote again to his sister and brother-in-law, even his son Lysander, who suffered from asthma, had managed to become a soldier and had joined two more grandsons (Lascassas and Leander) in battle on the Rio Grande. Gideon wrote,

> There were but 12 grown men in the family when the war commenced. One, Capt. Campbell, <u>dead</u>. The balance, except the detailed physicians, Leander and Lucullus, in the Service. So you may imagine that we have a lonesome time of it. We should doubtless feel lonesome were it not for the fact that we live where the two great thoroughfares of Middle Texas cross. Few nights pass without company. They are generally soldiers; and to them our house and cribbs are always open, free of charge. We have fed away to them three heavy crops and though it has reduced our means to a pretty low ebb, we are nevertheless sorry that we are not able to do more. All I have shall go free as water to sustain our cause. What would a life in the South under Negro equality and Yankee rule be worth?

At this point an editorial note is in order. One of the editors of this book is a direct descendant of the man who wrote those words, and all three editors have spent so much time reading and thinking about his personal correspondence that we feel more comfortable referring to him in print as "Gideon" than as "Lincecum." However, no one is more distressed than we are by the harsh and strident racism he voices in some of his letters. At times he was so extreme that we were tempted to delete his dehumanizing words. But out of respect for the historical record and with faith that knowledge can be a step toward understanding, and understanding a step toward progress, we chose to let Gideon reveal himself fully, warts, biases, racist rhetoric, and all. Moreover, any accurate account of the sociopolitical culture of "Middle Texas" in the 1860s would show how widespread was the view that African Americans were an inferior race for whom chattel slavery provided the best possible conditions.

Gideon was all too representative of Texans and Southerners in his outrage at Northern attitudes and actions toward the South, its states' rights standard, and its "peculiar institution." He may have gone to an extreme in totally demonizing the "Yankee" adversary, but most of his feelings about the Union government, its army, and its society were widely shared across the Confederacy. Even as high-minded a person as Capt. Elijah Perry of Texas, who had determined to be a free man or a dead man and died at Pleasant Hill, wrote that like Hamilcar, the legendary general of Carthage who was defeated by the Greeks in the fifth century B.C., "I have sworn my children to eternal hostility to the Yankee race."[8] Though less elegant, Gideon's formulation, in a letter to his son Lysander in 1864, was equally strong: "It would be a gratifying thing to my feelings, to be certified that every man, woman and child in the bounds of the confederacy had taken a solemn oath that to die fighting is far preferable to submission, and that so long as they have life and strength to damage a yankee in any manner or form that they will continue to do so. And also to swear eternal hatred to the infernal heartless race, and that they will teach their children, to the tenth generation, to hate and kill the damned yankees on all favorable occasions and never to trade with them to the amount of one cent."[9] Such strong feelings would obviously persist long after the Confederacy's surrender. Those whose task it was to design and implement Reconstruction needed to take those persistent attitudes into account; that they apparently attached little importance to the attitude of the defeated population may account in part for the subsequent failures and shortcomings of Reconstruction.

Despite their being common to slave-owning Southerners, the views Gideon expressed about African Americans and the institution of slavery are even more to be deplored than his opinion of "Yankees" and their government.[10] He was not alone in invoking racial stereotypes to support his opinions, for at the same time Gideon ridiculed as unscientific the contention by Northern abolitionists that an African was a "white man with black skin," in England Charles Kingsley asserted Celtic inferiority by writing, "I am haunted by the human chimpanzees I saw [in Ireland]. . . . I don't believe they are our fault. . . . But to see white chimpanzees is dreadful; if they were black, one would not feel it so much."[11]

It is noteworthy as well that these letters reveal a number of warts on Gideon's fellow Texans. He was increasingly disturbed by evidence and reports of shirking and speculation, fraud and corruption, especially among state authorities and politicians. In one letter to his sister and brother-in-law, he used ironic humor to express his indignation:

> But you, in your letter, complain at the few scattering rogues which infects your Country, who are occasionally appropriating to themselves a beef or a poney. That is a mere trifle when compared with our Country. Here, the rogues come prepared with written authority to take your truck [miscellaneous articles]. These papers are made out and signed by some Commanding general, quarter Master, or the president, Secretary of the treasury, or the lord, or devil—some high authority; and they go to peoples houses with these papers, and after some strutting and bombastic parade, the people become frighten[ed] and the rascals apropriate whatever

> they take a fancy to, particularly if there is no man at the house. All of this goes to show that yours is the preferable Country to dwell in, for while you encounter an occasional rascal, and they wide scattered, we dwell in the midst of thousands, all cut and dried and ready to apropriate any thing from the fruit of a henroo[s]t to a good saddle horse. Your rogues do business on their own hook; ours on governmental authority, and they are more greedy. Yours steal and run off. Ours steal, provoke you to prosecute, gain the property, and make the owner pay the cost of suit.[12]

It was enough to make him long for anarchy, though it is hard to fathom how that would have been an improvement.

On the brighter side, Gideon's letters give ample testimony to his fervent support of the Confederate cause; indeed, though he was too old to fight, he was a cheerleader to the end, feeding and entertaining troops in his home, writing many letters to the fighting men, and never losing hope until the last guns were silent. With his pen he encouraged other Texans to see the crisis as an opportunity as well as a challenge and to invent, experiment, and devise ways to meet the needs of the community, the state, and the nation hard pressed by war and blockade. The zeal and the resourcefulness Gideon and a number of his correspondents showed to achieve self-sufficiency for Texas and the Confederacy through factories, home industries, and changes in agriculture under the stimulus of wartime necessity and the Northern blockade give a hint as to how Texas might have fared had the Republic chosen in 1845 to continue on the path of independence rather than on that of annexation—a "what if" that is both fascinating and futile to conjecture.

What else can be learned from these letters is for each reader to determine, enriched, we hope, through having participated vicariously in the Civil War by peering over the shoulder of Gideon Lincecum as he wrote.[13]

[1] Barr's essay is included in B. P. Gallaway, ed., *Texas, the Dark Corner of the Confederacy: Contemporary Accounts of the Lone Star State in the Civil War*, 3d ed., p. 276.

[2] Gideon's sister Emily was the wife of Daniel Boone Moore. See the appendix for biographical notes on Lincecum family members.

[3] The Civil War broke off Gideon's correspondence with many of these scientists, including Charles Darwin. See Jerry Bryan Lincecum, Edward Hake Phillips, and Peggy A. Redshaw, *Science on the Texas Frontier: Observations of Dr. Gideon Lincecum*, chapter 1.

[4] The Gideon Lincecum Papers at the Center for American History in Austin fill thirteen boxes, the bulk of them containing Gideon's correspondence in holograph plus transcriptions in typescript. Lois Wood Burkhalter's assessment of the transcriptions is apt: "The bulk of the letters have been typed and placed in as nearly chronological order as possible. The typed material is bound in fifteen volumes of almost 5,000 pages, frequently unnumbered. The typing, done in 1931 and 1932 by the National Youth Administration and through the courtesy of the Texas State Medical Association, is in many cases unreliable—names are wrong, Lincecum's handwriting has been misread, addresses are omitted. Copies should be checked against originals; and the originals are difficult to locate" (Lois Wood Burkhalter, *Gideon Lincecum, 1793–1874: A Biography*, p. 327). By the 1990s, the holograph originals, which were letterpress copies (the nineteenth-century equivalent of carbon copies), had deteriorated to the point where one is grateful that the typescripts, erroneous as they are, were made when the originals were more legible. Without the typescripts, some of the originals would now be indecipherable. Only when the original and the typescript of a given letter have been compared can the researcher feel confident of having come as near to Gideon's original message as possible. The editors

have gone through that painstaking process for every letter and excerpt that appears in this volume.

[5] Born in Georgia in 1793, Gideon was raised on the frontiers of Georgia and South Carolina, for his father Hezekiah loved the bordering life. According to Gideon's autobiography, his only formal schooling came when he was fourteen years old, and it was limited to five months with a drunken schoolmaster. However, while clerking in a trading post, the boy was befriended by a traveling bookseller, "Parson" Mason L. Weems, who made him an agent for Weems's "flying library" and encouraged him to read all the books in it. He read voraciously and thus educated himself (Jerry Bryan Lincecum and Edward Hake Phillips, *Adventures of a Frontier Naturalist: The Life and Times or Dr. Gideon Lincecum*, pp. 29–32, 36). Although Gideon corresponded with highly educated people who valued his ideas, opinions, and scientific observations, his neglect of the mechanics of writing gave pause to a few of his correspondents. For example, after receiving two letters from Gideon, which he eventually published (after some editing), Charles Darwin wrote to a colleague, "The whole letters are so odd that they are almost worth your reading,—such spelling—such grammar! He evidently speaks the truth that he was never educated" (Lincecum, Phillips, and Redshaw, *Science on the Texas Frontier*, p. 27).

[6] According to Mary Elizabeth Massey, in *Ersatz in the Confederacy*, "the state that suffered least from shortages was Texas" (p. 169). For more information about conditions in Texas, see Richard N. Current, ed., *Encyclopedia of the Confederacy*, *s.v.* "Texas," 4:1583–87, and Robert L. Kerby, *Kirby Smith's Confederacy: The Trans-Mississippi South, 1863–1865*, pp. 64–72, 258–62. Gideon's letters show that his family suffered from a variety of shortages and exercised considerable ingenuity to come up with substitutes. For example, for a time he slept under a blanket woven from Spanish moss on a loom built by his own hands.

[7] Gideon Lincecum to S. B. Buckley, Long Point, Tex., 24 December 1865. Lincecum Papers, Box 2E364, Center for American History, University of Texas at Austin (hereafter cited as LP). This letter appears in chapter 7 below.

[8] Norman D. Brown, ed., *Journey to Pleasant Hill: The Civil War Letters of Captain Elijah P. Petty, Walker's Texas Division, CSA*, pp. 300, 325.

[9] Gideon Lincecum to Lysander Lincecum, Long Point, Tex., 5 July 1864, LP, Box 2E366. This letter appears in chapter 6 below.

[10] To place Gideon's views on slavery in context, see Randolph B. Campbell, *An Empire for Slavery: The Peculiar Institution in Texas, 1821–1865*. See also James Oakes, *The Ruling Race: A History of American Slaveholders*, in which portions of Gideon's "autobiography" are summarized in order to cite both Gideon and his father Hezekiah as prototypes of the small slaveholder, a group that Oakes argues has been neglected in previous studies of slavery. Gideon did not raise cotton, and by the standards of Washington County, which had some large farms, his slaveholdings were small indeed: according to slave schedules in both the 1850 and 1860 Census, he owned fewer than a dozen slaves (including several children age twelve or under). In 1860 his son-in-law James Matson owned thirty-two slaves, while three of Gideon's sons owned a total of fifteen.

[11] Gideon Lincecum to E. Durand, Long Point, Tex., 13 January 1861, LP Box 2E366, this letter appears in chapter 2 below; Kingsley quoted in Lewis P. Curtis, *Anglo-Saxons and Celts: A Study of Anti-Irish Prejudice in Victorian England*, p. 84.

[12] Gideon Lincecum to D. B. and Emily Moore, Long Point, Tex., 9 March 1865, LP 2E366. This letter appears in chapter 7 below.

[13] Except for modernizing Gideon's punctuation (to facilitate clear communication), we have chosen to publish his writings verbatim, including occasional misspellings and incorrect grammar. In short, we have tried to convey simply and accurately what Gideon wrote, except for minor changes to avoid misunderstanding. Our annotation identifies as many persons, places, and events as we could locate and points out textual discrepancies and problems.

CHAPTER 1

FORESHADOWINGS OF CONFLICT

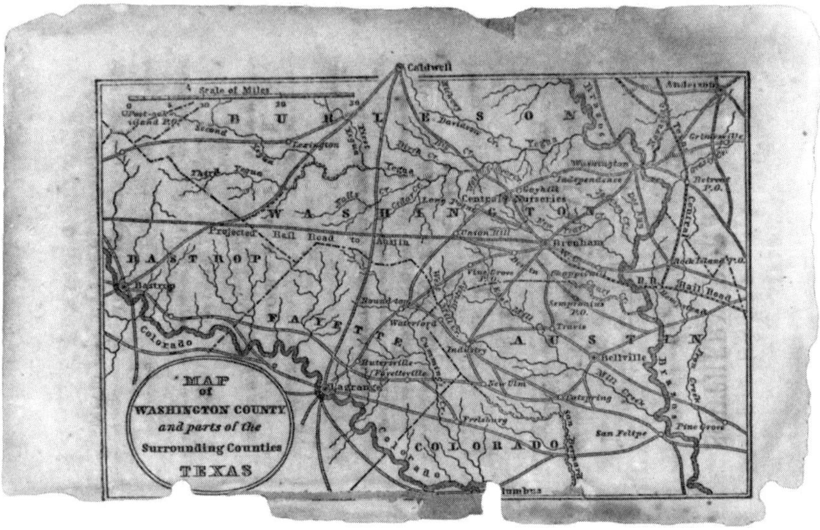

Reprinted from *Affleck's Southern Rural Almanac, and Plantation and Garden Calendar for 1860*, by Thomas Affleck (published by David Felt, New York, and H. G. Stetson & Co., New Orleans). Courtesy Center for American History, University of Texas, Austin.

Six days before his sixty-seventh birthday and almost exactly one year before the fall of Fort Sumter, Gideon Lincecum wrote an affectionate letter to his nephew in Louisiana.[1]

Long Point. Texas. 16 April 1860

John P. Lincecum
Bear Creek, La.
My Dear John.

I plead guilty and I know you will excuse me, when I confess and explain a little.

I only allow myself to write of nights, and having a very extensive correspondence, I am of course, pretty generally behind hand. I have a box in which I place all the unanswered letters as they come to hand, filing them in order so that each one may be ground out of the mill according to its turn. This evening, on examining the letter box, I was proud to find that there was but one left in it, which when I read it over, turned out to be your letter of 29th January. Then I did not feel quite so glad. How it got to the bottom I cannot conjector. I received it a day previous to going to Galveston, for my well boring tools.[2] I was gone three weeks, during which, a good many letters came for me, which I suppose were placed in the letter box without regard to the order in which they came. But a great many letters have arrived and been replied to since my return from Galveston, and somehow or other yours still remained till today. Well, it did not have its turn, and though I cannot, to myself, satisfactorily account for it, I hope you will overlook the delinquency, and forgive the delay that has, unavoidably, supervened.

We are all well here but your old Aunt.[3] It seems that she can't pass the spring season without a spell of sickness. She has been right sick. She is better this evening.

Your father was some better at the time you wrote; we all had hopes that he would recover but have had no news from him of a later date. We feel disposed to scold a little, because you might have written, whether we answered your letter or not. How did you know, but some of us had been smitten with paralysis? Or do you, like the fanatic followers of the creedal religions of the day, become miffed at slight derelictions of what you conceive to be the duty of other folks, and abandon them to the tender care of old Nick and brimstone hospitality? Did you not know that I am 70 years of age?[4] You might have excused me on the score of old age and its accompanying weakness and consequent imbecility. But I could not justify myself on that ground, for I write perhaps not so well but with sufficient facility to keep pace with a large number—perhaps 100—severe scientific, philosophic and theological correspondents, many of them requiring lengthy communications, scattered from Salt Lake City to New York, and some even in London. And having the same indomitable thirst for knowledge that I had when I was a boy, I prosecute my studies, investigations and experimentations with as much eagerness and energy. Having the full use of all limbs I work and go about extensively. I have engaged to collect, this year, for the Academy of Natural Sciences at Philadelphia, specimens of all the shrubs and forest trees that are to be found in the range in which I circulate, and it's a pretty wide one. To do this properly requires strength and activity; a man that can climb—and yesterday—Sunday—had you [been here you would] have found me 40 feet up a tree. To procure blooming specimens from the pecans, oaks and hickories, I am forced to do some tall climbing.

Sarah has engaged to collect, for the same institution, specimens of all the grasses and herbaceous plants.[5] She has already collected near 200 species and has them papered and marked. I have but 80 species yet; but the trees do not bloom so early as the herbs and grasses, and besides they do not include near so many specific characters.

I am also keeping Meteorological tables for the National Observatory; upon these tables I enter three times a day the reading of various meteorological instruments. The Barometer, the Thermometer, Ozonometer, Anemometer;[6] there are two of these latter: one marks the force of the wind and the other gives its velocity. In addition to all these I record the amount of cloud, foggy mornings, smoky days and any other phenomena of the heavens, and I intend to record the amount of rain, if that should ever occur again. So you see, all these little things, and the boring of my well, is just about enough to employ my daylight; and the attention I pay to my correspondences, my night time.

My well boring machinery works finely. The steam engine I had made for the purpose is one of Rham's best.[7] It works eight horse powers and moves like a thing of life. I am boring with a rope, instead of poles, and as it is a new thing under the sun, there are of course, many predictions and opinions about the ultimates. All I can say now about it is, if I can procure rope enough, I'll fetch water over the surface.

There is no use in your talking of moving to this country. You have waited too long; the grass is nearly eat out, or rather ploughed out—and good lands are selling at from $25–$35—and numbers of our citizens would not give up their places at that high figure. They are, however, trying to ruin our glorious country by Railroads and other ruinous, unnatural projects. But there is no help for it. The common mass of the people positively do not possess intellect enough to feel safe without a leader; and there is not honesty amongst those who are willing to assume the leadership, to prevent them from riding the poor devils as soon as they break them to lead gently. Well, that's no crime. I consider it, however, a hell of a misfortune. Besides, it adds so much to the arrogance and rampant vanity of the priests, lawyers, doctors and all the self-set professions.

You was expecting to hear me say something of Electricity in your father's case, and you ask what I think of it?[8] I have often used it in paralytic cases, indeed, in nearly all I ever treated; and I cannot now say that the patient ever derived any advantage from its application. I am sure that I never succeeded in relieving a case of any form of disease by doing violence to the patient, either by the use of poisons, abrasions or shocks. Health is the positive and disease the negative condition; and when we find one in the negative condition, we must draw near like a friend, and warm them up into the positive—if we can, without violence in our action.

Present me affectionately to your father and mother, and all the connection. Especially to the associate of my boyhood, old Lewis.[9] Love to your Lady, to yourself.

Your Uncle, Gid.

[1] John P. Lincecum is the son of Gideon's brother Grant. Biographical notes on relatives of Gideon are provided in the appendix. Hereafter these relatives will be identified for clarification only.

[2] The year 1860 was one of extended drought in Washington County, and the shortage of water led Gideon to devote several months to an unsuccessful attempt to drill an artesian well on his plantation at Long Point (Lincecum, Phillips, and Redshaw, *Science on the Texas Frontier*, pp. 114–15).

[3] Sarah Bryan Lincecum, Gideon's wife.

[4] Gideon's age was actually just shy of sixty-seven, not seventy. He had a habit of exaggerating his age.

[5] Sarah here is his daughter, Sarah Matilda Lincecum (Doran).

[6] Gideon's instruments for collecting weather data included the ozonometer for measuring levels of ozone in the air and the anemometer to gauge wind speed. The ozonometer used small slips of special paper that changed color according to the concentration of ozone. When a strong norther brought in high concentrations of ozone, the ozonometer reading might go as high as 7. See the following letters for details: Gideon Lincecum to Swante Palm, Long Point,

Tex., 20 October 1859, and Gideon Lincecum to Col. C. G. Forshey, Long Point, Tex., 29 March 1860 (both in LP, Box 2E364).

[7] Gideon had ordered an eight-horsepower engine made by Phillip Rahm of the Eagle Machine Company of Richmond, Virginia. It cost him $850 (Burkhalter, *Gideon Lincecum*, p. 138). Gideon addressed two letters to Rahm about the engine (Gideon Lincecum to Phillip Rahm, Long Point, Tex., 16 September 1859 and 28 September 1859, both in LP, box 2E364).

[8] In the early decades of the nineteenth century, the eclectic school of reform medicine advocated a form of treatment that included the use of galvanic and faradic currents to stimulate the spine or certain organs of the body (John S. Haller Jr., *Medical Protestants: The Eclectics in American Medicine, 1825–1939*, pp. 114, 168–69). While practicing medicine in Mississippi in the 1830s, Gideon himself had experimented with therapeutic uses of electricity (Jerry A. Harlow et al., *A History of Monroe County, Mississippi*, p. 77).

[9] Lewis Shellhouse (later Lewis Shellhouse Lincecum) was a Lincecum slave at this time. See the appendix.

There is only a slight reference in the letter above to the mounting crisis between North and South that would lead to secession and war within the next twelve months. But for the previous three or four years Gideon's letters had reflected his growing animosity toward Northern critics of Southern institutions, especially slavery. Gideon lashed out with his pen (and no doubt with his tongue) at Yankee abolitionists, especially if he thought they were in league with ministers of the gospel, whom he (a self-proclaimed "Infidel"), usually referred to as "priests," regardless of their denomination.[1] *The following sampling of his letters from 1857 to 1860 reveals the heat of his growing resentment toward the North, a resentment that made him suspicious even of his Northern scientific friends.*

By 1857 Gideon had become enamored of the idea of castration as a deterrent to antisocial behavior, including agitation against slavery, especially by Northerners. He expressed his views to a number of correspondents, including this unidentified gentleman in Milliken's Bend, Louisiana:

Long Point. Texas. 17 May 1857

Dr. Sir.

From the newspapers, I am informed that a certain E. R. Smith, alias R. E. Smith, has been meddling with the negroes of your parish by distributing amongst them incindiary papers, etc.[2] We of Texas have a very potent antidote for the negro loving mania of those fellows; and we will apply it to any man, when it is satisfactorially proven that he has been making an effort to excite the spirit of insubordination in our slave population. It is a little rough, it is true; but not too much so, when applied as a preventive and a remedy to that species of lunacy that is in a thousand ways seeking opportunities, and insidiously trying secret plans for cutting the throats of our wives and innocent children.

The inclosed papers will explain to you the Texas plan to remedy crime and outrage.[3] We have, as you will see, memorialized our legislature on that subject of changing our modes of punishment, as being useless and of no avail; but whether they favor our views with legislative enactment or not, we are determined, in all such cases as is said to have occurred in your Parish, to assume the authority and apply emasculation, regardless of the consequences. Talk about "tar and feathers" indeed. Those fellows glory in such proceedings, and brag about it when they get home. It is capital for them to work with. If you Louisianians are too faint hearted to protect your families, by putting into practice the only remedy for northern negrophobia, just send them over here, and we'll break them from sucking eggs. Let us hear from you.

Very Respectfully
Gideon Lincecum

P. M. [Postmaster]
Milliken's Bend
Madison Parish, La.

[1] A popular alternative to traditional religion in early nineteenth-century America, Infidelism shared with Unitarianism and Universalism a skepticism that denied the hegemony of orthodox forms of religion and also challenged key ideas at the very heart of Christian thinking. The several forms of Infidelism—deism, rationalism, humanism, atheism, and so on—turned away from the religious life toward more human-centered philosophies that tended to denounce all religion, attacking in particular the dictates of Christian orthodoxy and protesting against existing churches. The weekly *Boston Investigator* newspaper was the unofficial publication of the Infidel movement (J. Gordon Melton, *Encyclopedia of American Religions*, 6th ed., pp. 121–23).

[2] E. R. (or R. E.) Smith has not been identified.

[3] In the mid-1850s Gideon stirred up a great deal of controversy when he submitted a "memorial" to the state legislature advocating a law providing for emasculation of males convicted of capital crimes. He mailed 676 copies of his memorial to lawmakers, newspapers, citizens, scientists, and doctors. Published in part in several Texas newspapers and in full in two of them, the *Colorado Democrat* and the *Ranger*, the memorial was tagged the "Lincecum Law." The memorial was presented to the legislature in 1855 and again in 1856 but never received serious attention. A copy of the memorial, dated April 1854, appears in the Lincecum Papers (Box 2E364), along with a list of persons to whom a copy was sent, their replies, and a list of those failing to respond (Burkhalter, *Gideon Lincecum*, pp. 93–96).

In a similar vein, Gideon wrote to an Alabama editor in November.

Long Point. Texas. 6 Novr. 1857

To the Editor of the Eutaw Whig[1]
Eutaw, Ala.
Sir.

Having seen an article in the Weekly [New Orleans] Delta, which was extracted from your paper, on the subject of a case of interference with the negro population of Sumter county by a couple of abolition scoundrels, I thought it would be nothing amiss for me to communicate to you the Texas plan of dealing with such heartless villians.

You talk of profiting the State by their labor eight or ten years in your penitentiary and seem to think that such a process will teach them a better sense of propriety and justice. But my dear sir, it will not do either. It will only produce capital for those they have left behind to work with and harp upon, and when their term of service is accomplished they will go forth from your prison doubly incensed and filled with the spirit of retaliation, go to work with the negroes again—it may be—more secretly, cautiously, and probably, more successfully. Apply the Texas remedy to them, and they will pester your negroes no more, and it will operate as a damper and a terrifier to the negro loving types of the white race every where.

I am aware that there is no clause in the criminal code of Alabama that would justify your courts in passing such a sentence on the poor devils, but a half dozen properly fixed masks on the right sort of faces could take them from the jail some night, and do the work for them. Do you hear?

The inclosed printed document is the form of a Memorial on the subject now before our legislature. It was presented during the last session, when the merits and powers of the movement was discussed at some length. It was finally referred to the committee on the judiciary, where it remains among the unfinished business of the present session, which convened last Munday.

The good of society has the right and they should entertain no scruples on the subject of carrying it into action in all cases where a few badly organized scoundrels are injuring the morals of our negroes and endangering the quietude and safety of our wives and children.

The Amative developments preponderated in the organism of all violators of order and propriety. To disarm amativeness will secure the peace, protect society, and prevent the propagation and increase of the villainous types of the race. There is no use in a moments hesitation on the propriety of carrying this plan for checking crime and protecting the innocent into action, when every body knows that there is no other reliable remedy that can terrify the wicked, and so effectually prevent the propagation and spread of the animal action in our species. It is the animal portion of our organization that leads to crime and violence. The intellectual, never. Disarm the beast and there will be no more sin. No more outrage . . . .

Very Respectfully,
Gideon Lincecum

[1] The *Eutaw* (Alabama) *Whig and Public Advertiser* was a weekly newspaper published by "Houston & Davis" in 1840. In 1852 its name was shortened to the *Eutaw Whig* (*Library of Congress Online Catalog*, <http://lcweb.loc.gov/catalog/>, 18 October 1999).

Although Gideon's main interest in these years was scientific investigation, he kept informed on the vital political struggle that was going on in Washington. To his congressman he wrote as follows:

Long Point. Texas. 25 Apl. 1858

Hon. Guy M. Bryan[1]
Dear Sir.

I am obliged to you for your attention in sending me congressional documents. We are by the newspapers furnished with such parts of the speeches in Congress as suits the present political notions of the Editor who publishes them. The whole action of the press leads to sectionalism, and will, if the people has no other chance for obtaining the true state of the affairs of our government, terminate in disruption. For my own part I prefer the oppertunity of examining the entire speeches. It enables me to analyze the range of thought and the motives of the speaker; and to weigh and measure, more to my own satisfaction, the organization of the man who produces them. I am however, much better suited at this stage of my protracted existance when any of my congressional friends so far favers me, as to send me "executive documents" such as explorations in the Geological, agricultural departments, or any scientific production under the direction of the government, whether on the land, wind, or water. I am quite an old man, but am still a student in nature's school, and should you have an oppertunity of distributing books of that character, for you to think of me occasionally will lay me under lasting obligations; beside confering an acceptable favor.

Most Respectfully
Your ob[t] Serv[nt]
Gideon Lincecum

[1] Guy Morrison Bryan, a nephew of Stephen F. Austin, served in the Texas legislature from 1847 to 1857 and represented the west-

ern district of Texas in the U.S. Congress from 1857 to 1859. He was an active secessionist leader (Ron Tyler, ed., *New Handbook of Texas*, 1:790–91 [cited hereafter as *New Handbook of Texas*]).

The prospect of disruption of the Union increasingly became a topic in Gideon's correspondence: first as a matter of concern, then as a warning, next as a threat, then a prediction, and finally as a desirable end.

To one of his "theological" correspondents who shared his interest in Spiritualism he wrote (in his wife's name),

Long Point. Texas. 18 May 1858

Mr. Charles Partridge[1]
Dear Sir.

I find by the paragraph in the Telegraph of May 1st that another year has rolled around, and that I am a delinquent subscriber. I thank you for the little blue pencil mark. It put me in mind of my duty to my self. Notwithstanding the fact that you and many others, north of 36° 30',[2] are often committing yourselves on a subject which you know but little about, your paper in other matter is fraught with high toned philosophy that is pleasant to contemplate. You often inculcate the doctrine—and I adhere to it—that we poor mortals are as liable to the suggestions of the evil as of the good spirits, and that we "should meet their commands with the demand—what use?" Spiritualism, if it continues to mingle itself with the politics of the reckless office seeker, will ultimate in a disruption of our union; and I demand—What use?—

Please find $2—and enter it to my credit as subscription money for the 7th volume, "Spiritual Telegraph." Send back numbers, as 2 or 3 numbers will be issued before this can reach you.

Very Respectfully thine
Sarah Lincecum

[1] Charles Partridge made his fortune as a match manufacturer and had embraced Universalism before becoming a Spiritualist editor and publisher. In the nineteenth century, Spiritualism, with its belief that spirits of the dead can and do communicate with mortals, became an organized religion in the United States. In 1857 Partridge became the sole editor of the *Spiritual Telegraph*, which was the longest lived and most widely circulated of the antebellum Spiritualist publications. Published weekly in a newspaper format, it was launched in 1852 by Partridge and Samuel B. Brittan (Bret E. Carroll, *Spiritualism in Antebellum America*, pp. 22, 35, 42, 69, 121–22, 161).

[2] In 1820 Congress had prohibited slavery north of the latitude of 36° 30' in the national territory between the Rocky Mountains and the Mississippi River, except for Missouri, which was admitted as a slave state. In 1854 the Kansas-Nebraska Act repealed the federal restrictions against slavery north of 36° 30', igniting a violent contest over slavery in Kansas Territory that helped lead to the Civil War (James M. McPherson, *Ordeal by Fire: The Civil War and Reconstruction*, 2d ed., pp. 2, 90–92).

Gideon was thinking of another sort of union when he wrote an old friend from earlier days:

Long Point. Texas. 22 Aug. 1858

Dr. A. Weir[1]
Harmony Hill, Texas.
My Dear Friend.

Your verry kind communication of 5th inst. came to hand today and as it assures me that you are yet in the land of the living, I was much gratified; for I had not heard of you in two years. The last account I had of you it was said by a traveller that you were verry ill, and had gone to the white Sulphur Springs in Virginia. Since then, I could not find out where you were; nor did I have any idea of your whereabouts, until the arival of your letter today. . . .

Your suggestion that the harmonic name of your little town would cause me to infer that peace and quietness was the reigning sentiment with its inhabitants is not based upon a knowledge of my experience in such cases.[2] We have a little town 5 miles west of this place, which bears the pacific name of Union.[3] And the every action of its sainted inhabitants declare it to be a deceptious misnomer. The village and its vicinity is made up of four or five different sets of sectarian fanatics, who know more about anything else than they do about union. But what else but misnaming and deception are we to expect from a people who worships a God who, in the management of his business with his chosen people here on earth, is forced to the disreputable alternative of making use of lying spirits as the best plan he could avail himself of to insure success? To make this part of my letter short, and therefore more interesting, I will here make the declaration—and I know what I am talking about—that all religions are false and injurious in proportion to their magnatude. And where ever any form of religion prevails, there humanity suffers and mourns over the wrecks of lost liberty and individual rights. Who would be a religionist? What independent thinker could consent to bear the name, when the very root and origin of the word signifies "to bind anew," and thereby debar him from his natural rights; cramp his mental freedom, and clog intellectual progress? . . .

I shall now close; making no remarks or apologies for what I have herein perpetrated. Neither do I intend to submit to a cross examination on the subject, for thus boring you. But I may say in style more pacific, that I remain as ever,

in Righteousness thine,

Gid

[1] Dr. Andrew Weir was a good friend of Gideon when he lived in Columbus, Mississippi, and they reestablished contact after Weir moved to east Texas, exchanging several letters. The 1870 Census

lists him as living in Titus County (northeast Texas) (U.S. Bureau of the Census, Ninth Census, 1870, Titus County, Tex., p. 002).

[2] The town of Harmony Hill, Texas, in northeastern Rusk County, near Tatum, was given that name in 1856, and the town flourished through the 1860s until it was bypassed by railroads. Finished off by a tornado in 1906, today it is a ghost town (*New Handbook of Texas*, 3:466).

[3] Apparently Gideon refers to Union Hill, a town located two miles northwest of present Burton, Washington County, on Yegua Creek. Named in 1841 for its location on a hill and the lack of discord among its residents, Union Hill in 1860 had a population of about 130. Bypassed by the railroad, it ceased to exist after 1871 (*New Handbook of Texas*, 6:624).

Abolitionism was not Gideon's only grievance against the North. As with many Southerners, he resented the imposition of tariffs that served primarily to protect Northern manufacturers against foreign competition at the expense of Southern consumers and exporters. He expressed his disgust with the system and the politicians behind it in this rich letter:

Long Point. Texas. 14 Oct. [1858]

Dr. C. B. Stewart[1]
Danville, Texas

Your kind favor of 15. ult. did not reach me until the 11th inst. I am not complaining—that would be useless—but it does seem to me that for a letter to be on the road 27 days, when the distance is but 80 miles, is something extraordinary in this fast world of ours. It is so however and we must make up our minds to submit to it, not withstanding the fact that we are taxed to the tune of 100 millions of dollars per annum to support the machinery of our government. Away with all tarifs and all indirect taxation. Give us free trade and direct taxation. It is a humiliating thing to think that our government hasn't sufficient confidence in her citizens to depend on them for support without cheating them into it. And that is not their reason for keeping up the tarif system. It is because that system affords them better oppertunities to cheat us. The chances for stealing by our public men are increasing at such a rapid rate and becoming so lucrative that the excitement among our office seekers, and the derangement in society at large, is greater than it was at the opening of the California gold mines. But, bad luck to them, that was not what I set down to write about, no how.

I intended to write, as well as I could, a good friendly, familiar letter to my Danville friends; instead of which I have growled out a whole page on a subject that no one takes an interest in, except the men of the four professions—Gamblers, Lawyers, doctors, preachers—. . . .

Present me affectionately to your family, and believe me most truly, and fraternally thine in all

Righteousness
Gideon Lincecum

[1] Dr. Charles Ballinger Tate Stewart of Danville, Montgomery County, Texas, was a signer of the Texas Declaration of Independence. Gideon considered him a fellow Infidel, and he was listed in the *Spiritual Telegraph* as an agent to receive payment for subscriptions. Later he was a collector of the Confederate Tax District for Montgomery County (James M. Day, *The Texas Almanack, 1857–1873*, pp. 591, 595, 603; *New Handbook of Texas*, 4:99; Burkhalter, *Gideon Lincecum*, p. 107n; *Spiritual Telegraph*, 13 September 1856, p. 1).

While each of those four "professions" was anathema to Gideon, he leveled his venom most fully at the preachers, or "priests." Consider, for example, the letter he wrote near the close of 1858 to a fellow Infidel:

Long Point. Texas. 20 Dec$^{r.}$ 1858

Robert Wallin, Sec'y
Cent. Ex. Com., Philadelphia
Dear Sir.

In accordance with the desire, expressed in your "special notice" published in the Boston Investigator, I send you my name as an open Infidel.[1] Having never advocated any other religious sentiment or principle, I am not—like bro. Barker, Sunderland and many others that could be named here—able to say that I know and feel, experimentally, the pleasures of being liberated from the thralldom of the wiley priests and their stultifying creeds and ceremonies.[2]

I am now nearly 70 years of age and as I always have, I do not glory in the title, "Infidel." It means just what I am to every institution, or principle that forbids or avoids the scrutiny of the earnest, philosophic investigator.

We cannot get up an infidel association in this vicinity. The spa[r]seness of our population, the suspicion that rests with our community ever since the days of "know nothing-ism" of every movement that comes from the north, with a considerable sprinkling of intellectual cowardice, precludes the possibility of an association here.[3] The intermedling disposition of northern fanaticism is another ism that will operate very seriously against the infidel movement in all the Southern States. Can't you see how you are about to increase your paupers?———

Fraternally, thine,
Gideon Lincecum

[1] The "special notice" referred to appeared in the *Boston Investigator*, 15 December 1858, p. 3. It was signed by Robert Wallin, secretary of the Central Executive Committee of the Infidel Association of the United States. Wallin was a bookseller in Philadelphia and an agent for the *Boston Investigator*. The *Boston Investigator*, called "the leading freethinkers' periodical," ran for seventy years,

from 1835 to 1904. Josiah P. Mendum was its publisher from 1838 to 1876. Horace Seaver was its editor from 1839 to 1878 (Frank Luther Mott, *A History of American Magazines*, 2:78). In 1858 it was published every Wednesday morning, and the subscription fee was "two or three dollars per annum, according to the ability or liberality of the subscriber" (*Boston Investigator*, 1 December 1858, p. 1).

[2] Joseph Barker and LaRoy Sunderland were prominent Infidel lecturers frequently featured in the *Boston Investigator*. What Gideon refers to is that each of them admitted to being a convert from traditional religious sects (*Boston Investigator*, 24 November 1858, p. 2; 8 December 1858, p. 4).

[3] The Know-Nothing or American Party, prominent from 1853 to 1856, was organized to keep control of the government in the hands of native-born citizens. Its name came from the fact that when questioned about their party's activities, members would say "I know nothing" (McPherson, *Ordeal by Fire*, pp. 86–89).

Three months later, in writing to an agnostic publisher in Yankeedom, Gideon expressed not only his animosity toward Northern abolitionists but also his belief in racial superiority and his support of slavery.

Long Point, Washington Co., Texas, 17 Mar. 1859

Barrington & Co., Publishers
335 Broadway, New York
Dear Sir.

Inclosed please find $2 subscription for the "Cosmograph." Send No. 1 [one subscription], 6 numbers, to Dr. L. R. Lincecum, and the other to your humble servant, the undersigned. Send the first numbers, the Apocryphal New Testament and the Infidel's Text Book.[1] We are pleased with the name you have adopted for your "Philosophic Monthly," and more soe with the contents of the first, which we see published in the Boston Investigator. Should have subscribed for the 12 mno. but we of the south are so often imposed upon by the Negro Stealers of the North that we are beginning—though too late—to be more cautious in the bestowal of our patronage. But we flatter ourselves that that "Cosmograph" will not turn out to be a negro advocate, until the white man is elevated at last to the sphere of mental independence. We encourage ourselves with the conclusion that any company of men who are capable of arranging, even the contents of your first number, must have attained the knowledge of the facts that there are many races in the genus homo, and that amongst the numerous races there are indisputably, well marked and distinctive specific differences to sustain the doctrine of superior and inferior types; that the superior types possess the natural, inherent right to and that they will so long as such type maintains upon our globe—in their benevolence and devoted spiritual desire for progressive development, never cease to direct, to control and to use the physical strength of the inferior or less perfectly developed types: that slavery in some form is by nature clearly indicated, and that chattel slavery is more natural, humane, elevating, and better adapted to the constitutional peculiarities of the low pitched types than any other form. We will continue our patronage and procure other subscribers if we like the Cosmograph.

Very Respectfully, thine.
Gideon Lincecum

[1] Gideon was responding to an ad in the *Boston Investigator*, 9 March 1859, p. 3, for Barrington and Co., Publishers. The ad stated that "persons remitting $1 will receive six numbers of the *Cosmograph* and *The Apocryphal New Testament* or any other $1 book they may order." *The Infidel's Text-Book* was identified in another ad as "being the substance of thirteen lectures on the Bible by Robert Cooper, first American edition republished from the London edition. Price 87 cts.; postage 12 cts" (*Boston Investiga-*

tor, 15 August 1860, p. 8). Dr. L. R. Lincecum was Lysander Rezin Lincecum, Gideon's son.

Such a strong racist view was shared by many, if not most, of Gideon's fellow slaveholders,[1] *though perhaps more than others he drew strength from his growing knowledge of and belief in a philosophy, if not a science, of evolution, a theory that his fellow naturalist Charles Darwin expounded that same year in London. Gideon was an early and appreciative reader of Darwin's seminal work,* On the Origin of Species by Natural Selection *(1859).*[2]

At about the same time Gideon wrote to another Yankee bookseller for a cookbook for his youngest daughter, Sarah (nicknamed Sallie), and neither the innocuous subject of the book nor its trivial price deterred him from interjecting his opinion of Northerners and blacks.

Long Point. Texas. 29 March 1859

To the Seller of the Little book,
on healthful cooking without powders,
or yeast.[3] La Grange place. Boston.

Please find the dime herein—Send the little book to the address of

Miss Sallie M. Lincecum
Long Point
Washington County
Texas

We don't care about the dime, nor do we care a great deal about any amount of money when we know what we are spending it for, or the kind of person who is to receive it. We have been so often imposed on by the enemies of the southern people—the northern people—that we have become more prudent in scattering our money. We have plenty of it. So plenty is the cash amongst us, that we never resort to any little trick for the sake of it. We seldom stoop to anything less than a nigger baby or a bale of cotton to procure money.[4] And if your little book had not been sanctioned by the Boston Investigator, we would not send for it.

No advertisement in any other northern paper has our confidence, and it thinks a little too much about the animal called the negro.

Respectfully
Gideon Lincecum

[1] Although only one-third of the South's white families owned slaves, many nonslaveholding whites had a strong stake in the slave system because it made them feel a part of the "master race" and gave them an "inferior" race to look down on (McPherson, *Ordeal by Fire*, pp. 35–36, 49–51).

[2] See Gideon Lincecum to Charles Darwin, Long Point, Tex., 29 December 1860 and 4 March 1861, both in LP, Box 2E366. For discussion of Gideon's correspondence with Darwin, see Lincecum, Phillips, and Redshaw, *Science on the Texas Frontier*, chapter 1.

[3] Gideon was responding to an ad in the *Boston Investigator*, 16 March 1859, p. 3, with the headline "Bread without powders or yeast."

[4] Gideon here alludes sarcastically to the idea that slaveholders were so heartless as to take their slaves' babies and sell them. Randolph Campbell, in *An Empire for Slavery*, documents that such action was highly unusual, although one case was recorded of a six-week-old female being sold for seventy-five dollars when the master was in severe financial difficulty (pp. 163–64).

Twelve days later, Gideon revealed that Sallie's mother shared his own mounting antagonism to Northern writers and publications when he wrote to cancel her subscription to the Spiritual Telegraph.

Long Point. Texas. 10 April 1859

Mr. Charles Partridge
125 Maiden Lane, New York
Dear Sir:

My Lady, Mrs. Sarah Lincecum requests me to say to you, that she has concluded not to take the Spiritual Telegraph any longer. She hardly knows how to do without it. She likes spiritualism, and also the style and spirit of a goodly number of your contributors, but with many others in your conference there are too many vulgar, and often malicious allusions to the subject of negro-dom.—She wishes her paper discontinued. She will not send you any money this year.

It was Dr. [illegible] in one of his speeches at the conference that furnished the straw that broke the camel's back, with the old Lady.[1] When she read what the doctor said, she threw down the paper and observed that she would patronize it no longer. That, however, is no more than what is being done by a great many people of the South. The everlasting slang-whangings and vulgar display of stupid ignorance on the subject of negrodom, which is daily emanating from the northern press, has at last caused us to turn our money—a good many of us—and the sentiment is growing daily—in another direction. We are inculcating the doctrine that it is wrong to send our money or produce to the north for anything. You won't let our negroes alone, but we can let you alone.

Very Respectfully,
Gideon Lincecum

[1] There were regular reports in the *Spiritual Telegraph* of the proceedings at weekly meetings of the "Spiritual Lyceum and Conference," held in New York City every Tuesday evening in Clinton Hall, 8th St. near Broadway. Probably Sarah was reacting to one of these reports.

Although Partridge's reply to Gideon's letter is missing, it is clear that he was upset by Sarah's cancellation and Gideon's letter. After hearing from him, Gideon wrote again, seeking to soothe his feelings but stating the Lincecum view at some length.

Long Point. Texas. 31 May 1859

Charles Partridge
New York, N.Y.
Dear Sir.

Your communication of 14th inst. reached me today. I am sorry that I disturbed you, for you are my consistent brother—the consistent brotherhood to quite a small family, and it pains me when I am the actor in any performance that will raise the dust, or perturb the clear waters of our common fountain.

I told my old lady before I wrote that it would not be necessary, that you would write "expired" on the last number, the paper would stop, and that would be the end of it. She didn't like that. Being pleased with you and all you say in your department in the "Telegraph," she did not wish you to think that it was on your account that she discontinued the paper. I read your letter to her today. She replied that she couldn't help it; that if she thought you needed it, she would send the money but could not agree to take the paper so long as it is filled up with the irrelevant fanatical articles of those ignorant, wanton disturbers of the national peace—those filthy amalgamators—who, while they derive the principal portion of their support from the Southern States, are saying and doing everything they can to slander and ruin us. She bids me say to you that she admires a free paper, will take no other; she delights in the interchange of views and opinions; has no objections or dislikes to those who differ with her; but she has it in her head that the thing she complains of is no mere matter of opinion, but a regular well-devised, systematized scheme for plundering the South, which cannot fail to disrupt the government. She said several other pretty tight thing[s] on the subject of the frequent conjugal unions that take place in the North, between the "White men with black skins, who had fled from their rightful owners in the South, and the [illegible] black women, with white skins["] &c but I will not write it here.[1]

Her conclusion as to the results that is to come out of the northern mind is doubtless correct. And what of it? If we cannot dwell together agreeably, separation is the only remedy. And when the two halves shall each get up their sectional splits, let them separate again and again, as the office seekers and theologians may find it necessary, until there is nothing left but an ugly tale of the sad affair.

The toiling portions of these United States are all democrats, desiring liberty and peace. They form one party. Among them there would arise no national divisions. But they are ignorant, illiterate, abhorring mental labor. Theology, politics (office seekers, that's politics), speculators, and all the professions, are opposed to a republican form of government—to liberty, to progress. Altogether—in private—they form one party. They possess good intellects, highly cultivated, but no honesty—no conscientious scruples as to the means to be employed in controlling the profits arising from the labor of the down trodden multitude. To ensure greater and more certain success, they make arrangements in secret or in packed conventions, divide themselves into two parties; these parties assume names which they at the time suppose to be best calculated to confuse and split up the strength of the laboring classes—some times they find it necessary to assume three or four party names to successfully carry their point—always with the secret understanding that they are in reality but one party. Thus prepared they go forth amongst the people and pretend that they are explaining the political wants of the masses by villifying & calling each other the proper names of the theiving schemes they have in secret conclave concocted to plunder community. After they have produced a sufficient loss of confidence amongst the people to prevent any of their number from becoming a candidate, the[y] call them to the polluted ballot box. As the candidates all represent the thieving party, it makes no difference with them who is elected. The people make a pretty close affair of it; think they have done well by using their judgment in choosing the least of two evils, and go home, to find themselves badly plundered one more time.

Such is the continual action of all the professions, mon[e]y and place seekers and the like, and any paper, calling itself "free," publishing and widely circulating their nefarious plans under the cognomen of mere difference of opinion, is but one of two things—unenviable.

I know you as an earnest, industrious worker for progress, Partridge, and enjoyed <u>your</u> articles in the Telegraph very much, particularly on the principles of Government. Also the general character of the questions and the democratic (I don't mean conventional democracy) manner in which the discussions are conducted in your weekly conferences; and can have no <u>right</u> to object to what anybody may say to that, or any other paper (that is, to their <u>right</u> to say it). I may say the same thing of a brier thicket: can't object to its thorns, snakes, or thieving vermin, so long as it keeps its mischief at home, but that's no reason I should go into it or remain silent in regard to its prickles and reptiles. A word to the wise, &c. . . .

Very Respectfully,
Gideon Lincecum

[1] On the topic of "amalgamation" (miscegenation), the *Boston Investigator* reported the following item, under the heading "Summary of News": "Amalgamation.—The Boston Traveller says that

within the last year there have been, in this city, some four or five marriages of colored men with white women, but not a case of the marriage of a white male with a colored female" (14 January 1857, p. 3).

Despite Gideon's seeming low opinion of the African race and his strong support of the institution of slavery, he was not without some tender feelings toward his slaves. A letter he wrote in January reveals a glimpse of this side of Gideon.

Long Point, Tex. 19 Jan$^{ry.}$ 1859

Mr. Joday Newsom[1]
Brazos County, Texas
Dear Sir.

While you were last in this county, I road the best part of a day trying to meet with you; but failed, and now I must make known to you the business I was after then, by writing to you. It will, however, make but little difference, as a knowledge of the matter can be obtained by the interchange of one or two short letters quite as well as if I had seen you.

My boy Philip is complaining sadly at the idea of losing his wife. I let him go to your place, so that he might ascertain the distance. He says its too far for him to visit her with any satisfaction, and he is daily begging me to buy her for him. I have, if it will suit you to part with her, consented to do so. Now in return answer to this letter, just state the terms for which you can afford to accommodate the negros, and if I can stand it, the negros shall still be man and wife.[2]

Do the best you can, for it will be no profitable speculation on my part, I assure you.

We are all in good health.

Very Respectfully
Your ob^{t} Serv^{nt}
Gideon Lincecum

[1] Joday Newsom is listed as residing in Boonville in the 1860 Census (U.S. Bureau of the Census, Eighth Census, 1860, Brazos County, Tex., p. 084).

[2] Apparently the arrangement Gideon sought did not take place, for Philip was still seeking to be with his wife in 1863 (Gideon Lincecum to K. Warnke and Joday Newsom, Long Point, Tex., 12 August 1863, LP, Box 2E366).

That his humaneness went no further than this was in part due to his conviction that slavery was an absolute blessing to this "inferior" race. He expressed this view fully in two revealing letters written in this year. In the first he is urging a Northern friend to come to view the paradise that was Texas:

Long Point. Texas. 15 May 1859

R. P. Hallock, M.D.[1]
New York
My Dear Sir.

. . . You will have to come to Texas. In which case you would not certainly fail to fight for [it], by the time you have passed over the intervening prairies which lie between you and the place where you would have to land on the gulf; snuffed the sweet odors which emanate from the millions on millions of the endless variety of pretty flowers, which at this season of the year bedeck our far reaching plains with every form and style in nature's catalogue, dressed in all the gorgeous colors and tints of every shade that old Sol, with his perpendicular rays and sevenfold threads of light, can untwist; the beautiful and gentle undulating fields of rich grass, spreading far out beyond the range of observation; thickly dotted with numerous herds of fat cattle, horses and rivers of sheep. Flock does not convey the idea; they do flow and disembogue from behind the little hills into the wide valleys like a river; fields of luscious corn—high and blooming now; big promise for another year's provision—with the sorg[hum] and sugar cane, and broad areas of the Gossypium [cotton], in which are found peaceful, agricultural hosts, of well disciplined, well fed, well clad, healthy, highly developed and very useful animals, supposed by the superficial observer to belong to the genus homo! Science admits him as a sub genus, species Africana—with strong muscles and gleeful hearts—sweeping away with their well ordered implements the noxious weeds, nursing the cotton plants and boasting in songs of loudest note that "with its silky tissue, the bully nigger shirts de world!" . . . I say, by the time you have passed over all these substantial realities, and a thousand other striking scenes which I forbear to write, and you at last find me, you will be so changed in every attribute and sentiment, that you will have to inquire of me, of what it was, about which we were to fight! And I won't tell you—But I can, and would soon show you, inducements that would produce the desire with you, for the presence of Gilee Ann and the children here; and you would say, "if they were here I would never return to New York"—that blotch of churches and sin. That's what I think about it. But if you are an Israelite, you might want to get back to the paints and pots, after all! . . .

In righteousness
I remain fraternally thine
Gideon Lincecum

[1] Robert T. Hallock, M.D., of New York City, was a socially prominent New York physician and Spiritualist lecturer who was part of the same circle as the editors of the *Spiritual Telegraph*, Charles Partridge and Samuel B. Brittan (Carroll, *Spiritualism in Antebellum America*, pp. 37, 121).

In a letter written three months later to a fellow reader of the Boston Investigator, *Gideon extended his idyllic view of slavery by proposing the extension of the institution to all Africans in the country, North and South, to benefit both races.*

Long Point. Texas. 12 Aug. 1859

M. C. Hamilton[1]
Austin, Texas
Dear Sir.

Published in the Boston Investigator, I notice a communication from you, dated 9th April 1859, which corresponds with my views on the subject it treats throughout. I have not the pleasure of a personal acquaintance with you, neither do I suppose that you have any knowledge of me and my proclivities. I cherish the hope, however, that we shall know more of each other ere long.

What you say of the African race is true. The negro cannot be elevated to a level with the white race. He at best scarcely attains above a sub-genus, and it exhibits an entire want of a knowledge of the nature and history of the races, to contend that they are capable, by any plan of culture or treatment, of being raised to the moral and intellectual plane of the more perfectly organized developments of the white species of our genus. But that is not the object and aim of the misdirected philanthropy that is meddling with this perplexity.

There is so much good sense contained in that short letter of yours—so much truth—and your two reasons for declining to become a subscriber are expressed with so much calm, sober firmness, that [I] was much pleased and intended to write to you immediately, but was prevented just then, and the subject slipped my mind until I came across your letter again this evening.

I have a project which I wish to communicate to you, and if you think well of it, I hereby solicit your aid in giving it shape and notoriety. I have been thinking of it a long time, and when I read your letter in the "Investigator," I set you down as the man that can—for I do not feel myself competent to carry out the plan of the project with sufficient force to satisfy my taste in such an enterprise—should it meet your views, render the necessary assistance.

Now, I have no thought that the project I am about to propose for your consideration can ever be consummated. The expectation on the subject goes no further than to excite thought, and to operate as a check upon the most [illegible] fanaticism which is, at this time, so prevalent North of the Mason & Dixon's line.

The proposition is this: What should be the results, if all the slave states should simultaneously memorialize congress on the subject of the inhumanity and maltreatment which has been for a long time and is still being exercised, by the people of the free states towards the negro race? And suggesting to that honorable body the propriety of their recommending to all the states, that instead of forcing the reopening of the African slave trade it would be far better for them, the states, to enact laws for the reenslavement of all the runaways and free negroes that shall be found in any state or territory within the limits of the U.S. after a specified date; permit only the negro to choose a white master, or on his refusal to do so, to sell him into bondage at public auction?

The memorial may also state, which is nothing more than the truth, that this proposition, carried into successful action, will restore the negro to his normal condition, render him in every way more happy, better provided and cared for, and more useful to himself as well as to the superior types of the genus. Considered on the plane of humanity, there is no comparison between the conditions of the well clothed negro in bondage, with his full belly, his gleeful songs, the good gusto with which he enjoys his banjo, his hearty dance and his tobacco, and the denuded, starving, lazy, thieving, improvident free negro, or negro in any state without a white man for a director.

On this phase of the subject with the enlightened ethnologist, very strong terms may be justifiably used and with no fears of successful contradiction, as to its scientific and philosophic character.

Be so kind as to favor me with your views of this proposition, with any addition or alteration you may see proper to suggest and oblige.

Very Respectfully
Your Obt. Servant
Gideon Lincecum

[1] Gideon was writing in response to a letter from Hamilton that appeared in the *Boston Investigator* and in which he defended slavery (18 May 1859, p. 2). Morgan Calvin Hamilton of Austin (1809–93) was born in Alabama but came to Texas in 1830 and worked in the War Department of the Republic of Texas from 1839 to 1845. Strongly Republican before and after the Civil War and brother of later Republican governor Andrew Jackson Hamilton of Texas, he served as state comptroller in 1867 and represented Texas in the U.S. Senate as a Radical Republican from 1870 to 1877 (*New Handbook of Texas*, 3:430).

Gideon's new friend Hamilton replied approvingly to the above letter, and Gideon wrote to him again at some length, not only pushing his idea of reenslaving free Negroes, North and South, but affirming the vital principle of states' rights in the process.

Long Point. Texas. 1 Sept. 1859

M. C. Hamilton
Austin. Texas.
Dear Sir.

Your highly esteemed communication of 20th. ult. came to hand last friday.

I experienced much satisfaction in the finding from it that in respect to our political sentiments we can fraternize in toto. "The great doctrine of state rights, raised by Mr. Jefferson, and elaborated by Mr. Calhoun" is the main thing—the foundation upon which the whole fabric and the stability of our government institutions are based;[1] and when the laboring classes shall recognize the principles and the bearings of this "great doctrine" they will cheerfully adhere to them—each type of our genus will take its place in the business and duties in the life stage without murmuring, and the deceptions, misrepresentations and strifes practiced by the office and place seekers will cease, because they will no longer pay. Even the General Government, exclusive of foreign relations, would have nothing to do; except perhaps an occasional arbitration by way of settling minor difficulties which might arise among the great sisterhood of states on points and phases of rights, of recent date, which would necessarily occur in the ever onward movements of ceaseless progress. But to bring about these much to be desired ultimates, centuries will roll by and many important changes must take place in our social system. Legislators and politicians must become honest. Fanaticism and superstition must be banished from our seminaries of learning. The people must understand the authority of individual rights. Deeper down yet, for the coming generations more suitable progenitors must be provided, more particularly the maternal parents. In short, the breeding portions of community must be purified. There is but one possible available power that can do that.

From your remarks on the subject of memorializing congress, I am led to think that you have misconstrued that portion of my project. Please examine it again and you will find that all ideas of meddling, by congressional enactments, with the sacred rights of the individual States is carefully avoided. Nothing further than for congress to recommend to the states,

&c. I agree with you, that excitement is the life sustaining aliment for fanaticism, and that under the influence of quiet repose it withers and dies. But would it produce great excitement for the slave states to solicit congress by respectful petition, merely to recommend a measure to the free states? Congress might and very probably would lay the petitions under the table, but the object would be attained; the thought would be opened up, and men from every State would hear it.

I am not however, married to the plan of this project; and if I was so much of a bigot, I should be, from accounts which I have received from different portions of the union since the writing of my former letter, forced to the conclusion that there can be no further use for the action of my old semi-torpid brain in the matter. From these accounts I find that quite a number of highly cultivated, master minds, have grappled with the science and the philosophy of this very grave question and are handling it with an earnestness that seems to me augers favorable ultimates. As yet, I have seen no sign of it, but if they had included the principles of my project in the program of their investigations and argumentations, my fears on the subject of the disastrous consequences which would inevitably result from disruption would rest more calmly.

On the same day that your letter reached me I received the Mississippi Democrat, and Debow's Review.[2] In the first is published at length Mr. Jeff Davis' address before the recent Democratic convention, in the City of Jackson, Mi.[3] In the latter, the speeches of Mr. Spratt of S.C. and Gov. Foote of Mi.[4] In the course of these three speeches, reference is often made to a number of other strong minds, who acting under the influences of various political schemes, seem to be honestly exciting their entire mentality for the purpose of quieting down the agitation among the states on the slavery question to a basis of philosophic equality. A majority of these active minds are decidedly opposed to the project of reopening the African slave trade; but they have suggested no plan for the relief—the restoration of the free negro population, to the humane and elevating plane of use: Slavery. The only condition in which the African species of our genus can be elevated above the animal developments, which naturally preponderates in his cerebral organization.

My desire is in some appropriate movement, calmly and sensibly, to introduce this wing of the negro question, and to place them upon the political arena, in the analyzing crucibles, with the rest of the negroes. I think it would tend to equalization.

I see also, in the "Day Book," a copy of which was handed me by a friend today.[5] The number of the paper is 42, and contains a notice, that Mr. Jacobs of Md. had published a pamphlet on the free negro question, and that the supply was entirely exhausted. I am told that Mr. Jacobs' pamphlet includes my proposition. If so, I may not trouble myself further about the matter, except perhaps, so far as to write a few letters to some of the purest advocates of States' Rights, and to a few rabid negro lovers—black men with white skins, in the north.

In the meantime should anything occur to your mind that would aid in placing this subject before the public, in proper shape, to elicit investigation, and feel inclined to communicate it to me, I shall be gratified, and shall esteem it a great favor.

You were "unwell." Are you an unhealthy man? If so, pay me a visit, prepared to remain with me a week or two, and it may be that I can suggest something to you on the principles of the laws of life that will be worth the trip to you at least. Please write again, and oblige.

Very Respectfully
Your Ob[t.] Serv[nt.]
Gideon Lincecum

[1] Gideon's "Mr. Calhoun" refers to Sen. John C. Calhoun (1782–1850) of South Carolina, the leading exponent of the doctrine of states' rights, which affirmed the sovereign right of each state to interpret for itself the limits of federal authority over it and its citizens, including its right of secession (Current, ed., *Encyclopedia of the Confederacy*, 4:1531–37).

[2] A newspaper named the *Independent Democrat* of Canton, Mississippi, was started in 1842 by J. Handy. In 1844 it moved to Carollton, Mississippi, and became the *Mississippi Democrat* (Library of Congress Online Catalog, <http://lcweb.loc.gov/catalog/>, 18 October 1999). Except for an interruption during the Civil War, *Debow's Commercial Review of the South and West* was published in New Orleans from 1846 to 1880 and edited by James D. B. DeBow (Mott, *History of American Magazines*, 2:384). DeBow was forced to flee New Orleans when the city was captured by Union forces in 1862. Although he established temporary offices in Columbia, South Carolina, publication of all journals and magazines in the South was hampered by a paper shortage. In the next three years he managed to get out only one issue, and that was in the final year of the war (Massey, *Ersatz in the Confederacy*, p. 142). For more information on DeBow's magazine and the views it advocated, see Current, ed., *Encyclopedia of the Confederacy*, 3:985.

[3] In his address to the state Democratic convention in Jackson, Mississippi, 6 July 1859, Jefferson Davis, then a U.S. senator representing Mississippi, decried the North's "fanatical hostility" against the South and its institution of slavery. He stoutly defended slavery, referred to blacks as a "subservient race," favored annexing Cuba, and feared a Republican victory in 1860 would result in an "irrepressible conflict" (Lynda L. Crist and Mary S. Dix, eds., *The Papers of Jefferson Davis*, 6:614).

[4] Leonidas W. Spratt, a Columbia, South Carolina, editor, was a leading proponent of reopening the foreign slave trade in order to increase the supply of labor (Steven A. Channing, *Crisis of Fear: Secession in South Carolina*, p. 149). Henry Stuart Foote (1804–80) was a former U.S. senator (1847–52) and governor of Mississippi (1852–54), who moved to Nashville, Tennessee, and served in the

Confederate congress (1861–65). Unlike Spratt, he opposed reopening the foreign slave trade (Clement Eaton, *A History of the Old South*, 2d ed., p. 234).

[5] The *Day Book* was a "Copperhead" (pro-South) journal published in New York by N. R. Stinson from 1849 to 1863 (Mott, *History of American Magazines*, 2:154).

There was no rush by blacks, in the North or South, to embrace Gideon's proposal of reenslavement; on the contrary, the year 1860 produced rumors and some manifestations of insurrection by slaves in various points of the South, including Texas. Gideon, an avid reader, was concerned by the reports and offered advice for deterring any outbreak. He encouraged direct action by a mob, if necessary, but instead of lynching or tar-and-feathering, he recommended castrating the agitators or rebellious slaves. Witness the following letter:

Long Point. Texas. 18 Jan. 1860

J. M. Taylor & J. M. Carter[1]
Marshall. Harrison County. Texas.
Gentlemen:

I find published in the Galveston News, notice of a meeting, held on 26th December last at the court house of your place, at which you two gentlemen were called to preside as chairman and secretary.[2] The object of the meeting was to consider the course to be pursued against E. C. Palmer, &c.,[3] and one amongst sundry doings was the appointment of a committee to memorialize the legislature to punish with death any person seeking to excite a servile inserection in the state.

I offer nothing from the spirit, nor desire to dictate; but I would most respectfully suggest that with the expectation of obtaining aid for the amelioration of the people, or for the protection and progressive development of community, it would answer as good a purpose for us to call on the man in the moon as on the legislature. Society has the right to rid itself of any nuisance. I would also suggest that tar and feathers, riding on a rail, and ordering out of the country is not the most successful and reformatory method in the treatment of these fellows for nigger-mania. All crime and villainy originate in the inferior portion of the posterior brain—Amativeness—and when you are pestered with one of those negro loving scoundrells, all that is necessary to break him from sucking eggs and ensure good behavior from him in all the future is to disarm Amativeness for him [by castration]. Think of it.

Very Respectfully
Gideon Lincecum

[1] Probably Gideon is referring to James F. Taylor, a state senator and leading Whig opponent of the Union, who in May 1861 became head of a public safety committee for Harrison County, ready to enforce order by vigilante means if necessary (Randolph B. Campbell, *A Southern Community in Crisis: Harrison County, Texas, 1850–1880*, p. 202). J. M. Carter has not been identified.

[2] There was a mass meeting in Marshall in December 1859, in part agitated by John Brown's raid at Harper's Ferry and perhaps by Brown's execution. Contrary to Brown's belief that he had a divine mission to take vengeance for enslaved black people, the meeting attendees declared slavery to be "ordained by God" (Campbell, *A Southern Community in Crisis*, p. 144). Another possible cause for the meeting was reported by the *Daily True Delta* (New Orleans): "The Courthouse at Marshall a few nights hence, was set on fire. Fortunately, it was early discovered and extinguished. It is thought to be the work of incendiaries" (24 December 1859, p. 1).

[3] E. C. Palmer has been described as "a local man" who was convicted "of being an abolitionist" by the "meeting of slave owners" held in Marshall in December 1859 (Wendell G. Addington, "Slave Insurrections in Texas," *Journal of Negro History* 35 [1950]: 420).

It may seem strange that as tough-minded, scientific, and agnostic as Gideon was, he was attracted to Spiritualism, as was his wife Sarah. When Spiritualist writers strayed into the zone of antislavery sentiments, they lost Gideon's support, as well as Sarah's, and raised his hackles, none more than the "Poughkeepsie Seer," Andrew Jackson Davis.[1] *Gideon addressed the following letter to the colorful, eccentric Davis:*

Long Point. Texas. 30 March 1860

A. J. Davis
New York
Sir.

It is myself instead of Sarah Lincecum who is the subscriber to the Spiritual Telegraph. I have received four numbers of the Herald of Progress, and with a good many of the articles published therein, I am pleased.[2] I am always pleased with the truth; but there are principles and bearings in your paper that are not true; and many articles published, that if their principles be carried out, must ultimate as a check to human progress.

Here is an extract from your own pen—"The love hearted and lion headed Parker."[3] This I consider to be an encomium with a bloody secret; and for A. J. Davis to pass it upon the man who earnestly recommends that one half of a highly progressed, superior type of the human genus would be doing no harm, aye more, it would be a virtue for them to encourage—aid and assist—a comparatively small number of an inferior type—the lowest and the blackest type of our genus—to kill and destroy the other half of the progressed type. You style all this as emanating from a "love laden bosom."

You give countenance to such foolish fixions as the Vision of Frances Ellen Watkins, which indicates that the god you worship, demands the same old fashioned sacrifices of blood! blood!! blood!!! and this you call a "fine vision of the triumph of freedom."[4] How common it is, in the world's history, for the founders of a new fanaticism to introduce fire and sword and bloody sacrifice as a sweet savor to their gods.

There are many other signs and indications in your paper which, to the advocates of real human progress, must be very objectionable. I state these things as disagreeable facts and not as a complaint at you and your paper; nor at how much you and your sanguinary associates may think proper to encourage the worship of the bloody god; for I know that you and them, and all the balance of organized things, are just as good, as perfect, and as intellectual as it is possible for them to be at this stage of our little planet's existance; and I would offer, as the highest thought suggested—by my so far advanced organism—that I do not think it would push the car of progress a single inch ahead for me to become a subscriber to your paper. It grieves me, but I have no alternative. Come what may, I am ready. Notwithstanding that I have weathered the frosts of seventy winters, I am still healthy and active. I was born in the smoke of the first American revolution, and I have no grounds for the hope that I shall not pass from the life state in the thunder and smoke of the second; that is, should the wrong, unnecessary progress-checking principles which you advocate be continued.

I have said nothing here from an unfriendly spirit. Yet I understand human nature well enough to know that you will be offended at what I have said. For nature has not produced the man yet, ignorant enough to commit a wrong, who is not bad enough to be offended if you tell him of it. Write what you please to me, but nothing in print.

Respectfully
Gideon Lincecum

[1] Largely because of the writings and activities of Andrew Jackson Davis (1826–1910), Spiritualist ideology took root in western

New York state in the late 1840s. Incorporating the ideas of Emanuel Swedenborg and François Fourier, principles of mesmerism, and the broader harmonial philosophy of which these ideas were a part, Davis published in 1847 *The Principles of Nature, Her Divine Revelations and a Voice to Mankind*. Another impetus came in 1848 when two sisters named Fox developed a code for communicating with a spirit that was producing strange knockings in their cottage at Lily Dale, also in western New York (Carroll, *Spiritualism in Antebellum America*, pp. 16–21).

[2] Davis founded the *Herald of Progress* in 1860 as part of his effort to separate his "harmonial philosophy" from Spiritualism, which he felt had become too sensationalized, obscuring the deeper religious meaning that had characterized its beginnings (Carroll, *Spiritualism in Antebellum America*, p. 179). The editor of the *Spiritual Telegraph* announced in the issue of 25 February 1860 that it was ceasing publication and that arrangements had been made to transfer subscribers of the *Spiritual Telegraph* to the *Herald of Progress*, which commenced its regular publishing on 3 March 1860. Even though Gideon had requested in April 1859 that Sarah's subscription to the *Spiritual Telegraph* be canceled, apparently she received several weekly issues of the *Herald of Progress*, and Davis must have sent a letter asking if she wanted to subscribe to the new paper.

[3] Rev. Theodore Parker of Boston (1810–60) was a prominent Unitarian minister who made impassioned speeches against slavery, helped fugitive slaves to escape, and wrote an abolitionist tract, *A Letter to the People of the United States Touching the Matter of Slavery*. He also served on the secret committee that aided John Brown in obtaining arms (Alice Felt Tyler, *Freedom's Ferment: Phases of American Social History to 1860*, pp. 80–82).

[4] Frances Ellen Watkins Harper (1825–1911) was a remarkable free African-American reformer, lecturer, and poet who spoke and wrote widely against slavery (Edward T. James, ed., *Notable American Women, 1607–1950: A Biographical Dictionary*, 2:137–39).

The worsening sectional crisis and the threat of a bloody conflict over slavery could not disturb Gideon's equanimity for long, as can be seen in a letter to his sister and brother-in-law, who lived on the edge of the frontier in south Texas.

Long Point. Texas. 2 April 1860

D[aniel] B[oone] Moore
Emily Moore
Hondo, Texas
Dear Brother and Sister.

I had heard and seen so many accounts of Indian depredation, and had had no news from you for so long a period, that I had given you up for lost; until today when Sarah handed me a letter which you had written on the 26th of march, and which she had just received from the P.O.

The account you gave of the dangers by which you are environed is somewhat startling. Under such circumstances one cannot avoid the feelings of anxiety, especially when so far away, that all the mischief, if any should occur, would be done and over before the news could reach us. To us who are surrounded with a densely populated country and all the paraphernalia of a prosperous people, it causes us to shudder when we contemplate the condition of the inhabitants of the wild, unprotected border country. We feel safe from the theiving depredations of the maraudering Indians, snakes and savage beasts; and we tell over with anxious, sad faces the disastrous misfortunes of those who are thus exposed—the murders, the kidnapping of women and children; stealing all the horses &c and indeed it sounds and looks very bad. Six men killed in your county in the course of two or three days.[1] It is, to be sure, awful to contemplate. But while we are thus horror stricken at the calamities which are occasionally befalling our distant frontier friends, we forget to look around us in our comparatively safe homes and to number the victims that fall a prey to the king of terrors, in almost every family; while the Indians are dispensing the fiat of death to six men in your country, five times as many are killed by scarlet fever and the doctors in this. Last summer while the Indians were killing an occasional man on the frontier country, to the number of 20 or thirty souls, and stealing a few thousand horses, the yellow fever killed as many thousand people[2] and the prayerful christian incendiary destroyed cities and an immense amount of property on the farms in the country by fire; besides we have almost as much shooting, stabbing and killing right amongst us as there are in any portion of the Indian infested countries. Last night, at Brenham, a man cut off his wife's head with an axe,[3] and we hear of as many or perhaps more killings in our happy, god serving community—where the hoarse croaking prayer ceaseth not, nor the sound of the church going bell quieteth never—than we hear of from the Indian range.

For my part, I feel just as safe in one country as another. Death is everywhere, slaying all who belong to him; he can slay no one else. I know that someday or other I shall die, at some place. That place is now existing, and [I] cannot die at two places; and until that place and the someday meets, I need not feel any anxiety as to what can be done to me by the murderous Indian, the assassin, or relentless disease.

Under the soothing influence of this irrefutable philosophy I am calm and easy as to the where death shall claim me. It is none of my business. So I pray not, neither do I sing psalms, yet the ranting devotee in all his howling glory can never know or feel the peace that calms, nor the quiet that reigns in my mind, on that topic.

But I have said enough on that dull subject. Better speak of something that will afford a more lively interest. I may say that thus far we have had a very favorable spring for the agricultural persuits. Though our lands have not been moistened to the depth of three feet during the last six years, and notwithstanding the fact that we had an exceedingly dry winter, but very little rain since the spring set in, and the ground now quite dry, our crops look very promising and so far advanced that we feel assured that if the rain god will vouchsave us a few sprinkles at the proper times, we shall be able to produce sufficient crops to carry us safely through the chilly recesses of another winter. Last year we had but one light rain after the first of May, during crop time, and though I did not gather a full half crop, we cribbed plenty to last us, with care, till corn comes again, if it should come.

Our branches are all dry, so are our wells, and have been for years. We have deepened all our wells ten or twelve feet and some of them are dry at that, and the best of them affords but little water and no prospect for them to have water in them this year. It would require a whole winter of constant rain to saturate the earth sufficiently to start the branches and fill up our wells to their former, useful supplies of good water.

With the view of remedying that obvious defect in our otherwise inimitable country, I sent off last fall and had a very fine 8 horse power steam engine made for the purpose of sinking an artesian well. I have had the engine home a month or more and have just completed the machinery that is to be worked by the engine for boring the well. It has been a very heavy job, the timbers are all so heavy and large. But we have got it done and it works very well. We run it a few hours, soon went down 55 feet, and finding that it operated to suit us, we cooled down the steam and laid up the implements for awhile. It is time of the spring to hunt up stock; and while Lysander and a young man who resides with us are attending to that business, the negroes can get the crop cleaned out and we shall be able to set to work in earnest at the well. I have made all parts of the machinery so perfect and strong and it works so well that if I meet with no insurmountable obstruction below, I feel very certain of success.

The machinery and the whole plan, tools and all, are on an entirely new principle. Instead of the old fashioned jointed, troublesome poles, I am using a rope. I took the idea from seeing some men last summer prospecting for water with a punch a foot long, which they called a drop auger, and a small line tied to it, and this contrivance they were dropping in a hole they had made with it; when it got full, they drew it out, cleaned out the dirt and let it down again; and by this simple means, they had penetrated the earth to the depth of 75 feet in three days and they had passed through some pretty hard sandstone with it. Seeing so much work done so quick with so small and simple means, it occurred to me that on a large scale with sufficient power and well regulated machinery, a body might work wonders. And so far as I have tried it, I am not disappointed. The contrivance I saw those men at work with cost them $2.50; mine as it now stands has cost me $1500.00. But I am all ready for the work, and if I succeed in obtaining a good, gushing column of water it will remunerate me a hundred fold. Everything about us have been suffering for water for several years; during all last winter, and it's so now, our cows, hogs and horses can get no water nearer than two miles of us. Hence you may see the cause of my extraordinary effort.[4]

Our country is rapidly filling up with wealthy farmers. A great portion of our prairie—and it had no fields in it worth naming when you left here—are now under cultivation. From Brenham to Chappell Hill, from Chappell Hill to Washington, and from Washington to this place, and all the way to La Grange is almost entirely under fence. We shall have no uncultivated prairie between our two rivers in 2 more years, and then our fine cow range is done. We have largely too many cattle now. They done pretty well the past winter, but if we keep so many, they will not do so well again. The country hereabouts is fast progressing every way. The cars are daily running to the Brazos five miles beyond Chappell Hill, and the railroad (except the bridge across the Brazos) is nearly finished to Brenham.[5] People are erecting fine houses and seem to be intent on settling themselves permanently.

Nothing out of the line of ordinary events has occurred of late date in our vicinity; Sallie will write to you, and she of course will tell you of the deaths and marriages. I may say here however, that neither has happened in our family in several years, but quite a number of births. Our family now, counting the old lady and myself, when they are all together make a pretty smart show, being 49 of us; exhibiting every type of character that is to be found in the Caucasian race, from ordinary to good middling. All except Cassandra are settled close around us, and are sustaining themselves quite creditably.[6] They are all sober, well to do, and there are no evil reports about any of them that I know of. But I must say that it is a hell of a gang for a progeny and me only just in the prime of life; only think.

The old lady bids me say to you for her that she had rather see you than any people in the world, and if the lord—I can't see how he can have anything to do with it—is willing, she intends to see you before another year rolls round—if the Indians don't kill you. She enjoys pretty good health and bids fair to hold out a good many years.

Accept of my prayers for your safety and believe me as ever, most affectionately,

Your Brother
Gid

[1] For accounts of Indian raids in southwest Texas immediately before and during the Civil War, see A. J. Sowell, *Early Settlers and Indian Fighters of Southwest Texas*. See also J. W. Wilbarger, *Indian Depredations in Texas*.

[2] Yellow fever epidemics were common in Galveston and Houston between 1839 and 1867. In Houston in November 1859, an esti-

mated 1200 to 1500 people were struck down by yellow fever, and 246 died; however, Galveston did not experience a severe epidemic that year. Mosquitoes are the carriers of the virus that causes the fever, and after 1867 improved sanitation and mosquito control decreased the number and severity of the epidemics (*New Handbook of Texas*, 2:877–78; David G. McComb, *Houston: A History*, pp. 61–62; David G. McComb, *Galveston: A History*, pp. 92–97).

[3] No published report of the axe murder case has been found.

[4] When Gideon abandoned the well-drilling project in November 1860 (after significant rainfall occurred), a depth of two hundred feet had been reached and the well produced water (but not artesian flow). The site of this well remained visible on the Lincecum homestead in 1993, although the well was not in use (Lincecum, Phillips, and Redshaw, *Science on the Texas Frontier*, pp. 114–15).

[5] The Washington County Rail Road Company was chartered in 1856 to construct a railroad from a connection with the Galveston and Red River Railway Company to Brenham. Construction began at Hempstead in 1858 and the railroad began operating in 1860, but it was another year before train service extended to Chappell Hill and Brenham. It remained in operation throughout the Civil War, thereby enabling Gideon and others in the area to receive regular deliveries of newspapers and other communications from the Texas coast. By contrast, Austin was relatively isolated and starved for reports on the progress of the war (*New Handbook of Texas*, 6:836–37).

[6] "Cassandra" is Cassandra Lincecum Durham, Gideon's daughter, who lived in Austin.

As the spring of 1860 advanced, Gideon was too busy with his scientific projects and well drilling to spend much time fighting the abolitionists, but he fired an occasional salvo to express his resentment of Yankee attitudes and aims. His link with Northern Infidels and Spiritualists was becoming more and more tenuous.

Long Point. Texas. 13th May. 1860

J. P. Mendum
103 Court St. Boston.

Inclosed please find $2—subscription for Volume 30. Boston Investigator.

I thought I would not take the paper any longer, but you have forwarded the first number of the New Volume. I took it from the office, and after reading it, concluded to send the money for it again, and that I would continue to take it until you and your religious, spiritual, and political associates shall spoil our good government; when I shall positively cease to subscribe to it, except you publish it on this side of the dividing line.[1]

I have no complaint to make at you, nor instructions to offer. Neither shall I grumble at you at any time for doing just what you "damn please"; but should your action in siding with the fanatic enemies of the American government get any worse, I can do as all good Infidel democrats would—just let you alone.

Religion and politics on both sides of the Mason & Dixon's line (I have allusion to the leaders only) are heartily opposed to a republican form of government; and he that takes sides with either of them is but one of two things.

The Editor of the Investigator has dealt out his billingsgate pretty freely to everyone who felt aggrieved and named it—at the course the paper had taken in politics—Negrotics—Well, let him go ahead.[2] I remain Infidel to all subjects requiring conventions, oaths, prayers, gods, devils, or spirits.

Gideon Lincecum 70.

[In fact his age was sixty-seven.]

[1] By 1 April 1857, the *Boston Investigator* (p. 2) was commenting on its loss of numerous subscribers from the South because of the issue of slavery. It is somewhat surprising that Gideon chose to renew his subscription in 1860.

[2] Gideon refers to the fact that Southerners who wrote to the paper complaining about its pro-abolition stance were given a stinging response by the editor. For example, on 19 December 1860 the editor printed a letter from a subscriber in Buckhorn, Mississippi, canceling his subscription: "I am well pleased with the paper, but as the Northern States have nullified the Constitution, viz., the Fugitive Slave Law, I think it high time for the South to withhold any sympathy from the Northern States." The editor commented as follows: "The orthography in Mr. Coleman's manuscript is laid aside, and the Northern style substituted, as we presume there is nothing in that, at any rate, that is constitutional. . . . It strikes us that if we were a subscriber to a Southern infidel paper, and liked it, we would support it, even though the state where it was printed repudiated her debts, or drove out Northern people from her borders, or destroyed Northern papers coming in the mails to her Post Offices, or advised secession from the Union—all which things are as much a violation of the Constitution as the nullification of the Fugitive Slave Law, or any other law. However, each one to his fancy" (p. 6).

Gideon's equanimity, as well as that of most Texans, was upset in midsummer 1860 by the report of a sizable slave insurrection in several parts of the state. Although in retrospect the insurrection seems to have been more imagined than real, the report gained credibility with the telling, as rumors spread rapidly from one community to another. Alarms were sounded, volunteers assembled, and vigilante "justice" was applied all too swiftly and indiscriminately. Whatever the facts of the plot were, most Texans (including Gideon), believed a dastardly rebellion, fomented by Northern abolitionists directly or indirectly, had taken place. Gideon described the disturbance in several letters:

Long Point. Texas. 15 Aug. 1860

D. B. Moore
Emily Moore
Hondo Valley, Texas
Dear Brother and Sister.

Your kind letter of 18th ultimo came to hand about a week since, finding us all well, and I should have replied sooner but we were at the time it came, passing under the ordeal of a negro insurrection, which required a whole week to suppress and ferret out the cause.[1] We have discovered that the negroes were instigated to make the attempt by traveling book agents, map peddlers, and Northern Methodist preachers. A good many of those godly negro lovers have already been hung up, and as many more are now under examination.[2] We also find that the germans were extensively concerned in it. But I will not consume my time and space, by giving the particulars of the frustrated outbreak, as the news papers are full of it, and to them I refer you. . . .

Fraternally,
Gideon Lincecum

[1] A number of fires did break out in midsummer 1860 in north and east Texas, touching off a wave of hysteria against slaves and suspected agitators; however, most of the fires were probably started accidentally, as weather conditions were very hot and dry. Several editors recklessly passed along the rumors, adding to the hysteria (Donald E. Reynolds, *Editors Make War: Southern Newspapers in the Secession Crisis*, pp. 97–116. See also William W. White, "The Texas Slave Insurrection of 1860," *Southwestern Historical Quarterly* 52, no. 3 [1949]: 259–85; Addington, "Slave Insurrection in Texas"; and Michael Phillips, "White Violence, Hegemony, and Slave Rebellion in Dallas, Texas, before the Civil War," *East Texas Historical Journal* 37, no. 2 [1999]: 25–35).

[2] One authority has estimated that there were at least fifty hangings (Reynolds, *Editors Make War*, p. 107).

Gideon gave further details in a letter to his nephew.

Long Point. Texas. 18 August 1860

Nephew John
Bear Creek, La.

Your very kind letter of 31st ult. came to hand three or four days ago. . . .

We are just passing through the ordeal of a negro insurrection here that has worried our young men considerably. The negroes were incited to rebel by a set of northern fanatics who are prowling about through the country, preaching, selling maps, mending clocks &c. &c. We have hung a good many of them, amongst whom were four or five preachers. As is the custom in the world's history of such matters, the insurrection and the mischief they done was all conducted in the name of the Lord. Poor Lord, he stands a bad chance to sustain a good character, for the damndest rascals perform their villainies in his name universally. In this portion of the state there was no mischief done but the negroes nearly all knew of the movement, and were prevented doing anything by the timely interference of the white people. It seems to have been a pretty general thing throughout the state, and some counties have suffered great loss from the fires that occurred from the influence of the infernal plot. Five or six towns in the upper counties have been almost entirely destroyed by fire, under circumstance that leaves no room for conjecture in the case at all.[1] Already 30 or 40 negroes and 10 or 12 white men have been hung or shot; our jails are full of prisoners and vigilent committees are making daily discoveries, & I have but little doubt of there being many more of the heartless scoundrels who will yet be detected. Preachers of the gospel are being looked upon with suspicion. . . .

Give my love to your mother and afflicted father with all the rest of the family, not leaving out old Lewis. And believe me as ever, in righteousness, thine

Gideon Lincecum

[1] Although much less extensive than Gideon believed, fires that contributed to the alarm occurred in Dallas, Denton, Pilot Point, Ladonia, Honey Grove, Belknap, and Henderson (Reynolds, *Editors Make War*, pp. 97, 101).

Many Texans remained wary and even trigger- (or noose-) happy for weeks after the alleged rebellion, as Gideon reported:

Long Point. Texas. 16 Sept. 1860

C. S. Cook[1]
Mason City, Ill.
Dear Sir

Your kind letter of 29th ult. came to my table yesterday, and I was pleased to hear from you and my old friend John G. [Douglas] and also that you were all doing well.[2] . . . there has been no sickness of any kind this year in our county anywhere that I have heard of. In this county we have barely made corn enough for bread, and it is said by travellers that the crops of this county are better than common. There is, however, no danger of a famine.

As to politics we hear but little said on the subject. In fact we have been too much engaged in hanging and cutting those reckless simpletons who are sent out here by northern fanatics—haters of a free Government—to disturb the peace of our negroes. They are the greatest fools in the land. Notwithstanding the fact that they have failed everywhere and have been hung up like dogs, by the dozen; our negroes every few days bring in a new one to be done the same way.

Nothing of interest having turned up since you left, I will close. Give my respects to Douglas, and receive for myself your prayers.

Gideon Lincecum

[1] No C. S. Cook was listed in the 1860 Census for Mason County, Illinois (Eighth Census, 1860).

[2] John G. Douglas was listed in the 1860 Census as residing in Mason City, Illinois (Eighth Census, 1860). Gideon wrote him a friendly letter at that address on 14 January 1860. See Lincecum, Phillips, and Redshaw, *Science on the Texas Frontier*, p. 108.

A month later, Gideon described the insurrection in more modest terms but leveled both barrels at those he was convinced were behind it:

Long Point. Texas. 12 Oct$^{r.}$ 1860

D. B. & Emily Moore
Castroville, Texas
Dear Brother & Sister.

. . . Our Negro insurrection has quietly subsided, and but few negroes had to be hung; none in our portion of the state. Some of them were severely punished, but no facts of importance have been ellicited by it. The real abolition movement was really confined to the upper and more northern counties. The performance with the vigilent committees are now principally employed in ferreting out the villianous white incindiaries who have been inciting our slaves to insurrection. They are picking up one almost weekly: they are all religionists and most of them priests. Damn the priests universally, for they are the cause of all the real sufferings among us, both civil and political; it is clearly attributable to them.

But that is too disagreeable a matter to put in a letter . . . .

Receive our best prayer[s]—and they are first rate—for your wellfare and long pleasant continuance here below.

Your Brother
Gid

Gideon's growing resentment over Northern agitation on the issue of slavery spilled over into his cherished field of science, souring his attitude toward some of the leading scientists in the nation, as the following letter to Benjamin Silliman and James Dwight Dana, distinguished professors at Yale, attests.[1]

Long Point. Texas. 5 November 1860

Messrs. Silliman & Dana
Gentln.

Your circular, accompanying the prospectus of the somewhat respectable and long established "Silliman's Journal," was handed to me by our worthy P[ost] M[aster] several days ago.

The circular is sufficiently polite and the prospectus promises enough. I have no fault to find in that direction. But how are we of the <u>South</u> to have faith in the hearty reality of the one or the honest fulfillment of the other? We think it quite soon, after the destruction of property over the South by hireling incendiaries from the "immigrant aid societies of New England," for the members of that society to solicit our patronage.[2] We have not forgotten that notorious "Sharp's Rifle."[3] Neither has it escaped our recollection that a certain "great" man figured as the distinguished leader in getting up that <u>great</u> memorial to Congress; and so on to the end of the chapter.[4]

I am in possession of ample means, but cannot consent to patronize a paper conducted by men whose want of political honesty permits them to sacrifice their philosophy to fanaticism or to sectional political purposes—men whose knowledge of Natural Science is so defective, so superficial, that they can see no impropriety in advocating and contributing material aid to the foolish doctrine that "a negro is a white man with a black skin," cannot possess the capacity to instruct "earnest" seekers of scientific truth to any considerable extent.

We are fond of and do labor in the extended planes and open fields of the natural and physical sciences; but we do not confound them with the desire to promote sectionalism, fanaticism, or incindiarism. Progressive science favors, not war but minds of the masses, not distrust and discord, but confidence in Union and fraternal reciprocality.

Don't be offended for you are wrong!

Very Respectfully
Your Obt. Servnt.
Gideon Lincecum

[1] A chemist and geologist, Benjamin Silliman Sr. (1770–1864), was a professor at Yale University for fifty-one years and helped organize Yale Medical School. In 1818 he founded the *American Journal of Science and Arts*, which was known as *Silliman's Journal* and became one of the world's leading scientific journals. His son, Benjamin Jr. (1816–85), worked with his father at Yale and served as assistant editor (and later as editor, 1838–85) of *Silliman's Journal*. He was also a professor of chemistry at Yale. Father and son were both original members of the National Academy of Sciences, founded 1863 (*Dictionary of American Biography*, 9:160–63, 163–64). James Dwight Dana (1813–95) was professor of natural history at Yale from 1856 to 1864, after which he served as professor of geology and mineralogy from 1864 to 1890. A son-in-law of Benjamin Silliman Sr., Dana in 1840 joined Benjamin Silliman Jr. as an editor of the *American Journal of Science and Arts* (*Dictionary of American Biography*, 3:55–56).

[2] Competition between the North and South resulted in organized efforts to encourage migration to Kansas. The immigrant (or

emigrant) aid societies were founded in the 1850s in New England and New York to promote the settlement of antislavery supporters in the Kansas-Nebraska territory (Current, ed., *Encyclopedia of the Confederacy*, 1:175–76).

[3] John Brown was furnished with Sharps rifles by abolitionist organizations, including some emigrant aid societies dedicated to keeping Kansas free of slavery. Brown used these rifles in his raid on Harper's Ferry in October 1859 (David M. Potter, *The Impending Crisis, 1848–1861*, pp. 206–7).

[4] The identity of the "certain great man" whom Gideon had in mind is uncertain, although it may well have been the antislavery clergyman Henry Ward Beecher, who said, during the struggle between pro- and antislavery forces, that Sharps rifles would do more than Bibles to enforce morality in Kansas just then. The guns became known as "Beecher's Bibles" (McPherson, *Ordeal by Fire*, p. 96).

This was strong, even reckless, language indeed, attributable not only to Gideon's characteristically blunt nature but also to the high temperature the sectional crisis had reached. The letter was written one day before Abraham Lincoln was elected to the presidency of a deeply divided nation.

Chapter 2

Secession

The election of the Republican Lincoln (or, as Gideon put it, the defeat of the proslavery Democrat, John C. Breckinridge), was the last straw that broke the Union. Within a week the South Carolina legislature unanimously called a state convention for the purpose of secession. Even before that convention met and took its fateful step on 20 December 1860, Gideon was ready and expecting Texas to follow South Carolina's lead. To his nephew he wrote,

Long Point. Texas. 3 Decr. 1860

Nephew John
Bear Creek, La.

Your kind letter of 4th ultimo did not come to hand until last friday. It was handed round amongst the connection and read with seeming interest, except the political portion of it. We are all opposed to submission in any form that can be named. It would make very little difference with us, which of the three, Bell, Douglas, or Lincoln shall be elected, as we would not tamely submit to the rule of either.[1] We are however, glad that the election has terminated in the manner it has, as it leaves no plausible excuse for remaining in the confederacy [Union].[2] The government has failed, almost in every instance, to comply with her part in the articles of annexation, and we have been wishing for an excuse for seperation for five or six years. We have a fair one now, and from the signs and preperations which are being had throughout our state, I give it as my opinion that we shall be cut loose by next 4th. of March.

We are very capable of sustaining an independent government, and with our very abundant rich resources, a very wealthy one. We know the value of our cotton and sugar, will engage the attention, and if we require it, the assistance of foreign powers; and we'll call them, most certainly, before we will agree to yield our necks to the yoke that has been prepared for us by Northern fanaticism. It would have prolonged our sufferings for either of the other candidates to have triumphed.

We are all in good health but as poor as Job's turkey. It has been so long since we made anything that we could spare, that there is no money in the country. And the crop of corn that was cribbed by them that made any to crib is not fit for a preacher to eat, mean as they are. . . .

We are all here excited to the highest pitch. Mass meetings, conventions, and minute men is all the go. Lone Star flags and blue cockades are fluttering to every breeze and glittering on every hat, as well as on the breast of many of our patriotic ladies.[3]

We do not desire any fuss or fighting; but we intend to withdraw from the federal Union, and we are organizing, arming, and equipping ourselves for the purpose of sustaining our republic in a stile that will deter invasion. We never have, nor do we ever intend to be, the aggressors in any contingency; and we are a people peculiarly adapted for being mightily in the way, and hellish troublesome to any people or party who may take it into there hands to molest us—that's all.

We have no dangue [dengue fever] or sickness of any type in this vicinity this year. Nothing but drouth, no deaths or marriages. We might have had some marriages; but when they tried they were so infernal poor that they possessed no adhesive properties, and so they could not be made to stick. I said above that we have had no deaths. I meant natural deaths. Of course we have a good deal of very nice deaths from the playful process of suspension [hanging], and the season for it is not over yet. So far the work has been confined to the gospel promulgators; and we have swung so many of them, it does not seem that there can be many more. As soon as we find that we are through with them, we shall have time to wait on their deluded flocks. But why preserve their contaminated flocks? There will be no danger of losing seed of the genus, if we swing superstition all up. . . .

Immigrants are crowding in upon us. They will see hard times the coming season, those who have not brought enough money with them to secure bread from our sea ports. They have run off with their negroes, most of them from the border states to get them out of the way of the hell-bent fanatics. I suppose they think it better to risk starvation here, than the loss of their property where they came from. What a damnable fix that is for a people to be placed in; and all done too in the name of the lord. Poor lord, his followers are no credit to him. For my part I wish him success, and I do hope he may think of it, turn honest, and earnestly try to get his affairs in a condition that will redound more to his credit. If he don't soon, he'd better quit.

Present me affectionately to your mother and father, and to all the rest—and my old playmate Lewis Shellhouse. Tell your good wife to think of, and you do the same—

Your Uncle
Gid

[1] John Bell (1797–1869), former congressman and senator from Tennessee, was the presidential candidate of the Constitutional Union Party, which appealed to moderates on the sectional crisis (James M. McPherson, *Battle Cry of Freedom: The Civil War Era*, pp. 221–22. See also Joseph H. Parks, *John Bell of Tennessee*). Sen. Stephen A. Douglas (1813–61) of Illinois had won the nomination of the Democratic Party but only after the Radical Southern Democrats had bolted from two conventions held in Charleston and Baltimore (McPherson, *Battle Cry of Freedom*, pp. 213–16. See also Robert W. Johannsen, *Stephen A. Douglas*).

[2] Although Lincoln was elected president, all of his 180 electoral votes came from Northern states. Douglas won only 12 electoral votes; Breckinridge won 72 and Bell, 39. In the popular vote, Lincoln re-

ceived 1,864,735, while the total for his opponents was 2,821,157 (McPherson, *Ordeal by Fire*, p. 129).

[3] Apparently, in Texas the flying of Lone Star flags was a widespread reaction to Lincoln's election. According to the *Galveston News* (22 November 1860), in a column headed "Public Sentiment in Texas," "the 'blue cockade and Texan star' have made their appearance on the streets of Houston." It also reported that "on the 16th at Brenham the citizens raised a tall liberty pole and from it the Lone Star flag floats." Another column noted that "so many 'Lone Stars' were never before seen in this city [Galveston]—not even in the days of the Republic—as have made their appearance with the past week, or since Lincoln's election has been known."

Gideon was not alone in his enthusiasm for the break from the Union. He wrote a description of the Long Point response a few days later:

9 December 1860

Editor—Brenham Inquirer.
What They Did at Long Point

The largest assemblage that has ever occurred at Long Point took place yesterday. It was occasioned by an appointment, previously made, for a meeting to organize a company of "Minute Men."

Quite early in the day, I observed three very pretty Lone Star flags at different points in the village, already hoisted and fluttering their tri-colored folds in the briskly moving South wind. Two of them were constructed after the pattern of the original Lone Star flag of Texas Republic. The other was a white flag; a crimson star, with a single blue stripe, lengthwise thru to center. I asked for the meaning of that single blue stripe. They told me that it was intended to represent that Texas can stand alone; and that sooner than submit to Black Republican rule, in any form that can be offered, she will try it.

On contemplating the two old Texas flags, as they gayly quivered to the wind, I could but reflect that there floats the emblem that was reluctantly hawled down when Texas was annexed, and as the Lone Star illumined the azure field, I was reminded of what Texas once was, and of what the misdirected, deluded people of the Northern section of these United States have forced us again to make it.

Both these old fashioned flags were bright and beautiful; and still more inspiring and endearing, on account of their being produced by private subscription and the handiwork of the patriotic ladies of Long Point and its vicinity. May they never feel the need of a protector.

Soon the people began to collect from all points of the compass. By 11 1/2 o'clock, the little town was full of men and horses. With the exception of three or four oppositionists, the Lone Star Cockade was to be seen on almost every hat, and all intent upon carrying out the object for which this meeting had been called. And now, at the fierce sound of the almost forgotten words, "Parade here, fall into ranks, men," the startled crowd dropped their various topics and filed into line. It was a pleasing sight; a sight that many of the brave looking young men, who stood up in the long line of determined spirits, had never before witnessed. There were three or four of them, however, whose flowing white beards and their easy, familiar manner of dropping into line indicated that they had seen service. Such for instance, was Col. S. D. Lauderdale, who during the continuance of the War of 1812 and 13 with the Creek Indians was the confidant of Genl. Jackson, and the active spirit among his staff officers.[1] [illegible] Belcher, who has always been here and fought through all the wars Texas ever had.[2]

The company at this, its first turn out, numbered 87. They immediately proceeded to organize, by electing the proper number of officers, which they soon completed, with harmony, and much apparent good feeling. And then, by vote, viva voce, still standing in ranks, they decided that the company should be a mounted Rifle Company armed with Hall's breach loading rifles and Colts Revolvers.[3] After which they appointed a committee to draft a set of by-laws, and also to designate an appropriate uniform. Many other regulations of minor importance was agreed to, and finally, the Captain requested the entire Company—and he also, extended the request, in the form of an invitation, to the quite numerous crowd who were spectators, and in hearing of his voice, to [attend] the mass meeting to be held at Brenham on the 15th. Instant.

And all this was so calmly and soberly enacted, and there was so much unanimity and chee[r]ful good feelings manifested by all the parties throughout the entire proceedings, that I, as a spectator of the performance, could plainly see that it was intended for no kind of child's play.

Gid.

[1] Samuel Lauderdale is listed in the 1860 Census as being age eighty-one and residing in Long Point (Eighth Census, 1860, Washington County, Tex., p. 152). Sam and his son James Lauderdale came to Texas in 1858 from Columbus, Mississippi (Burkhalter, *Gideon Lincecum*, p. 141n).

[2] Isham Belcher is listed in the 1860 Census as residing in Gay Hill (Eighth Census, 1860, Washington County, Tex., p. 150).

[3] In his rifle works along the Shenandoah River, John M. Hall (a native of Maine) developed a system of tools, machinery, and gauges that succeeded in establishing economical methods by which common workers could fabricate identical rifles (Current, ed., *Encyclopedia of the Confederacy*, 2:739–40).

There was some opposition in Texas to secession, especially in the northern counties and in the German settlements, and Gov. Sam Houston was loath to break the cord, but

Gideon was confident that the will of the majority favoring secession would prevail. To an old friend from earlier days east of the Mississippi he wrote:

Long Point. Texas. 12 Dec$^{r.}$ 1860

H. M. Thompson[1]
New Orleans, La.
My Dear Friend.

I was speaking yesterday of your protracted silence, and laid off to write a letter to you, enquiring the cause, in the evening; but we had company, and I, as a matter of course being consigned to the music stand, lost the time for the consummation of what I most desired. And so the matter was laid over to be fulfilled this evening. But while I was this morning at 10. o'clock engaged, compiling and writing out the notes of my observations on the laws, religion, works, manners and customs of the quite numerous, and extremely interesting forms of little animals, denominatd in "Holy Writ"—by way of derision as [I] suppose, "Pismire" [ant],[2] Sarah came tripping into my study and deposited on my table your welcome letter, bearing date of 4th. instant.

I am glad to find that you are still active, a condition that my mind was beginning to contemplate with some degree of doubt. Its all right now however, and I, in place of sorrying in uncertainty, am inditing, as well as I can, a communication to my long esteemed and never-to-be forgotten friend—associate and companion of my youthful amusements and sprightly plays. Well, in this long continued and intimate brotherly familiarity, I have, candidly, nothing to accuse you of, that will give his Satanic Majesty a chance at you; and so when they fire the reserection gun, there will be no use in calling me to the Witness Stand on your account.

I read the two discourses which you sent me, of the two New Orleans clergymen with deep interest.[3] I had seen both in the Delta of last week. I think well of the men and their political sentiments. The time has arrived, when men possessing such exalted talents should speak. They have done so, in a stile that must meet with the entire approbation of every man, who has not consented to become a slave to Northern arrogance.

So far Texas stands up pretty well. We were just now, based on information from all the counties, making an estimate of the proportion of the opposition to secession in our State. We made it out 9% with our Governor at the head of it. Volunteer companies are being organized in every portion of the State, and the people of all the counties are calling on their Chief Justices to order an election, for the purpose of electing delegates to a State Convention; Object, to take into consideration the proper course to persue &c in the secession movement. To avoid the daily application for him to make a move in the business, old Sam [Houston] has left his station at Austin, and is now off lecturing in favor of submission. On this account the people have taken the affairs of the State into their own hands, and from present manifestations, I think it quite probable that we shall have a State Convention, fresh from the people, on the fourth Monday of January 1861.[4]

Texas will secede, and would feel proud to have the whole South with her. She will fraternize with any number of seceding Southern States, but should all the rest submit, she will go alone.

The subject of secession is one with which the Texans are quite familiar. It has been discussed amongst us during the past four or five years. As one of the conditions in the Compact of annexation, the U.S. government obligated itself to protect our frontiers, for which we gave up the revenues from custom houses under the Lone Star Republic; we relinquished our arms, our navy, surrendered the power to levy war, and the means for its prosecution, on condition that we should have adequate protection from the general Government; and has not every stipulation been violated on the part of the Government![5] Forced to carry on our own wars, we must assume the means of prosecuting them, by controlling the resources arising from the imports. For this purpose, we are forced to return to our former nationality. This is a topic well understood here, and it has been the subject of discussion, with the people for several years. If their had been no excitement on other accounts, if the Government of the U.S. had continued to turn a deaf ear to our demands for justice another 12 months, secession would have been the consequence. So you see we are quite ripe for such a movement. We know it will better our condition, and we are sure to consumate secession. You may count us out now if you like.

Could you see and contemplate the meaning of the ten thousand Lone Star flags that are flutering to the winds, in every town, village and hamlet, over the whole State, you would think that to be the proper conclusion.

Believe me most sincerely,
Thine,
Gid.

[1] In an earlier letter to Thompson, Gideon indicates that they have known each other since 1822 and liked to send one another published material, such as the sermons enclosed by Thompson (Gideon Lincecum to Hugh Thompson, Long Point, Tex., 20 April 1858, LP, Box 2E364).

[2] Gideon studied ants for twenty-five years and published a number of articles. For a listing of his writings on this subject, see Lincecum, Phillips, and Redshaw, *Science on the Texas Frontier*, appendix 5.

[3] The two pro-secession clergymen in Louisiana were probably Dr. Benjamin M. Palmer and Dr. W. T. Leacock. Both defended the institution of slavery and upheld the right of a state to resist the

"Black Republican" North and to sever connections with a Union that intimidated and hampered the economic well being of that state. According to them, since compromise was impossible, the road ahead was clearly marked: Louisiana must secede (John D. Winters, *The Civil War in Louisiana*, p. 8).

[4] Ignoring Gov. Sam Houston, pro-secession leaders called for a state convention, and 92 of the 122 organized counties selected delegates. On 28 January 1861, the convention met in Austin in the house chamber, with slightly fewer than 180 delegates present. On 1 February the convention voted for secession, 166 to 8, but submitted the ordinance to the people, who ratified it on 23 February by a vote of 46,153 to 14,747, with more than 62 percent of the electorate voting (Walter L. Buenger, *Secession and the Union in Texas*, pp. 141–43, 148, 174).

[5] It is not hard to rebut Gideon's claim that the U.S. government had violated "every stipulation" of the annexation treaty. For example, the government had erected many forts and stationed many troops on the Texas-Mexican border and the Indian frontier to protect the Texas population. With irony, the *Boston Investigator* printed a contrary view on this subject with the heading "The Right of Secession": "The New York *Evening Post*, in discussing the pretence that a state has a right to secede from the Union at will, thus puts the case in a way that needs no answer:—

'Texas, when she came into the Union after we had paid many millions to discharge her debts, and other millions to go into her coffers, was and is, according to this theory, entirely at liberty to secede with the booty. Each and all, the states carved out of the Louisiana Purchase, for which we paid such an immense sum, may do the like'" (*Boston Investigator*, 21 November 1860, p. 7).

Gideon's family and neighbors in Long Point shared his enthusiasm for leaving the Union, as he described in another letter to one of the newspapers:

[undated—mid-December 1860]

Long Point. Minute Men

Mr. Editor:

Pursuant to adjournment of last Saturday, the Long Point Volunteers met today in full force; enrolled three new members; had the names of five more, who could not attend this meeting, sent in to them, which now raises the list to between 95 and 100 strong.

After maneuvering and drilling about an hour, they received an invitation to form in front of the dwelling of L. L. Lincecum,[1] which they did in good stile, and from thence the ladies of the village came out and present[ed] the company, through their representative, Miss Sallie Lincecum, with a very pretty flag, which was made after the pattern of the old flag of the Texas Republic. And while in the act of handing the flag to the Captain of the company, she delivered the following charge, — (I shall not insert it here, as it is herewith enclosed.[2] She handed it to me this morning; it is in her own writing, and she bids me say, that you are at liberty to publish it if you think it worth the trouble). The Captain politely received the flag; complimented the ladies, and in the name of his company assured them that the charge just received from their fair representative should be obeyed to the letter. He then with a few, but appropriate, remarks, passed the flag to his ensign. When the company gave three hearty cheers for the ladies, three cheers for the flag, and three cheers for the company; when they marched to the Company's Rooms, and resolved themselves into an organization for business, by calling C. B. Shepherd to the chair.[3] The committee which had been appointed at the previous meeting for that purpose reported a pretty rigid set of bylaws, which were read and adopted unanimously. Then they voted "Long Point Minute Men" as the name of the company and adjourned.

[signed] A Spectator

[1] Leonidas L. Lincecum, one of Gideon's sons.

[2] Among the loose papers in Box 2E363 of the Lincecum Papers is the following undated item, on two pages of a folded piece of notepaper, written in a different hand from Gideon's. It is signed with the initials "S. L." at the bottom, and while it may be addressed to another group of soldiers, we believe it is at least the analog of Sallie Lincecum's address to the Long Point Minute Men:

> *Lieut. Shepherd & Gentlemen of the Davis Mounted Riflemen.*
>
> *From time immemorial it has been the custom for the ladies to present banners, and make speeches of encouragement in time of war, to the military of their country. But now when peace and liberty, the shrine of each patriot's devotion, lie bleeding at our feet; when our whole country is moved with the excitement of a call to arms, to meet a heartless foe, whose only incentive is rapine, and plunder; whose watch-word, for the encouragement of their brutalized myrmidons, is beauty and booty, and whose beastly acts on the occasions they have met with opportunity to manifest them, would shame the veriest savage, it is not to be wondered that the angel of vengeance even, should wave his flaming wings over the confederate states, until the last spark of resentment shall be kindled in the coldest heart. It is no wonder then, that we see the gatherings, the running to and fro, and the great manifestation of the martial spirit of the young braves of our lovely country; for if ever there was a cause for a universal movement, among any people, that cause is ours. If there be such a thing as the principle of justice, that too is ours, and should be inscribed in letters of terror to the dastard foe, on every banner that waves over the victorious armies of the Southern Confederacy. I speak that as a <u>prophetess!</u> And now receive this banner with my blessing, Go brave men to the battlefield, not doubting for one moment the justness of your cause. Go into the fray calmly but determined never to turn from the foe, till you see them bite the dust. May the Laurels you win never wither, nor the star of your glory grow dim.*

Tis on the battlefield forsooth,
The bleaching bones of age and youth,
Lie mangled by the ruthless hand
Of some low dastard lawless band.
And e'er anon is heard the sigh
My country bade me, and I die!—S.L.

[3] C. B. Sheppard [*sic*], age forty-seven, is listed as residing in Union Hill in the 1860 Census (Eighth Census, 1860, Washington County, Tex., p. 168). The census lists as part of the household two sons, Chencey [*sic*], age seventeen, and Seth, age thirteen. Burkhalter identifies the father as Chauncey Berkeley Shepard, who served as state senator from Washington County from 1856 to 1864 (Burkhalter, *Gideon Lincecum*, pp. 152n, 260n). The elder son, Chauncey, served on the staff of Gen. Tom Green and was killed at the Battle of Mansfield in 1864 (Marcus J. Wright, comp., and Harold B. Simpson, ed., *Texas in the War, 1861–65*, p. 6). Seth served in the Confederate army during the last months of the Civil War and went on to become a state legislator (*New Handbook of Texas*, 5:1014).

Separation from the Union would not necessarily be a blessing to Gideon, for it might sever some of his scientific contacts in the North. To his friend, Yankee-born Samuel Botsford Buckley in Austin, he mentioned the prospect.[1]

Long Point. Texas. 19 Dec$^{r.}$ 1860

Prof. S. B. Buckley
Austin, Texas
My Dear Sir.

Your very welcome letter of the 16th instant reached me this morning. In my reply to its contents, I shall be guilty of patronizing a figure in holy writ, by attending to the "last first and the first last."

No, I have not sent my plants to Philadelphia yet;[2] and under the present aspect of our national affairs, I am of opinion that it would not be strictly in accordance with a prudent degree of self respect for me to do so, until I know what kind of people it is, who are to receive them. If they are Black Republicans, they cannot be expected to be endowed with a sufficient amount of correct intelligence to instruct community on the subject of the natural and physical sciences. This much I must know before they can enjoy the benefits of my researches. When I am certified that they are men of a true liberal stamp; there is nothing that would give me so much pleasure, nor is there any employment that would be so freely performed as that of making up contributions in aiding the progressive sciences. And so it must stand with me. . . .

If those fellows at Philadelphia should turn out to be of the Black Stripe, what good reason is there, why Sarah and myself should not bestow our 800 specimens on our own State?

What though the poor fellows at the North are ignorant? have embibed that ignorance and consequent aptitude to wrong doing, from the breasts of their priest ridden mothers; it is meaness nevertheless, and I have no disposition to encourage it by withholding from them my knowledge of the damnable facts.—Anyhow, what is there to prevent us of Texas from setting up for ourselves! When we again unfurl the Lone Star Banner, we'll do that. You and I can start it now, by a careful collection and preservation of specimens of every thing we can get hold of belonging to the natural science first; and then—

I know where Dr. Cartwright's Formica resides.[3] Our cutting ants are in all respects, equally interesting. They too, practice in all its ramifications, what our theiving brethren of a portion of the North, in their ignorance of ethnologic facts, are pleased to term the "peculiar southern institution," and there are no black republicans, or sneaking, hireling incindiaries, working with their slave population. They are, within their own kingdoms, or communities all honest, have perfected their Government; and this is made manifest by the notable fact that every one knows his place and his duty, and will maintain and perform it or sacrafice his life in the attempt. This is far in advance of the highest developments of the genus homo; and to my mind, is satisfactory evidence, that as a race, they have occupied the Earth much longer than the human; for he has not perfected his government, by a million or two of centuries yet. Wouldn't you hate to be a spirit, and have to wait all that time for men to become honest to let you alone with your ants and bugs and grass and weeds and things? Write often—

Thine in Christ.
Gideon Lincecum.

[1] Samuel Botsford Buckley (1809–83) was born and educated in the North but did most of his research in the South. He came to Texas in 1860 and later became Texas state geologist. He and Gideon became active correspondents and friends (*New Handbook of Texas*, 1:803–4).

[2] Despite his hesitation, Gideon did send the collection of plants to his friend (by correspondence) Élie (Elias) Magloire Durand (1794–1873). Born in France, he came to the United States in 1816 and in 1825 opened in Philadelphia a pharmacy that became an informal clubhouse for scientists. He was elected in 1824 to the Philadelphia Academy and to the College of Pharmacy, and in 1854 to the American Philosophical Society (*Dictionary of American Biography*, 3[1]:538–40).

[3] Formica is a Latin term for ants. Dr. Cartwright has not been identified. Here Gideon mixes comments on politics and politicians with a subject and a species he found more congenial, the ant.

Despite the possible loss of his association with Northern scientists, Gideon was full of anticipation of the secession of his state. But he was concerned that Gov. Sam Houston might prevent it, as he wrote in a letter to his son-in-law:

Long Point. Texas. Dec$^{r.}$ 20 1860

G. J. Durham
Austin, Texas
My Dear Sir.

I was told this evening that the Governor has issued his proclamation to convene this Legislature on the 17th of January.[1] I shall not attempt to question his reasons for doing so; but there may be mischief in the movement; and I hope that the simultaneous and unanimous call of the people from every portion of the State for a State convention will not, now it is progressing so vigorously, be retarded by it. As far as the election of delegates to the convention is concerned, there must be no attention paid to his proclamation, if it is true that he has issued one.

The movement for getting up a state convention, which was started at Austin, has been everywhere responded to. It was the men and the manner the call was made that excited the cheerful and willing response. And now if it is true that there is a proclamation for convening a state legislature, it can produce nothing but procrastination, and of that we are already sick. I suggest that yourself and Johns, Rector Fry, White and as many of those clever boys as you can get together, who had a hand in getting out the call for a convention, meet again and get out another, of encouragement to the people to go on with the election.[2] It is their own business and must not be stopped.

Thine.
Gid

[1] Actually, the governor called for the legislature to convene in special session on 21 January 1861, hoping that it would slow down

or stop the steamroller that was rushing toward secession (Buenger, *Secession and the Union in Texas*, p. 143).

[2] "Johns" is identified as Clement R. Johns of Hays County, "Rector Fry" as J. E. Rector of Travis County and James H. Fry of Webberville, and "White"as George W. White of Travis County in Burkhalter, *Gideon Lincecum*, p. 140n.

The next day Gideon, full of enthusiasm, wrote to a German friend residing in a nearby community who, unlike some Germans in Texas, supported the Confederacy.[1]

Long Point. Tex. 21 Dec[r.] 1860

G. W. Willrich[2]
Independence, Texas
My Dear Friend.

Your kind letter of 19th inst. did not reach me until about sunset this evening. . . .

I give honor to the patriotism, if you please, especially to the Ladies. May they always find protectors. It is the same way here. We are all secessionists, and our Ladies are daily employed making Banners and Lone Star Cockades for our large company of "Minute Men," which now numbers 95, and will at our next meeting be greatly increased. The Germans are enrolling their name freely. You ask for my opinon of the government. Well, <u>disruption is certain</u>. If we manage it on the true basis of our reserved rights, we shall have no war. Splits in our own ranks will encourage invasion. Let us stand firm. Compliments to your good Lady, and believe me thine in these wars.

Gideon Lincecum

[1] For a discussion of Texas German dissent from the Confederacy, see James Marten, *Texas Divided: Loyalty and Dissent in the Lone Star State, 1856–1874*, pp. 27–28, 31–32, 113–21.

[2] G. W. Willrich is listed in the 1860 Census as residing in Independence (Eighth Census, 1860, Washington County, Tex., p. 153).

Not all Texans were as eager for the break as Gideon. Some advised caution, and others hesitated. Gideon was impatient with such timidity. To a gentleman in the largely German community of Round Top, he wrote,

Long Point. Texas. 27 Decr. 1860

Aurelius G. Ledbetter[1]
Round Top, Texas
My Dear Sir.

Your favor enclosing the letter of Judge McFarland was received today.[2] For it you are entitled to my hearty thanks, and also for your frank declaration that the letter expresses your views on the subject upon which it treats. It enables me to know how you stand in regard to the propriety or impropriety of a judicious and timely preparation for coming events.

I agree with the Judge as to the propriety of calmness, deliberation, and united action amongst us. But how are we, if we make no general movement in that direction, to find out whether the people are united or not?

The Judge's answers to the question, "What are the wrongs of which we complain?" are a long way short of existing facts, and if it is not his intention to retard the progress of suitable preparation, whereby to enable ourselves to be ready to meet the pressing emergencies, which are actually threatening us on every side, I cannot imagine what he does mean. What harm can there be in organization? How can it damage our cause, for us to be ready to defend it? Does he fear that it would make a fuss? And what are you afraid of?

With great Respect,
I remain as ever.
Gideon Lincecum.

[1] Aurelius G. Ledbetter is listed in the 1860 Census as residing in Round Top (Eighth Census, 1860, Fayette County, Tex., p. 282).

[2] Judge McFarland is identified as Judge Isaac Burton McFarland in Burkhalter, *Gideon Lincecum*, p. 142.

Amidst all this excitement and concern, Gideon found time to write a long letter to his fellow naturalist Charles Darwin in England. He expressed his own views on the theory of natural selection and cited in considerable detail his research on Texas ants. Before closing the letter, he stated, "I am a native American, born in the smoke of our first revolution; was raised and have always been a dweller in the wild border countries, and now, I think the chances are pretty good for me to make my exit in the turmoil and smoke of another revolution."[1]

Early in the fateful new year of 1861, Gideon wrote at length to one of his favorite "Infidel" correspondents in north Texas and gloried in his independence from religion and, in all probability, from the Federal Union as well:

Long Point. Texas. 4 Janry. 1861

John A. Rutherford[2]
Honey Grove, Texas

Yes. Standing barefoot—as is the rule—in the doorway at the first gleam of dawning light, christmas morning; I performed, three times over, the "christmas tune" etc.[3] That made the fiftieth time without missing a single christmas. It's getting to be somewhat of a serious affair with me. It brings around me crowds of bright faces—I can see their very eyes, and hear their joyous words—that are long gone, passed away to be seen no more. No. I shall never more behold any of them. Decomposition has had charge of them, and scattered the atoms of which they were built up, into their original elements; and there mixing with the atoms of millions of similar and dissimilar organisms, has placed it beyond the reach of possibility even, for the powers of recomposition ever again, either intentionally, or by accident, to gather up those atoms; the atoms of which my dead friends were composed and build them up again. No, no, no they are gone to be seen no more, in this, or any of the other worlds. As to the bible promise, that we shall be renewed and fitted for the enjoyment of a higher life, it is as physically impossible, as it is philosophically foolish. Stop the pay from the makers and venders of these foolish falsehoods, and soon, very soon, the gospel trump would cease to sound. Or do as you say, obliterate the bible and the impression it has made on the world's mind, and we should have peace on earth until they made another bible for us. But that however, wouldn't take them long. The material for such false books to rest upon is always here with us. It's the undeveloped condition of the masses—ignorance. We shall always have full crops of this, rain or shine, so long as the rights of society are so little understood as to allow them calmly to permit the ill-shaped, immoral specimens of the races to produce their kind. Another thing which stands in the way of progressive mental development is the historical fact that there have been in all ages men born with superior abilities; men who knew how and were sufficiently dishonest to profit by the errors and the ignorance of the masses. Priests of all religions have lived in idleness and fattened on the fears of the undeveloped multitude. In opposition [to] these progress checking, long faced, misanthropic rascals, in all ages and countries men have appeared who dared to speak the truth. But what could the feeble voice of truth effect against errors imbibed at the breast of a priestridden mother? . . .

Like begets like. The laws of hereditary transmission cannot be overruled. When the horse and the mare both trot, the colt seldom paces, as the saying goes. I never have gambled, or bet on anything in my life; but to show you how much confidence I place in my knowledge of the unvarying laws of hereditary transmission, the power inherent in the organism of the parents to impress, mould and shape, both the physical and mental systems of the embryon[ic] fetus, in utero, as well as after its birth, I am willing to hazzard a few hundreds on a bet that I can send an order to any of the New England states, and have a pair of people—male and female—bred, to fill any description of fanatic that can be written, from the moderate admirers of the odor that eminates from the inguinal regions of the lusty negro, to the enthusiastic ranter who would, in an ecstasy of delight, snuff his stink and wallow in unnatural conjugal union with him; and as one of the conditions in the bet too, I will obligate that all this shall be done in the name of the Lord. In case of such a bet, I should require that the parents be native New Englanders, belong to some church; the mother, during the period of gestation, from a few weeks previous to conception, must have the visits of a healthy abolition priest; the children, as soon as they are old enough, must go regularly to the Sunday schools and preachings, and at the ends of twenty years the judges shall decide who is the winner. All this and thousands of other conditions, some called good, and others bad, in the animal and vegetable kingdoms, that cannot be named in this letter, are the natural subjects of physiological law, now well understood by many investigators of the natural sciences. And there is no more God in it than I am in it. Not quite so much—for I am 180 pounds in it. He is nowhere!

I am glad to hear that you are all well, that you are expecting the return of your long absent sons, and that your friend "Gus" is married; may his union in the conjugal state improve the type.[4]

Gus did write me a long letter, stating the fact of his having married a religious companion; how he could get along in it

&c. I wish him well, but cannot agree on his politics. What harm can there be in organizing our military strength? How can it damage our cause for us to prepare and hold ourselves ready to defend it? Is he afraid that if we do our own business in our own way that it will raise a fuss with some of the other states? If we make no movement for the purpose of ascertaining our strength, how shall we know, when the time comes, whether we ought to go back or forth? But everybody knows all about this matter, and I will not discuss it here. As to my fears of the danger of leaving our families in care of the negroes while we go to war, I may say to you that I entertain vastly more confidence in the negroes than I do in any of the infernal, fanatic, abolition race. I shall be proud if all the slave holding states shall withdraw from the federal compact. If seven or eight, if two or three only, I shall be glad and shall be with them. If Texas alone declares her independence, I am still pleased and will hang to her destiny. But if she too submits, I shall have but one alternative left me. And that is to declare independence within the boundary of my own domain and maintain it as long as I have life. I'll do that if the worst comes.

I have not replied to all the points in your letter, please excuse me. We are all well. We have suspended operating on the well, on account of having to carry our cattle off where we could find water and grass.

Fraternally thine
Gideon Lincecum

[1] For the full text of this letter, see Lincecum, Phillips, and Redshaw, *Science on the Texas Frontier*, pp. 23–26.

[2] John A. Rutherford was listed in the 1860 Census as residing at Honey Grove (Eighth Census, 1860, Fannin County, Tex., p. 176). Born in Tennessee, he was sixty-one and had a wife and two sons, ages sixteen and thirteen (both born in Texas). His occupation was "Gentleman" and his real property was valued at forty thousand dollars. In *First Settlers of the Republic of Texas*, edited by Carolyn

R. Ericson and Frances T. Ingmire, he is listed as having been granted a league and a labor of land (2:100). He and Gideon exchanged numerous letters, and with good reason Gideon often addressed him as "Judge Rutherford": he had served as justice of the peace for Red River County from 1836 to 1838, was appointed chief justice of Lamar County on 18 December 1840, and served as justice of the peace for precinct 9 of Lamar County in 1843–44 (*Compiled Index to Elected and Appointed Officials of the Republic of Texas*, pp. 106–7).

[3] Gideon's "Christmas tune," so-called because of his annual ritual of playing it at daybreak on Christmas morning, was the ballad "Killiecrankie," which celebrated a Scottish victory over English forces in 1689. See Chris Goertzen, "Gideon Lincecum, 'Killie Krankie,' and Fiddling in Early Texas," *Between the Cracks of History: Essays on Teaching and Illustrating Folklore*, ed. Francis E. Abernethy, pp. 11–31.

[4] Gus is Augustus G. Stobaugh. He is listed as residing in Honey Grove in the 1860 Census (Eighth Census, 1860, Fannin County, Tex., p. 173). Another fellow Infidel, he published a letter that was headlined "The Resurrection" in the *Boston Investigator*, 9 May 1860, p. 2.

Gideon's "Infidelity" had its limits. When Northern Infidels dared to voice opposition to slavery and Southern secession, Gideon cut them off. To the editor and publisher of the Boston Investigator, *he wrote,*

Long Point. Texas. 7 Jan^{r}y. 1861

Horace Seaver
J. P. Mendum
Gentlemen.

It goes hard with me, but it is your own faults. I have taken your paper a long time, but I claim nothing from you on that account; and if I am behind hand with you for anything, forward the bill, and if it is just, I will honor it.

I am quite an old man, have been all my long life an Infidel, that is an unbeliever in wrong doing of every discription. You have done wrong, and therefore I am infidel to you also.

I know not but it may be a pleasing thing to you, to have an old man who is as you well know an unflinching advocate of righteousness, to withdraw his name from your subscription list. Well, be it so; I pester you no more. You have managed badly. Your paper has become an eye sore to me. In the name of righteous infide[l]ity your paper carries in its pages the hidden design of the liberty destroying priesthood. The ultimates will be blood!

Therefore stop it. I don't mean stop printing your paper. That's none of my business. Just quit sending it to me.[1]

Regretfully,
Farewell.
Gideon Lincecum.
Always Infidel.

[1] Gideon had remained a subscriber longer than many other proslavery Southerners, and the fact that he had previously published two items in the paper may have contributed to his reluctance to end his subscription. In the 15 July 1857 issue, Seaver had commented as follows on a letter from Gideon that the paper published three weeks later: "Your communication shall appear the first opportunity. The general view which you take of the subject is very fair and candid, and agrees with our own but it is difficult for us to make ourselves understood in regard to it. We endeavor to be liberal in respect to free inquiry and free discussion, but when we would carry it out according to our idea of the largest liberty, we are sure to run afoul of somebody's prejudices, and then we are greeted with fault-finding and —'stop my paper!'" In May 1859 Gideon had sent ten dollars to Mendum to enroll a new subscriber (B. B. Seat of Brenham) and to pay for five books and eight tracts that had been advertised in the *Boston Investigator* as "Standard Liberal Works Sold at the Investigator Office." He concluded as follows: "And for

the remainder of the money, if any, send such publications as you think will make the best impression amongst our intellectual cowards" (Gideon Lincecum to J. P. Mendum, Long Point, Tex., 25 May 1859, LP, Box 2E364). A letter he wrote to Mendum and Seaver in September 1866 indicates that they had recently sent him two numbers of the *Boston Investigator*. He replied, "I thank you kindly for the papers you were so thoughtful to send me, and as soon as I can get a little ahead of my actual necessities, I intend to subscribe for and take it again" (Gideon Lincecum to J. P. Mendum and Horace Seaver, Long Point, Tex., 6 September 1866, LP, Box 2E364).

Gideon was somewhat more hesitant to break his ties with Northern scientists. To his friend Buckley he wrote,

Long Point. Texas. 10 Jan^{r}y. 1861

Prof. Buckley
My Dear Doctor.

And you had to tell Durand of my scruples in regard to the propriety of my sending on my specimens of plants until I knew their sentiments in respect to the prevailing fanaticism of the northern section of the confederacy.[1] Well, that was right and has saved me the trouble of making inquiry myself. I have more confidence in his answers to your interogateries. I mean the members of the institution: as to Durand, I did not doubt him at all. The open frankness in the manner of his communications to me satisfied me that he is no fanatic. Yet, his remark, "that men of science seldom meddle in politics," is not strictly in accordance with my experience on that subject. The Sillimans, and the members of that institution, for instance. I could name a smart sprinkling besides, but it would [be of] no use here.

I admire Durand very much and had made up my mind, before I received your letter a few minutes ago, to send my little contribution to him, individually, notwithstanding the fact that he had instructed me to direct it to the academy. As I am now satisfied, I will put them up and forward them in a few days, in accordance with his instructions. . . .

Present my respects to Dr. Moore, and receive for yourself my best prayer, to all the gods, for your success in developing Scientific truth.[2]

In christ, thine ever.
Gid.

[1] For a fuller account of Gideon's hesitation about sending specimens to the Philadelphia Academy at this time, see Lincecum, Phillips, and Redshaw, *Science on the Texas Frontier*, pp. 29–30.

[2] Dr. Francis Moore Jr. (1808–64), born and raised in New England, migrated to Texas in 1836 and settled in Houston, where he was a newspaper editor and served as mayor. He became interested in geology and was state geologist from 1859 to 1860. He returned to the North when the Civil War broke out (*New Handbook of Texas*, 4:817–18).

Several days after writing this letter, Gideon sent a large box of botanical specimens to his friend Durand in Philadelphia and stated frankly his hesitancy. This turned out to be his last contribution of specimens to Northern scientists until the war ended.

Long Point. Texas. 13 Jan. 1861

E. Durand
Philadelphia, Pa.
My dear Sir.

. . . I have, as you instructed, directed the box containing the plants &c to W. C. Hensly Drugst &c. Care of Dean, Randle & Co. Galveston Texas.[1] It would have been sent off today, to the depot 30 miles distant but for the rain, which fell to the depth of 3 inches, a thing that has not occurred in this vicinity before in six years. We are all alarmed about it, it looks so strange to see and to hear the roar of the waters in our creeks and rivulets. There are some children here, old enough to go to school, that never saw the like before. Our old negroes look wise and say there must be some sign in it. Irony aside, the box will be sent to the Depot by the first wagon; from thence it will have to shift for its self on its own credit.

I communicated to our mutual friend Prof. S. B. Buckley, some time ago, my scruples about the propriety of sending my specimen until I could know about certain consurgencies &c, but I did not know until a few days since, that he felt concerned enough about it to write you on the subject. In a letter to me, which I received from him five days ago and which was written at Austin, Texas, he copied from your letter to him, what you wrote in regard to that matter. I thank you for your frankness. As to yourself, since I saw and examined your autograph, and considered the familiar, friendly stile of your letters to me, I have had no doubts. A fanatic could not write nor dictate such letters. But I knew nothing about the other members of your institution and did not feel willing to do anything that would aid or please such men as have shown a willingness to excite insubordination among our negroes, for the bloody purpose of butchering and ravishing our innocent women.

In your letter to Prof. Buckley, speaking of myself you say, "Tell him besides that men of science seldom meddle in politics." Strictly speaking, that may be so; And then our Silliman's, Dana's, and many more that I could name, who contend that a negro is a "white man with black skin only," are to be classed amongst the unscientific pretenders. Well, be it so, I am content. The foolish doctrine they so enthusiastically maintain in respect to the negro group is not the only blunder they are guilty of in the Natural Sciences. I do not however, attribute that it is a crime, but simply to defective mental development. . . .

You must not think amiss of me for the course I have taken in respect to sending my specimens, for I am persuaded that, if you knew the infernal work that has been perpetrated and is still going on here, by those ignorant, priest-driven fanatics of the Northern section of the Confederacy, you would not blame me at all for being a little reluctant in doing favors for such inveterate enemies.

With liberal-minded gentlemen, anything that I can do, in my small way, that will add a single line to the record of the natural—the only true—sciences, shall be done as free as the water flows.

With much Respect
Gideon Lincecum

[1] Gideon and his daughter Sarah sent specimens of "682 species or varieties" of plants. See G. Lincecum, "A Collection of Plants from Texas," *Proceedings of the Academy of Natural Sciences* 13 (1861): 98.

While not yet ready to sever completely his ties with Northern science, Gideon was fully ready to cut his ties with the Union. To a more cautious correspondent he wrote,

Long Point. Texas. 20 Jan. 1861

Aurelius G. Ledbetter.
Round Top, Texas
My esteemed young Friend.

Your very polite letter of 14th. instant. came to hand day before yesterday.

If there had been no antagonism to the action of those men who held the reins of Government in "their own hands," your fears would be well founded, and your arguments valid. As the facts stand, there is no real cause for your expressed fears, neither are your arguments tenable.

If you are afraid to trust the prominent men in the present movement, name those that you may think would do better; they may suit me too. As to the "death [k]nell of human liberty," that has been already sounded by the Black republicans. It is the business of the South to let them sound it on their own side of the line they have drawn, as long as they please. As to the women and children being driven from pillar to post, it is our business to be about, and to throw sand in their eyes when they undertake that.

Let our fears be based upon what grounds they may however, there is no chance now for anybody who is a friend to the interests of the South, and to liberty, to mistake the fact that it is the intention of Black Republicanism to enslave the Southern States; and if we fail to be united and face the music with unbroken front, they will carry their vile intent into execution. There is no use in argument; there are but two ways in it now. Resist firmly, or submit to degradation. I go for resistance and I am ready.

Very Respectfully thine
Gideon Lincecum

Most but not all of Gideon's neighbors were ready also, as he described to a member of his family:

Long Point. Texas. 2nd Feby. 1861

Richard Powell[1]
Dripping Springs
Hays County, Texas.

. . . Lysander says that you are desirous for me to write to you. I am willing to do so, but see not how I shall be able to write a letter that can interest you in the least. I am the same old thing, following the same pursuits, investigations, and studies that engaged my time and action while you were here, and should I write off, at this sitting, a long account of the small subjects that plays upon and pleasingly engages the peculiar developments of my little mentality, it would be but a dull affair. It could not serve for amusement. You have perhaps forgotten that the subjects that most fully attracted and afforded the greatest degree of agreeable excitement to my organic arrangements are but seldom sought after or are considered of any importance to other minds.

I am such a poor hand to delineate character or to describe the actions and doings and grand display of unmeaning words and foolish notions which occurs in the crowds of avaricious, deceitful, timid, wavering, and even frightened specimens of the hypocritical genus homo that passes my vision daily, that I need not try it; for I am sure I could not interest you. It would, as to the interest I could excite in your mind, be no less a failure on my part, for me to attempt to write out the historical facts in relation to the sudden ebullition of the spirit of patriotism, that seemed to kindle and boil in every breath; how they slammed together as one mind, like a shackling door on a windy day; and they kept on slamming; making and hanging out lone star flags, and hurrahing and snorting about war—bloody war—until they had gathered and organized themselves into a company of 107 minutemen, all extremely ready and more than willing to lay down their property and their sacred honor, in defense of the holy altars of insulted liberty; how they paraded up and down the road; how they held meetings, passed resolutions, formed a constitution, by-laws, and voted a tax on the company to procure a uniform dress for the company and arms and ammunition which, altogether, would not amount to more than twenty five hundred to three thousand dollars: nothing, with men who were wrought up to such a patriotic pitch and who were so willing to sacrifice everything, sooner than submit. How they met again and paraded and marched and formed lines eye-right, and how they marched and formed in the street before the dwelling of Dr. L. L. Lincecum, and while in that position, how they were presented with a very pretty Lone Star Banner, by a Lady, who, while in the act of presenting the flag, delivered a short, but appropriate address;[2] and then, how they squealed and raved; how they marched back again to the committee rooms, and passed more resolutions, and in this enthusiastic fire and zeal of their unquenchable fervor in the cause of liberty, made an appointment for the company to assemble at 9 a.m. the next Saturday at the Mount Vernon Springs, for the purpose of paying a visit to, and showing off in grand style, Brenham.[3] This order was promptly obeyed and all marched with old Sam Lauderdale and myself, wearing the blue cockade, placed at the head of the company by way of ornament, as we had no music; and how the long line marched into dumbfounded Brenham, reaching from the lower tavern up to McIntyres when they halted;[4] and how at that sang out, three or four voices, froglike, "hurrah for Long Point."

How the company was then dismissed to the court house, where they met, pretty near, the balance of the people of the county; heard several fine stirring speeches, passed resolutions, considered every man in the house a candidate, and all voted for whomsoever they pleased for delegates to a state convention; which resulted in the election of Dr. Robertson & Oldham for county delegates, and James E. Shepherd and Jon. W. Dancy as floaters for this county and Fayette.[5] This election only selected them as candidates to be voted for again by everybody, on the 8th of January. Which election accordingly took place, without opposition. And how the Long Point minute men assembled again, at the appointed time, called the roll, crossed half the company for non attendance; how the balance drilled and fired platoons, one gun at a time—half the day; and being so well pleased with themselves they appointed another day to muster and fire platoons. How they met again; called the roll, crossed three fourths; officers highly incensed; held a meeting in the committee room; consulted as to the best measures to persue; found that the people are poor; not able to arm and equip themselves; got up a memorial to the Legislature, offering their services to the State, also praying the State to arm and equip the company, and to pass laws to enable them to force attendance from the delinquents. And at this point the movement now stands. But the last move—the petition and proposition of service to the State—looked too much in earnest for some of them, and they have slipped in and made private applications, to withdraw their names.

How some of our loud talking citizens has never made their appearance at any of the public meetings that have taken place. Esqr. Hines, all the Kerrs, and many more too mean to name on this paper.[6] Another thing worth speaking of, which shows how the wind blows; none of the regulators, except John H. Dawson, has had anything to do with the movement at all.[7] The Morrises and the Union Hill gang of regulators have all stood aloof.[8] The whole of the Long Point folks, without exception, have enrolled their names in the company. George Gentry and Vincent are quite conspicuous in their patriotism and for once, when the election came on, voted with the Long Point Ticket.[9] We must not however, complain at any of them; all have their motives for their actions and with themselves, no doubt, they are good and valid. And, although we make apology for them and forgive their sins, we must not forget how much they weigh, where to place them, and how much to estimate them at, in cases of emergency, and occasions calling for pluck and true men. And hereafter, when the excitement is over, and peace and quietude shall reign again; when men shall crowd the political arena once more, calling for the sufferages of the people; we must not in our charity towards our fellows in time of peace, forget the cold heart that throbs in the bosoms of these shirking men. Neither must we keep secret for them.

We have had pretty fair rains this winter; tho' the prairie branches are not yet running, the ground is more deeply saturated than it has been during the past seven years. In november, the amount of rain was 4 1/2 inches. December 3 5/8 inches. January 8 inches. What lands we had plowed is well drenched; that which has not been plowed is wet 3 or 4 feet. The rain have not been washy rains, but falling very gently, has been mostly absorbed. We had broke up and fenced in ten acres in the prairie above the house, including the live oaks before the rains had commenced, and notwithstanding that we have had over 11 inches of rain on it, since it was plowed, there has been no water running off from it, showing that it has all been drank up by the thirsty soil.

Our forage of every discription is about out, and our horses and oxen are beginning to look badly. We had two or three warm days two weeks since, and everything began to spring forth, so much, that the cows and horses had began to pinch at it a little, but within the last ten days we have had two icy northers and all is black again.

There has been no new comers or changes in the place except Lawrence has taken Cronin's houses, Wood [has taken] Jo Brown's and Donzar has gone with his family to Houston for this year.[10] We are all well—

With much respect.
Gideon Lincecum

[P. S.] So there is no fun in this letter after all, as I expected exactly—

[1] Because of the drought in Washington County in 1860, four hundred head of cattle branded "GID" and belonging to the Lincecums were driven to Dripping Springs in Hays County, where water and grass were more plentiful. They were left in the care of

grandson Cassianus Lincecum and his stepbrother Richard Powell. Richard Powell, age sixteen, is listed in the 1860 Census as residing in the household of G. Lincecum, age sixty-seven, in Long Point (Eighth Census, 1860, Washington County, Tex., p. 151). Burkhalter identifies him as the son of John Powell, who married Martha Lincecum, the widow of Gideon's son Lycurgus (Burkhalter, *Gideon Lincecum*, pp. 136–37).

[2] The "Lady" referred to is Gideon's daughter Sarah.

[3] Mount Vernon, also known as Mount Vernon Springs, was a town located six miles northwest of Brenham in Washington County. Established in 1841, it was briefly the county seat (*New Handbook of Texas*, 4:870–71).

[4] A family named McIntyre is listed in the 1860 Census as residing in Brenham (Eighth Census, 1860, Washington County, Tex., p. 143).

[5] "Dr. Robertson" is Dr. Jerome Bonaparte Robertson (1815–90), who served in the army of the Republic of Texas in 1837 and settled in Washington County that same year, serving as a coroner. Elected to the Texas house in 1847 and the senate in 1849, he was also the first Texan to raise a company for Confederate military service, and it became part of the 5th Texas Infantry, Hood's Brigade (*New Handbook of Texas*, 5:617–18). Dr. Williamson Simpson Oldham (1813–68) was a native of Tennessee who moved to Austin in 1849. He served as editor of the Austin *State Gazette* from 1854 to 1857. In 1859 he moved to Brenham and was elected to the secession convention in 1861. The Texas senate elected him to serve in the Confederate senate in November 1861 (*New Handbook of Texas*, 4:1134–35). James E. Shepard (1817–94) came to Texas from Virginia in 1840 and settled in Washington County, where he was a lawyer and district judge. He was an alternate to the "People's Convention" in 1861 (Burkhalter, *Gideon Lincecum*, p. 141n). "Dancy" is identified as John Winfield Scott Dancy in Burkhalter, *Gideon Lincecum*, p. 141n.

[6] Lois Wood Burkhalter identified "Esqr. Hines" as James R. Hines and "all the Kerrs" as Hugh Kerr and Alfred B. F. Kerr (Burkhalter, *Gideon Lincecum*, p. 142).

[7] John H. Dawson is listed in the 1860 Census as residing in Brenham (Eighth Census, 1860, Washington County, Tex., p. 223).

[8] "The Morrises" are identified as Dr. Thomas Morris and T. W. Morris in Burkhalter, *Gideon Lincecum*, p. 142.

[9] George W. Gentry is listed in the 1860 Census as residing in Long Point (Eighth Census, 1860,Washington County, Tex., p. 152). He later bought some of Gideon's land (Burkhalter, *Gideon Lincecum*, p. 73). "Vincent" is identified as Joseph Vincent in Burkhalter, *Gideon Lincecum*, p. 142.

[10] The Eighth Census, 1860, for Washington County, Texas, lists three individuals named Lawrence. Benjamin (p. 191) and Claiborne (p. 192) are listed as residing in Doddville. G. W. (p. 151) is listed as residing in Gay Hill. Philip Cronin (p. 152) is listed as residing in Long Point. "Wood" is identified as Silas Wood, an old friend of Gideon, in Burkhalter, *Gideon Lincecum*, p. 87. The 1860 Census lists both Silas Wood and Joseph Brown as residing in Gay Hill. A possible match for "Donzar" is Charles Donsit, also listed as residing in Gay Hill (Eighth Census, 1860, Washington County, Tex., pp. 150–51).

Gideon found much more fun in writing on science than on politics, but the latter subject was hard to ignore at this time. In writing again to Élie Durand on 6 February, he commented,

Long Point. Texas. 6th Feb. 1861

E. Durand
Philadelphia, Pa.
My dear Sir.

. . . As to politics and religion, I know nothing about either. I am not yet through with my investigations and experimentations with <u>natural things</u>, and have had no time to spend with the so called supernatural. In my estimation, politics and religion, to the people who have to support them, are about the same thing. But abolitionism—Black Republicanism—is neither the one nor the other of these. It is what you have so justly stiled it, "An infatuated mob, led by fanatics and dishonest politicians." Their plan is "rule or ruin." Well, I for one, would prefer the latter. But the men will most likely fall upon themselves. . . .

I remain,
Very respectfully & truly thine,
Gideon Lincecum

As the Union was breaking up, Gideon became more interested than ever in urging Texas to develop its natural resources and become self sufficient. To an enterprising Texan who was interested in establishing flour mills in the state, Gideon wrote,

Long Point. Texas. 11 February 1861

Hiram Close.[1]
Galveston, Texas.
My Dear Friend.

. . . In your letter you allude to your extraordinary success in mill making. Thats something worth feeling proud of. Something that benefits society in good earnest. Did you every think of it? A mill is the teeth of [a] community; and so in regard to the successful experiment you have made in mill making, we may set it down, that you chew grain for the multitude. . . .

Your views in regard to the proper course for our people to persue in case of secession, accords with my own in all respects. To be independent we must produce not only our own bread and meat, but as far as we possibly can, everything else that we may consume. The Northern section of the late confederacy can be of no possible advantage to the Southern section. Within the limits of the southern states, we have the soil and the climate to produce everything that can be produced on any portion of this little whirling globe; then why should we put ourselves to any kind of inconvenience to conciliate, or even court the friendship of any people who do not wish to keep company on fair grounds with us. Let us draw into the limits of our own resources, which are ample; economise a little for a few years, and hold our heads steady, and we shall be the most powerful nation on the globe. We have nothing in the world to dread on account of any outside pressure. All the danger to our ultimate, complete and triumphant success, lies within; amongst ourselves! Let us not pester our cerebral organs about this matter, for we may comfort ourselves with the consoling reflections that turn which way it may, let there be peace or bloody, devastating, disasterous war, there is not the slightest danger of losing seed of the villianous genus homo. Don't be uneasy of that account at least.

My best regards to your good lady and family. For yourself my most fervent prayer—to whatever one of the holy celestial gentry that claims the management of your destiny—for your wellfare and success in business, particularly Mills.

Gideon Lincecum

[1] Hiram Close was a merchant in Galveston. In 1859 Gideon purchased an iron sugar mill from the firm of Close and Cushman (Burkhalter, *Gideon Lincecum*, pp. 121, 144).

Three days later Gideon wrote a letter to the Galveston News *strongly supporting a survey of the state's natural resources.*

Long Point. Texas. 14th Feb. 1861

Editors of the News.[1]

From the newspapers I discover that during the late extra session of our Legislature, an attempt was made to abolish the

State Geological Survey. We do hope that the frenzy of party spite may not further meddle with this matter, and that the survey may be permitted to go on uninterrupted; because now more than ever, the resources of Texas need to be developed. Let the future be as it may, we wish to know and understand the agricultural resources and mineral wealth of the state. The survey will, if no more, give direction and stimulous to individual enterprise; teaching us where we may expect to find useful ores, coal, and other valuable minerals, as well as where they are not to be found. The late discovery by the State Geologist (Dr. Moore) of an Iron mountain in Llano County, equal in quality and quantity, as I understand, to the celebrated Iron mountain of Missouri, is of more value by far than the entire cost of the survey.[2] It is known that the Iron mountain of Missouri gives millions of wealth, not only to its own state, but to all the states of the upper Mississippi. What would the great state of Pennsylvania be without its treasures of Iron and Coal? We say let the Geological survey be continued by all means.

Gideon Lincecum

[1] The editor (and publisher) of the *Galveston News* was a former Yankee, Willard Richardson (1802–75), who came to Texas in 1837. He assumed ownership of the *News* in 1845 and became a great promoter of Galveston. He was pro-secession and bitterly opposed Sam Houston (*New Handbook of Texas*, 5:572. See also Earl W. Fornell, *The Galveston Era: The Texas Crescent on the Eve of Secession*, pp. 140–47, 153–54).

[2] Gideon is perhaps referring to an item from the *Boston Investigator* (30 April 1856, p. 4), which referred to the discovery, a few miles from Pilot Knob, Missouri, of mountains containing iron ore sufficient for "the next 300 years."

That same day Gideon learned that Tennessee, unlike Texas, was reluctant to secede.

Long Point. Texas. 14th Feb. 1861

G. J. Durham[1]
Austin. Texas
My Dear Sir.

. . . I was at Brenham today, and saw a handbill—which I suppose will reach you tomorrow—stating that Tennessee had opposed holding a convention by an overwhelming majority & by many it is feared, that that will be the case with all the border states.[2] What can they be thinking of? . . .

Very Respectfully,
and truly thine.
Gideon Lincecum

[1] George J. Durham, Gideon's son-in-law.

[2] The vote in Tennessee for holding a convention to *consider* secession was far from overwhelming: 69,387 against; 57,798 for. However, an overwhelming majority did express opposition to secession: 88,803 against; 24,749 for (Potter, *The Impending Crisis*, p. 509).

Tennessee would not vote to secede until eight weeks after the Civil War began, but Texas voters took the fateful step on 23 February, at a special election called by the state convention when it met on 1 February. With the issue no longer that of secession but rather of possible war, Gideon wrote a letter exactly twenty-five years after the fall of the Alamo.

Long Point. Texas. 6th March 1861

Richard Powell
Dripping Springs, Texas
Dear Sir.

Your communication of 10th ult. in, but there has nothing occurred since, that would interest you, and now, I only write to prevent you from wondering why I don't do so; for I can't think of a single thing that will be worth saying to you. We are all well, but that being always the case, nobody expects to hear of our being sick. As to saying anything on the subject of politics, I shall forego that topic, for the newspapers everywhere have nothing else in them, and I am heartily sick of it. I may however, give it as my opinion, based upon the general aspect of the movements in every part of our troubled country, more especially amongst the black fanatics of the Northern states, that we shall have no war. Fighting is not a very desirable occupation, even to a hot-blooded southerner, and to the frigid souled North-man, it is too fatiguing. I don't think, from the shape of their recent program for the performance on the abolition stage during the coming four years, that there is much fight in it. I think very seriously, however, that a little depletion would be of great benefit to them.

There was a call on this county for a company of Rangers to go and help them keep the fort and arsnel at San Antonio.[1] They camped at Shepherds last night and left very early this morning. They were well equipped. Vincent, Jo, and Jim Polk formed a mess.[2] Mr. Paul got ready and followed on this morning and he said he would get into Vincent's mess if he could.[3] They had their election in Brenham yesterday. They made McIntyre captain. McPhale first Lieutenant.[4] I don't remember any of the other officers, except Jo and Vincent. Jo is first corperal, and Vincent flag bearer; which will exempt them from standing guard and fatigue parties. There are sixty in the company and five or six more followed on today. I don't think however, there will be anything for them to do, and likely they will be home again in two or three weeks; unless affairs runs contrary to my calculations of the signs of the movements at Washington. We shall know now, in a few days, all about it. If the North should hold on to the fool notion that she can coerce the cotton states into submission to her despotic plans, and undertake a war with us, she will be brought to bed with a most disastrous disappointment. For we won't be satisfied with thrashing them, but it will then, be their turn to submit to such terms as the exasperated southern confederacy may think proper to grant them. Civil war is a ruinous affair, and if they will persist and bring it on, we must make them pay the damages. But if they begin it, they will not be long before they will have explanations and manifestations of Southern prowess that will demonstrate to them in a most satisfactory manner that they have embarked in a heavy speculation; a speculation that won't pay. We tell them plainly now, that the seceding states will never join them again. If there is any fighting to be done about it, it shall not be our fault, and if they raise it, they must pay the expenses of it; we will see to that particularly.

While I am writing, news has reached us from the convention, now in session at Austin, that there will be no need for the men we sent from this county. So we may look for them back in a few days. It's well enough. The experiment shows who we may count on in case of actual necessity, and also shows who would not do to depend on in the hour of peril. I shall spot them, Morrises and all. . . .

Very Respectfully I remain
Gideon Lincecum

[1] Almost three weeks before the Texas ordinance of secession was ratified, Ben McCulloch called upon citizens of southwestern Texas to collect their firearms and rendezvous with him a few miles north of San Antonio. His troops surrounded the Alamo as well as the headquarters of Gen. David E. Twiggs, commander of the Department of Texas in San Antonio. On 16 February 1861 General Twiggs surrendered all Federal forces and stores of his command to state troops under McCulloch (Gallaway, ed., *Texas, the Dark Corner of the Confederacy*, p. 79).

[2] Joseph Lincecum is Gideon's grandson; Jim Polk has not been identified.

[3] Mr. Paul was probably Aaron Paul, a twenty-three-year-old teacher living with James Matson, Gideon's son-in-law, in 1860 (Eighth Census, 1860, Washington County, Tex., p. 166).

[4] The 1860 Census listed Hugh McPhail as residing in Brenham (Eighth Census, 1860, Washington County, Tex., p. 142). On 4 September 1861, at age thirty-one, he enrolled as a captain in E Company, 5th Regiment, Texas Mounted Volunteers, under Sibley's 1st Texas Cavalry Brigade (National Archives and Records Administration, *Compiled Service Records of Confederate Soldiers Who Served in Organizations from the State of Texas* [microfilm], roll 34, "Hugh A. McPhaill") (hereafter cited as National Archives, *Compiled Service Records*). In this very active regiment, he became a major, serving under Col. (later Gen.) Tom Green (Wright, comp., and Simpson, ed., *Texas in the War*, p. 24).

With Texas out of the Union, and no war having commenced, Gideon continued to write to his botanic friend, Élie Durand, in the North.

Long Point. Texas. 12 March 1861

E. Durand
218 South Ninth St.
Phila[delphia]
My Dear Friend.

Your very kind, friendly, and truly gratifying communication reached me in nine days. Its date is 28th Feb. For the familiar, friendly contents of that letter, and the enclosed speeches of your Mayor and President of the councils of your city, addressed to Mr. Lincoln, you are entitled to, and I do hereby tender, my most hearty and sincere thanks.[1] I very much admire the tone and stile of those two speeches. They embody the stile and character of the charge of a just judge to a jury of doubtful probity. Fixing his eyes on the Mayor, he seemed not to notice the surging throng. It was amazement that had fixed Mr. Lincoln's gaze. It was the first time the poor fellow had encountered honest men. Men who did not flatter; but who dared to open up before his astounded senses. The true conditions of our government and its suffering subjects; truths perhaps, that he had never before heard from his friends. I pity Mr. Lincoln. By the assistance of his heartless coadjutors, he may—though I think it doubtful—he may succeed in stirring up war; but he has no power to control or profit by it, when it comes. Enough on politics; and I would not have said this much, but to show you that I had carefully considered that portion of your very acceptable communication. I think I can treat of subjects, which to two old fellows, organized as we are, will be more congenial. . . .

Present me respectfully to your family, and believe me

Dear sir, most sincearly Thine

Gideon Lincecum

[1] Alexander Henry was mayor of Philadelphia at this time and throughout the war. His remarks in introducing Abraham Lincoln upon his arrival were respectful and moderate (*New York Times*, 22 February 1861, p. 1). Theodore L. Cuyler, who was president of the Select Council of Philadelphia in 1861, received Mr. Lincoln at Independence Hall the next day and introduced him there (*New York Times*, 23 February 1861, p. 1). President-elect Lincoln's speech at Independence Hall on 22 February was a very moving tribute to the Founding Fathers and the principles they set forth in their great Declaration of 4 July 1776. He pledged his adherence to these principles even if it cost him his life (see Roy P. Basler, ed., *The Collected Works of Abraham Lincoln*, 4:238).

Gideon never wrote much more about Abraham Lincoln. It is a pity he did not really know him. One has a hunch these two frontier individualists, free thinkers and avid readers, might have liked each other.

Chapter 3

War

Hours before South Carolina troops under Gen. Pierre Beauregard opened fire on Fort Sumter in Charleston Harbor, Gideon fired a salvo of his own, laced with sarcasm, that would break the union between him and the Louisiana Lincecums:

Long Point. Texas. 11 April 1861

Nephew John
[Bear Creek, La.]

Your letter of—no date—came to hand in due time, as did a previous letter, the date of which I have forgotten. Neither of them contained anything of interest and do not merit a reply. Had you not seemed to wonder why I had not replied to your previous letter I should say nothing now.

In your last letter, if I understand it, you signify that the union men of La. are largely in the majority and that the defeated and disappointed, office seeking democratic minority have swindled Louisiana out of the union!!! What a terribly bad set of fellows those Louisiana democrats must be; those enemies to the abolitionist, black republicans and their sectional president. Bad fellows; mighty bad.

Well, as I never offer advice to grown people, I cannot say what you are to do about it. I may, however, be permitted to suggest that it might produce some consolation and relief to your sorely wounded pseudo-patriotism for you to take your poor old sin smitten father and move away to your people, beyond the Mason's and Dixon's line.

Remember, that is only a suggestion; not a request, or advice, or order. Do as you think best about it.

Your Uncle
Gid

Although Gideon's hot-tempered salvo led to temporary disunion in the family rather than to war, Beauregard's shot touched off four years of bloody fratricidal conflict. Gideon seems to have written little about the war during its first six weeks. Of course, little fighting occurred after the opening bombardment until the Battle of Bull Run (First Manassas) in July 1861. Besides, Gideon was heavily involved in scientific research and correspondence in those early weeks and was also applying himself diligently to the long deferred and challenging task of translating hundreds of pages of notes. This great volume of information had been dictated to him by a Choctaw sage during Gideon's residence in Mississippi, and it comprised the traditional history of the Choctaw Nation.[1] It is also possible that some of Gideon's correspondence for this period has been lost or was never copied.

Not until late May did Gideon write about the war, at which time he addressed the following letter to his son-in-law in Austin:

Long Point. Texas. 27th May 1861

G. J. Durham
Austin, Texas

I had bearly finished the perusal of your letter of 22nd. inst. when San rode up looking quite healthy.[2] [He said:] "Can you find time to rejoice with me in the successes of our cause thus far?"

[My answer was] "Why certainly." And so far, apart from the action of a few crouching, southern cowards, I see nothing seriously to complain at. Its all rolling on a great deal better than I had expected. Our enemies are performing much good service for our side of the question, and it is to be hoped that they may continue their favors until we shall no longer need them.

It is true that they are vigilently engaged, and that their preparations are magnificent and very great. In addition to all this the whole people north are united, and laboring under the highest possible degree of warlike excitement. This I consider, however, to be a very favorable indication for our cause. We all know that the most ardent fever comes soonest to its acme, and the reaction, to the patient, is always dangerous in proportion to the degree of the excitement. At this time, with the Lincolnites, the excitement has gone up to complete mania, and if full, perfect insanity, which I think quite probabl[e], does not shortly supervene, an abatement of the symptoms of the present stage of their diseased condition will. I would much prefer the latter, for should the aberation of mind under which they now suffer develope [into] perfect mental derangement, they wouldn't let us alone, and we should be forced to [the] horrible necessity of slaughtering a nation of lunatics. But turn which way it may, they've got to be whipped.

I am still studying and investigating the grasses of Texas; and the ants, so closely, that I shall hardly have time to fight much, if the war does come. . . .

Our crops are very fine. Had rosting ears ten days.—everything else in proportion.—We would like to visit you and see your fine grapes, and shall do so if I can make a rise of a couple of good, suitable horses. . . .

Thine
Gideon Lincecum

[1] Lincecum and Phillips, *Adventures of a Frontier Naturalist*, pp. 95–101. See also Cheri Lynne Wolfe, "The Traditional History of the Chahta People: An Analysis of Gideon Lincecum's 19th Century Narrative," doctoral diss., University of Texas at Austin, 1993.

[2] "San" is Lysander Rezin Lincecum, Gideon's son.

Four weeks later, Gideon described something else that was occupying his mind—something that might be of real help to the Confederate cause:

Long Point. Texas. 24th June 1861

Messrs. Leeds & Co. Iron Founders[1]
New Orleans, La.
Gentn.

In these perilous times, it behooves every one that harbors any love for human rights to think of and to examine every subject and thing that seems to promise any aid or strength in fortifying and resisting successfully the unholy crusade of insane robbers by which we are daily threatened.

A man like myself, a back woodman, might think of something very valuable, or on the other hand, it might be useless. But having no one that knows anything about such matters, to whom such thoughts and their results could be profitably communicated, they fade away from the mind of the originator without affording him or any one else the satisfaction of ever knowing whether they would, or would not, be of service to the causes that had set his mind in motion.

For several months my mind has been working at a missile, the which, if it can be produced at a cheap rate—a price that will warrant its use—would in a field fight render a six pounder equal to a twenty four pounder gun, to say nothing of the advantages and facilities of working the light gun on the battlefield. But I will bring no arguments. If the missile can be produced, it will suggest all the uses to which it will be applicable. I am not sufficiently familiar with the extent of the creative powers of the iron foundry to know whether it can be produced at all. But if it can, it has a fourfold power. On this account I did not intend to give information to the enemy by making enquiry through the papers; nor did I know who to address on the subject until last evening, when in conversation with Mr. Wesley Broadwell, formerly of your city.

He informed me of your establishment and remarked that if any men in America could perform the work, it could be done at your establishment. From his high recommendations of the gentlemanly owners, I have ventured to address your firm.

The whole subject resolves itself into a single question, and to men of your knowledge and experience on the iron it may even look foolish. To me it has weight, which may be quieted by your having the kindness to answer my question as soon as convenient. I aim at no speculation, no patent.

Can not iron balls, perfect globes, weighing one ounce or thereabouts, be produced in large quantities, as cheap or nearly so, as ordinary castings?

If they can be produced, on the principles of making the leaden dropped shot, they would take the globular form, they would fly straight, and on the open field or decks of vessels would when fired from a good six pounder, do a deadly work 300 yards and would be equal to a six pounder or four six pounders with the ordinary cannon shot.

Your reply to this question will oblige a man, who was born with the constitution of the United States—in the smoke of one revolution—have lived long enough to see that constitution trampled underfoot; and now very probably shall make my exit to the good hunting ground in the thunder and smoke of another revolution. I am ready, if you can make the iron drop shot.

Very Respectfully
Your ob[t] Serv[nt]
Gideon Lincecum

[1] Leeds & Co. Iron Founders of New Orleans was one of the first-class foundries and machine shops in the South. It made forty-nine guns for the Confederacy before Union forces occupied New Orleans in late April 1862 (Current, ed., *Encyclopedia of the Confederacy*, 1:98).

Gideon thought of other ways he could help. Earlier he had been an official weather observer for the federal government and had continued to submit quarterly weather reports to the Galveston News. *After some hesitation, he submitted a report at the end of June and added a comment:*

Long Point. Texas. 4th July 1861

Richardson &Co Editors
Galveston News
Gentn.

As war begins now to pinch a little closer, I had thought that reports from my meteorological Journal could not find place in your crowded paper, and on that account had omitted to forward it at the end of the last quarter. But thinking again, I came to the conclusion that as there is nothing in it of greater importance than driving off a set of robbers, it isn't worth while to stop every little thing on account of it, and so I send you four months this time. . . .

Thine Truly
Gideon Lincecum

On 4 and 5 September 1861 men from Washington County were mustered into Companies E and F of the 5th Regiment, Texas Mounted Volunteers (Cavalry). These men would be a part of Gen. Henry Hopkins Sibley's New Mexico campaign.[1] *Among the soldiers were Gideon's grandsons, Cassianus and Josephus, and son-in-law George W. Campbell.*

That the war was beginning to "pinch" in Texas was largely owing to the naval blockade of its coast. Shortages of various articles resulted, including distilled spirits. In response to a sudden demand for stills, Gideon, who was for the most part a teetotaler, replied, with sarcasm, to an inquirer:

Long Point. Texas. 7th October 1861

C. C. Frusel[2]
La Grange, Texas
Sir.

Your note of 5th. inst. came to hand to day.

I am sorry that I am unable to comply with your request. There is a thoughtful gentleman who is engaged in setting up a distillery at Bre[n]ham; and to him I have already sold my still.

There is another gentleman at Bastrop county who is about to erect a distillery. He had heard of, and wrote to me in relation to the purchasing [of] my still, two weeks ago. He also was too late.

It is, however, very encouraging to know in these troublous times that so many gentlemen are thinking of preparing themselves for the production of the greatest and best, most popular and most loved article of which the cruel Lincoln blockcade has deprived us.[3]

Let us all strive for it; let us sedulously persevere in the great work until every little creek and ravine throughout the state shall be made pe[r]fectly redolent with the sweet savor, that eminates ever, from the soul saving still house.—I know of no other still in this vicinity—

Very Respectfully,
Gideon Lincecum

[1] For a discussion of Sibley's career, see Ezra J. Warner, *Generals in Gray: Lives of the Confederate Commanders*, pp. 276–77. Sibley's New Mexico campaign will be discussed below.

[2] A possible identification for "Frusel" is Conrad Frosh, listed in the 1860 Census as residing in La Grange (Eighth Census, 1860, Fayette County, Tex., p. 288). Perhaps Gideon misread the handwriting.

[3] Ten states of the Confederacy, including Texas, passed some sort of legislation prohibiting the distillation of liquor, because the

grain was needed for bread (Massey, *Ersatz in the Confederacy*, p. 48).

In a far more serious vein, Gideon wrote again to New Orleans to promote his idea of the new type of missile the South could produce and use effectively in the war.

Long Point. Texas. 18th October 1861

Dr. Carter[1]
New Orleans, La.
Dear Sir,

If I have been correctly informed, you are engaged in an enterprise that will enable you to examine and judge of the value, or uselessness, of a subject I have had on my mind several months. It is a misile to be used with cannon in field fights, and for raking the decks of vessels in engagements at sea.

I wrote on the 24th of June last. to Messrs. Leeds and C° of New Orleans. They replied that my projectile could not be made. I am not satisfied with the answer of those gentlemen; and as I have not made the thing known to any one else, but have been waiting to make the enquiry of some person in whom I could place confidence. I was please[d] to hear of your being engaged in a business that will afford you the oppertunity to finding out whether it can be made or not. I know enough about the nature of projectiles to be assured that it will raise the destructive powers of a six pounder, in a range of 400 yards at least, to that of four six pounders with ordinary canister shot, if it can be produced. And I think it can.

Cannot Iron Balls, weighing one ounce, be produced at as little cost or nearly so, as grape shot; I mean, by the pound. Leeds and C° say they cannot be made at all. I know, however, that the Yankees can make cast iron waistcoat buttons and very small buckles. Please examine the subject and let me hear from you.

Most Respectfully.
Gideon Lincecum

P.S. I am not seeking a pattent—

[1] Dr. Carter has not been identified.

Although Gideon found no "takers" for his missile plan, his mind was full of ideas. As he told his friend, Col. S. D. Hay, "I am always at home, and constantly engaged at one thing or other, trying to hold up through the glorious, humanity renovating war" (Long Point, Tex., 26 October 1861, LP, Box 2E366).[1] He described one of the "things" he was "engaged at" in a letter the next day to a young Texas botanist:

Long Point. Texas. 27 Oct. 1861

W. A. Wilson[2]
Caddo, Texas
My Dear Friend.

Your letter of 21st instant came to hand day before yesterday, accompanied by Mr. Palmer's "vindication of Secession and the South."[3] It is a high order of state paper, dilivered in a stile of language, on a plane of thought that cannot fail to put to silence the Reverend Breckinridge and all other Monarkists.[4] I perused it with a high degree of satisfaction, and feel very thankful to you for sending it to me.

The late war news is all favorable. Ere this you have heard how the boys of New Orleans done up the Lincolnites at the head of the passes.[5] I suppose by this time they are ready to pitch into them again. Wasn't that a daring exploit?

People from hereabouts are all gone to the war; and the soldiers having appropriated all my blankets, I have succeeded in inventing a machine to spin the long moss. The intention is to supply my bed with a substitute for my absent blankets, and I am cleaning and spinning it every day. Lincoln will not be able to freeze me into subjection, so long as the gray Tillandsia usneoides [Spanish moss] floats to the breezes beneath the branches of our venerable forest trees. . . .

I have no news, that you will not see in the papers, as soon as you will see this sheet. All's well!

In Christ I am thine.
Gideon Lincecum

[1] "S. D. Hay" is identified as Samuel D. Hay in Burkhalter, *Gideon Lincecum*, p. 144n. The Texas legislature in 1854 authorized him to establish a cotton and woolen mill in Huntsville, Texas.

[2] No W. A. Wilson was listed in the Eighth Census, 1860, for Caddo, Texas.

[3] Benjamin Morgan Palmer, identified as one of the "golden orators of Southern rights" (John D. Winters, *The Civil War in Louisiana*, p. 8), published "A Vindication of Secession and the South from the Strictures of Rev. R. J. Breckenridge" in various forms. It appeared in the *Southern Presbyterian Review* in April 1861 and was published as a forty-six-page pamphlet by Southern Guardian Steam-power Press in 1861 (*National Union Catalog*, pre-1956 Imprint, 438:673). One of his sermons in support of the Southern cause was also reprinted in the *Galveston News*, 8 December 1860.

[4] Robert Jefferson Breckenridge (1800–71) was a lawyer and Presbyterian clergyman who during the Civil War put forth all his fiery zeal in support of the Union. He was President Lincoln's chief advisor in Kentucky. Perhaps Gideon's calling him a "monarchist" referred to Reverend Breckenridge's allegiance to Lincoln. So uncompromising was his opposition to Southern sympathizers that he refused to save members of his own family from Northern prisons and firing squads (Current, ed., *Encyclopedia of the Confederacy*, 1:215–17, 2:887).

[5] On 12 October 1861 a small and light flotilla of Confederate

vessels turned back and sent fleeing a much larger and heavier Union fleet that was trying to take control of the Head of the Passes of the Mississippi River, where the river divided into three channels across the delta into the Gulf. It was a humiliating setback for the Union, but it turned out to be only a temporary one. See *Official Records of Union and Confederate Navies in the War of Rebellion*, series1, 16:3–20 (hereafter cited as *Official Records of the Rebellion*). See also Raimondo Luraghi, *A History of the Confederate Navy*, trans. Paolo E. Coletta, p. 105.

Another of Gideon's ideas involved some new ways Texas could alleviate a paper shortage caused by the Union blockade. He submitted his thoughts on this subject to the Galveston News.

Long Point. Texas. 10th Nov[r]. 1861

Editors of the New[s].

Having noticed sundry well said articles, going the rounds of the newspaper, on the subject of making an effort to establish a paper manufactury in our state; and from the half and quartersheet papers that are issuing from the press everywhere, I cannot avoid the feeling of wonder, that they have not said a great deal more about it; and that companies are not already organizing for the purpose of establishing one or more of the much needed paper mills.

We need not wait for the termination of the war, with the expectation of procuring supplies of paper from the discomfitted yankies. Doubtless, by that time they will be ragged enough to fall under the legitimate claim of the paper makers; yet they will not be in a condition to spare their rags, nor the paper mills to make them into paper: nor would we buy it, if they did.

Texas must have her own paper mills. There are plenty of enterprising men and sufficient capital. And as I conjecture, they are only deterred from embarking in it from a want of the knowledge of the resources of the country, and encouragement to begin. Let a company be organized; and then send a commission to some papermill that is now in action in the confede[r]acy, for instructions; and a few mechanics, to aid in constructing and starting the mill as soon as may be, and the trouble is over—the night mare dies.

The lack of sufficient material has been suggested as an objection by some of the writers who have alluded to this topic. It does not seem to me that this objection is founded upon a careful examination of our resources in that direction. I have been making observation on that wing of the supposed difficulty, during the last two months. It is surely groundless.

A very considerable amount of excellent material would of course be at once picked up about the wharves, ships, storing establishments, cotton presses, &c &c at Galveston, Houston; all the shipping ports; and gin houses. Also from our slaves; a wonderful amount of rags can be collected by them. I have talked with a number of them on the subject, and it takes well with them; many of them say that they could save a hundred pounds of rags every year; and upon my telling them that they would soon be able to realize 3¢ per pound for clean washed rags, they have already commenced laying them away.

In the vegetable kingdom Texas is rich in plants containing long fibre. I have a shrub growing in my yard now, that with the proper cultivation, on our ordinary poor, timbered lands is capable of yielding a ton or more [of] fine silky bast per acre; with no labor necessary after the ground has been once properly set with it, but to gather the crop two or three times a year. One planting would suffice for ten or fifteen seasons or more, owing to the quality of soil.

I feel well assured that ample amounts of good materials to supply the state with all the paper of every discription that may be required can be had on terms that will do away all danger of failure in that direction.

Herewith enclosed, please receive, for your chemists to experiment with, specimens of the bark and wood of the shrub alluded to above.

Texas produces spontaneously a very great variety of the Asclepias family (milkweed family), all of which yield heavy crops of fine bast fibre. The Malvaceous plants[1] also abound in Texas, one of which, Malva Texana (Spanish apple), surpasses all the rest for its wealth of fibre and cheapness of cultivation.

Cross and longitudinal cuts of the wood of my shrub, under a powerful microscope, after exposure to the chemical reagents, seem to contain almost as great a wealth of bast fibre, with long ribbed cells, as does the bark; and not sufficient incrusting matter to increase the cost of the cells, by the labor that will be required to reduce it to fine paper pulp; adding to this, that the natural whiteness of the wood, will require but a small amount of chemicals, and little labor in the processes of bleaching. It is my opinion, and what I have to say about it results from a somewhat extended observation on the physiological functions of this plant, that its woody cells which allways abound in the two years growth in a twofold proportion to the quantity of bark; and being soft and easily torn to pieces, will be, by the paper maker, considered equivalent perhaps to the bark itself.

My observations on the woody fibre of this plant, however, have not been of a nature to decide its true character and value; only sufficient to enable me to make hopeful suggestions. I leave its further analyzation, to the tests of better chemicals, and a higher order of scientific experimenters.[2]

The enclosed bark specimens are of two kinds. The white was peeled off, and subjected to a little hammering this morning. The dark colored specimens had been hanging out exposed to the weather, where I had tied up some vines with it, ever since early spring, and had become mildewed. This is termed the rotting process, and with this article, when the rotting is properly conducted, it leaves the fibre quite fair, requiring small expense of agents in the bleaching processes.

By proper tests, and a good microscope, it will be seen that this bark contains a greater amount of irregular shaped cells and less incrusting matter than hemp, and these are the qualities which are prised highest by the scientific paper producer.

Gideon

[1] The Malvaceae are a family of herbs with some shrubs and trees in which the leaves are palmately veined, often lobed, and rich in mucilage. Examples include *Gossypium* (cotton), *Hibiscus*, and *Malva* (mallow) (Michael Allaby, ed., *A Dictionary of Plant Sciences*, 2d ed., p. 267).

[2] Ironically, it was not until 1911 that pulp paper was first successfully manufactured on a commercial scale in Texas. Approximately one hundred years after Gideon's proposal, in the 1960s, it became a prosperous industry in Texas (Burkhalter, *Gideon Lincecum*, p. 146n).

The shortage of paper was one factor in some shrinkage of Gideon's extensive correspondence, which now fell below his pre-war level. Another factor, of course, was the severance of lines of communication with his correspondents in the North. He continued to express his views at some length, however, to friends, officials, and some soldiers on his own side of the Mason and Dixon line. To one of the last group he wrote the following:

Long Point. Texas. 14th Novr. 1861

Joseph C. Sniveley[1]
Lockhart, Texas
Dear Sir.

Your wellcome communication of 3rd inst. came to hand several days ago. I could not reply sooner; having several grass letters to answer. . . .[2]

As to Lieut. T. J. Wood; though he found hospitality about my house as a hunting companion with Durham, he did not succeed in placing himself in my estimation as a reliable defender of our form of government.[3] His aristocratic notions in regard to best bloods, first families and the like were features too prominent in his every day conversations to set well on my political stomach. From the conclusions I had formed in relation to Mr. Wood's aristocratic proclivities, I should have been surprised to have heard that he had thrown his sword into the confederate scale. Lieut. Wood is a man of moderate capacity. Durham is vastly his superior in all respects intellectually; and he is willing to serve as orderly Sergeant. But Durham understands and practically advocates the true principles of states and individual rights. Wood did not, nor could he be made to understand it. He had, if he ever understood the rights of the masses, been incapacitated for its recognition in common life at the West point school which has certainly damaged more men, in relation to the true basis of a free government, than any other American institution except theology.

I do not feel surprised at the condition of affairs as I find them manifested by the genus homo, at this period of the earths existance. On the plane of the rights of property, and reciprocal good will, and peace towards our fellows; he is but slightly in advance of the dog. Like that animal, he snatches and appropriates to his own use the sustenance of the helpless, and the fighting element that is in him is offered mutually; and becomes the test of justice. I ask, wherein does that differ from the dog race? . . .

Things are going wrong and to ruin everywhere, now adays. The most flattering anticipations are frustrated and the fondest affections are torn apart and blasted. And all this has been brought about and pressed upon us by a set of fanatics, who have been begot, bred, born and trained for the purpose by the infernal theologians who are now, demonlike, urging the fools they have thus created and prepared for the slaughter, to cut each other's throats on both sides of the Mason and Dixon line. Well, I am becoming accustomed to it, and shall soon be able to look upon it as a natural inconvenience only. It has prevented Durham's annual visit, and though it was a gratifying thing to us, knowing the cause of the failure now, we bear it without excitement or attaching blame to them.

In righteousness, I am thine
Gideon Lincecum

P.S. Interlineations make the paper hold out.

[1] Joseph C. Sniveley (or Snively) was distantly related to Gideon's family and to that of his son-in-law James Matson (Burkhalter, *Gideon Lincecum*, p. 158n). Joseph Culbertson Sniveley enrolled 7 March 1862 as a private in Capt. James G. Storey's company of Wood's Regiment, Texas Mounted Volunteers, and was mustered in 1 May 1862 at Camp Salado, where he served as a hospital steward. He is also listed as a prisoner of war on an undated roll, and his parole certificate was dated 26 July 1865 (National Archives, *Compiled Service Records*, roll 176).

[2] Having published articles on Texas native grasses in the *Texas Almanac* and the *Southern Cultivator* in 1861, Gideon was corresponding with several people on the subject. See Lincecum, Phillips, and Redshaw, *Science on the Texas Frontier*, appendix 3, pp. 163–67.

[3] Thomas J. Wood was a friend of Gideon's son-in-law George Durham. A graduate of West Point, he became a major general in the Union army (Ezra J. Warner, *Generals in Blue: Lives of the Union Commanders*, pp. 569–70).

The next day Gideon wrote to his son-in-law, giving an interesting and colorful perspective on the war in Texas.

Long Point. Texas. 15 Novr. 1861

G. J. Durham
Austin, Texas
My Dear Sir.

Your favor of 3rd inst, was received a week since. I withheld my reply until Lon had returned from Galveston, thinking that he probably might bring some accounts that would interest you.[1]

Billy, his son, had gone down as a volunteer, and being so well equipped, young as he is [14 or 15], he was received.[2] He, however, soon became diseased, with that scourge of the camps, Diarrhea.[3] The doctors would not relieve him. He was discharged and Lon went down to bring him home; which he did, and he is now cured of the complaint, but looks badly.

While down there he, Lon, made observation on the forces collected there around Virginia Point, and their preparations for defence &c.[4] He reports them badly armed at Virginia Pt. Many of them have no guns, some revolvers, and nearly all have knives. Their batteries are all in place, but most of the guns small and short range—He looks upon the soldiers as a very fine set of men, and has full confidence in their firmness and determined bravery. He has no doubt, if a landing should be attempted, but that the boys will fight them to the death with such weapons as they have. He is fearful, however, that they could not manage to hold their ground against any considerable force of well armed men. Upon the whole, however, since the news of the attack on the forts about Savannah and Charleston, the people begin to speak of an attack on Galveston as being unlikely to occur soon.

The papers on our side have been taken to lying as bad as the robbers beyond 36° 30' N. We can get nothing that is reliable now, except perhaps, such as comes from a few responsible travellers. Our near neighbor, Mr. Fullerton, who is able to bear the expense of such a trip, returned three days ago from a visit to the [Confederate] army of the Potomac.[5] He reports the army as being well provided in everything and healthy, with the exception of the Measles, which is pretty bad. He also states that they were in hourly expectation of a great battle; for which the greatest anxiety prevailed throughout the entire army; and that it would result favorably to the C. S. A. No one entertained the least doubt--Fullerton is in high spirits; he passed through a great portion of the encampments. He is a pretty good writer, and I think it likely that he will publish some of the things he saw.

Our county has sent off nearly all her efficient men, and a good many of her inefficients. The consequence is that some of them have been sent back, and we hear of others who have sunk down from exhaustion and are too feeble to bear the travel home. We see, nevertheless, about the usual number of Buggies passing the road, but a close inspection reveals the somewhat curious fact, that they are leighted only with women and children & with an occasional silver gray who, like the old war muskets, had been laid away as useless, [but] are now being rubbed up by the ladies to fight the home battles in place of better guns. It is quite amusing to observe the old fashioned flint locks, now they have been change[d] to percussions, performing their antics and popping caps only, around a carriage load of the fearful steel banded shells. They smile and hobble around mightily I tell you.

I find everybody yelling to pay "the war tax", but very few of them can say how they are to raise the money for it.[6] Our state bonds were looked to, to aid us in time of need; but as the state government, by her refusal to receive them for state taxes, she has thereby depreciated her bonds to a very low rate. Who is to be benefitted by this high handed, official swindle? People are beginning to speak of it in terms not very flattering to the performers of it; and besides, it is operating as a severe damper upon the patriotism of the masses, upon whom the burthen is intended ultimately to fall. It is not worth my while to say anything about it, but I can see already that if the coming legislature fails to raise the credit of the state bonds, though nobody hopes to pay the war tax with them, the collection of the war tax will drag heavily. Nobody but the southern branch of the northern oppressors and robbers would or could consent, at this critical time, to attempt a discouragement of the patriotism of our people by speculation of this kind.

I am for myself, however, aware of the knowledge of the fact that our ills are a northern production; war and devastation are the natural outcome; and like the wave to the storms & [illegible] as best we can. I hope the war may not cease until the oppressed people everywhere may be crowned with a full satisfaction from the instigators of their troubles. The priests and politicians, who are but the same party, have been working forty years to get up this war. They have succeeded; and now like a set of demons, as they surely are, are encouraging their poor, deluded dupes, on both sides of the line, to cut each other's throats as fast as possible.

And these are the self stiled promulgators of the will of God. Poor lord. Under the circumstances, what can he do? Like the said bonds, he is in the hands of the speculators and going at a low figure. But to stultify the laboring strugling masses further, and more effectually; we find, coming up from the heads of the swindling departments, proclamations, setting apart certain specified days, for thanksgiving and prayer. Pshaw!—How supremely ridiculous. Don't they all get drunk? and play the devil generally?—To sustain the credit of the state, would be a much better business, and much more acceptable to any of the good gods. More especially, if they entertain a desire for honesty and fairplay among the denizens of this little revolving clod of sand and rocks, and brimstone and thunder. . . .

The news of the loss of Port Royal and Hilton head[7]—and General Gid Pillows brilliant victory near Columbus will reach you before this will.[8]

Thine.
Gideon Lincecum

[1] "Lon" is Leonidas L. Lincecum, Gideon's son.

[2] William (Billy Lon) Lincecum, Gideon's grandson, was listed as being thirteen years of age in the Eighth Census, 1860, Washington County, Tex., p. 150.

[3] For a confirmation of Gideon's opinion that diarrhea and other diseases were a major problem for Civil War armies, see Paul E. Steiner, *Disease in the Civil War: Natural Biological Warfare in 1861–1865*.

[4] Virginia Point was on the mainland in Galveston County, several miles west of Galveston, where the bridge crossed from the island. During the Civil War Union forces blockaded the Gulf Coast. The Confederacy stationed troops along the railroad from Galveston to Houston, and Virginia Point was fortified (*New Handbook of Texas*, 6:760).

[5] John Fullerton is listed in the 1860 Census as residing in Long Point (Eighth Census, 1860, Washington County, Tex., p. 152). During the first year of the war, the Confederates referred to their forces in northern Virginia as the "Army of the Potomac," but on 1 June 1862 that force was officially designated the "Army of Northern Virginia," to distinguish it from the Union army of the Potomac (Current, ed., *Encyclopedia of the Confederacy*, 1:76).

[6] The Confederate government attempted to finance the war primarily through bonds and treasury notes, a policy that was only partially successful. In addition, the first of four principal tax acts was enacted 19 August 1861, in the form of a direct tax of fifty cents upon each one hundred dollars' valuation of certain kinds of prop-

erty, including real estate and slaves. This is undoubtedly the "war tax" Gideon is referring to in this letter (E. B. Long with Barbara Long, *The Civil War Day by Day: An Almanac 1861–65*, pp. 726–28. See also Douglas B. Ball, *Financial Failure and Confederate Defeat*).

[7] On 7 November 1861 a Union fleet under Flag Officer Samuel DuPont, with troops under Brig. Gen. Thomas W. Sherman, seized the fine harbor and roadstead of Port Royal in South Carolina by capturing Fort Walker on Hilton Head Island and Fort Beauregard at Bay Point on Phillips Island, which commanded the entrance. This was a major loss to the Confederacy, as Port Royal provided the Union navy with a major base for its blockade of the Atlantic coast. For a detailed account, see Daniel Ammen, "DuPont and the Port Royal Expedition," in Robert W. Johnson and Clarence C. Buel, eds., *Battles and Leaders of the Civil War*, 1:671–91. See also McPherson, *Ordeal by Fire*, p. 180.

[8] Brig. Gen. Gideon Johnson Pillow (1806–78), a veteran of the U.S.-Mexican War, did manage to win something of a victory at Belmont, Missouri, on 7 November 1861, over no less an opponent than Ulysses S. Grant. However, his victory came not from any brilliance on his part but from a blunder by Grant after victory was in his grasp (Bruce Catton, *U. S. Grant and the American Military Tradition*, pp. 68–69). Grant gained revenge the following spring when he conquered Pillow's forces at Fort Donelson.

Billy Lincecum was not the only member of Gideon's family who was serving with the Texas forces in the war. George W. Campbell, who married Gideon's daughter Leonora in 1851, was with the force under General Sibley that had been sent out to hold west Texas, guard the Rio Grande border, and bring the New Mexico Territory under Confederate control. Gideon wrote to him in late November.

Long Point. Texas. 29 November 1861

Capt$^{\underline{n}}$ G. W. Campbell

El Passo

My Dear Sir.

Two or three days after Allman, who came up from Brenham for the purpose, had delivered the miniature, two letters and $20—Leonora received another letter from you, stating that you had sent the above named articles by the hands of the said Mr. Allman, and that you had made a forward movement, in the direction of El Passo.[1]

Those letters found all well, with the exception of little Sallie.[2] She is mending, however, and will ultimately get well. . . . All the balance of our children and their mother are in good condition. I hear no complaint that they are in need of anything.

Lysander is here yet, and except actual invasion should occur on our sea coast, I do not think it likely that he will leave home this winter. He visits your house every day, and I notice that he attends to the milling and furnishing firewood to Leonora, as often as she needs it. Nothing <u>shall</u> go amiss in that direction. . . .

Things are moving along about as they were when you left us. As yet there has been no demonstration at Galveston. Leonidas has just returned from there, and reports the army as being extremely orderly and civil. They are fortifying themselves at Virginia Point. That is, the soldiers from up the country. In the city they are actively making all the preperations they find means to work with. The large guns that were sent on by the government have not yet arrived. They are however, expecting them daily. That has been a badly managed affair. Billy Lon had got sick of a bad type of diarrhaea; the doctors failed to relieve him; he was discharged and Leonidas went down after him;[3] [that] was his reason for going to Galveston at the time he did. . . .

As you will get the papers earlier than this will reach you,

I shall not attempt to post you on the subject of the general news. From the papers of today, I am satisfied that the balances are preponderating in favor of the south; and that we shall ultimately succeed. The whole army of the north, as they are constantly changing and displacing their Generals, must be in an unsatisfactory condition.[4]

They unceremoniously threw Fremont overboard, and from the demonstration made in his favor by 20,000 men, in grand convention, torch light processions, &c when he arrived in St. Louis on his return from the army, would seem to indicate that Lincoln will have trouble in that quarter soon.[5] Fremont denounced Lincoln and his administration, and at the mass meeting they unanimously adopted many very resolute resolutions. Amongst them that they would sustain Fremont. We shall hear in a short time how that movement will work. If Fremont has the soul of a man in him, I predict that he will not brook the insult offered him by the Lincoln government, but will hold on to his party and seek satisfaction. If, however, he does not carry the Soul of a man in him, which I think most likely, he will sell himself to the best bidder. And as we have no use for such men, Lincoln will have to buy him back.

I am glad to hear that at Savanah they have hoisted several black flags. I should like to hear that the black flag was adopted by our entire army. The object for which they are invading the south is, of all crimes, the most diabolical, and postively does not deserve quarter in battle, or any where else from us.—

As ever.
Gideon Lincecum

[1] B. F. Allmon is listed as a private in the muster roll (as of 4 September 1861) of 5th Regiment, Texas Mounted Volunteers (Cavalry), Company E, mustered in Washington County. He was listed as sick on 31 October 1861 and discharged 6 November 1861 (Martin Hardwick Hall, *Sibley's New Mexico Campaign*, p. 270; National Archives, *Compiled Service Records*, roll 32).

[2] "Little Sallie" was Leonora Lincecum and George Campbell's daughter, Gideon's granddaughter.

[3] See the appendix for details of William (Billy Lon) Lincecum's military service, which did not end with his first discharge.

[4] There had been a number of changes in the Union command by late November 1861. George B. McClellan assumed command as general-in-chief, replacing Irvin McDowell and Winfield Scott, Nathaniel Banks took over from Robert Patterson, and David Hunter replaced John C. Frémont after the latter was relieved of his command. Many more changes would follow before Lincoln finally found a winning team in late 1863 (McPherson, *Ordeal by Fire*, p. 213).

[5] As a general, John C. Frémont (1813–90) was flamboyant, insubordinate, and ineffective. Despite his having been hailed in earlier days as "the Pathfinder" and nominated for president by the Republicans in 1856, Frémont was removed from his command in the West by President Lincoln in November 1861 and replaced by Maj. Gen. David Hunter (Warner, *Generals in Blue*, pp. 160–61; see also Shelby Foote, *The Civil War: A Narrative*, 1:86–90, 95–99).

Waving the black flag of "no quarter" may seem somewhat out of character for Gideon, who was more aptly found under the banner of "no surrender," a motto he carried to the end.

As the year drew to a close, Gideon wrote to two members of Jefferson Davis's cabinet, providing good news to one and offering advice to the other. To the treasury secretary, Gideon wrote,

Long Point. Washington County. Texas. 14th December 1861
C. G. Memminger[1]
Secretary of the Treasury
Sir.

To your published circular requiring information in relation to manufacturies, and other industries, which did not exist, having sprung up during the existing war, &c I reply; that it is a subject, on the promotion of which I feel the deepest solicitude; and have taken some pains to encourage it, and to ascertain the amount of new effort that is making in this country to sustain our independence.

Except a few cabinet, wagon and carriage makers shops which are still carried on, we have had no manufacturing establishments. We have however, since the existing war commenced—having been in operation only five or six weeks—three spinning wheel factories, doing good business. The loom makers are busy; the ladies everywhere who can procure wheels are spinning both wool and cotton. Some of them have already produced long pieces of woolen janes, beautifully colored, and their patriotic husbands are proudly wearing it. The true spirit of independence prevails with so much resolute determination in the courageous heart of the Texan female throughout the families: it is easy to see that another year of war will clothe our population in substantial fabrics of their own production. Our ladies seem proud of the oppertunity, and they say so, of showing the yankee vandals that they ask no odds of them.

There are several shoe shops, perhaps a dozen, springing up in our county, and two distilleries in active operation.

Having been born in the subsiding smoke of our first revolution, I am old and can't do much of anything. However, on account of the warrior boys having appropriated all our blankets, and to show the Texans what may be done with our natural resources, I constructed a machine to spin the long moss (Tillan[d]sia usneoides) of our climate. Also, a loom to weave it, and have succeeded in producing a blanket composed entirely of the cleaned moss, that is valued by those who have seen it, at $20. It is indeed a superior article, weighing 18 pounds.

Carpets, rugs, bed blankets, saddle blankets, and if Kentucky had remained out of the confederacy, cotton bagging of a superior quality, could be supplied from this abundant natural production. It is quite strong and very durable.

In this report I speak only of Washington county. In Colorado county, at Thralesburg there is a tanery, which was in successful operation on a small scale previous to the war; within the present year they have enlarged considerably. I hear of other taneries about going into operation in several of the eastern counties.

In the adjoining county (Austin) there is a pottery which has been doing a small business, for perhaps a twelve month previous to the war. It is now in a flourishing state and still improving.

Should the blockade remain unbroken, which I most heartily hope may be the case, until it is ruptured by the confederate forces, a short period will develope manufacturies of all discriptions over the entire state.

Most Respectfully,
Gideon Lincecum

[1] Christopher G. Memminger (1803–88) of Charleston, a leader in South Carolina's secession from the Union, was secretary of the treasury of the Confederacy from 1861 to 1864, when he resigned under fire because of the poor condition of Confederate finances (Current, ed., *Encyclopedia of the Confederacy*, 3:1022–26). For a full study, see Ball, *Financial Failure and Confederate Defeat*.

To the secretary of war, Gideon once again put forward his missile proposal.

Long Point. Washington County. Texas.
17th December 1861

J. P. Benjamin[1]
Secretary of War
Sir.

On a subject, of what seems to me, of some importance, I

wrote on the 24th. of June last, to Messr. Leeds & Co., New Orleans. They replied to me discouragingly, stating that a certain misile, which I shall discribe presently, cannot be produced from iron. I am certain they are mistaken, and do not feel discouraged at what they have stated to me about it. I am acquainted with the principles of the subject of which I speak, and I am very certain that the misile I propose [can have no equal] in a field flight to protect batteries against charges of overwhelming number; and to sweep the decks of vessels and their rigging in a sea fight. It will too raise the capacity of a six pounder gun to that of a twenty four pounder, or four six pounders. A canister for a six pounder contains from 28 to 31 four ounce shot. I propose ounce shot, and even half that size for distances under one hundred yards. Not to supercede the ordinary canister shot, for the range to which they are suited, but for shorter distances. Say for the ounce shot, from one to three, and even four hundred yards. There being four times the number and equally destructive to life and limb, it is easily understood that the sweeping, devastating powers of the ounce would be four times as great as that of the quarter pound shot. Under one hundred yards and in an attempt to charge a battery, the half ounce shot would exercise an eightfold power in their sweeping influence.

If ounce and half ounce shot can be produced at a moderate cost, there is no mistake as to their great power, for the uses and distances I have named. If they cannot be produced at some foundry within the confederacy, it will not be safe to let the Yankees get the idea, for they can make cast iron waistcoat buttons at 20¢ the gross.

The reason assigned by Messrs. Leeds and C^{o} Iron founders at New Orleans for not being able to make them was their small size. That reason however, is not terrible; for there are millions of cast Iron buttons having five holes through them, less than a dram in weight.

Knowing as I do the wonderful destructive power of the misile I have suggested above, after my disappointment with Messr. Leeds and Co I did not think proper, or consider it safe to write again to them or any other iron foundry. And on that account have ventured to tax your time and patience with the matter.

My object for having maintained this matter as a secret is not the expectation of a pattent, or any kind of speculation or remuneration. I was born with the constitution of the U. S. that was; I have outlived it; and from those who caused the disruption and now are trying to throw the blame on us, I seek satisfaction.

I hope you may succeed at least so far as to make an experiment with the shot I have suggested. I have no fears as to the results. They will prove satisfactory.

Very Respectfully
Your Ob[t] Serv[nt]
Gideon Lincecum

[1]A remarkably able man, Judah P. Benjamin of New Orleans had been a U.S. senator (1853–61) before he joined Jefferson Davis's cabinet as attorney general. By this date he was secretary of war and finally would become secretary of state (Clement Eaton, *Jefferson Davis*, pp. 130–31; see also Eli N. Evans, *Judah P. Benjamin: The Jewish Confederate*, pp. 115–322).

As 1861 came to a close, Gideon submitted his final meteorological report in a letter dated 31 December to the Galveston News *and closed it saying, "And now, this last day of the year, we have green grass, flowers, butterflies and the hum of the industrious honey bee like spring."*

It had been a good year for Gideon and his family and, in most respects, for the Confederacy as well. But what lay ahead?

CHAPTER 4

1862

On the first day of the new year, 1862, Gideon Lincecum was confident that what lay ahead was ultimate victory for the Southern Confederacy, but he knew that the road to victory would not be an easy one. On that day he wrote to one of the local soldiers sent to defend the coast near Galveston and offered encouragement as well as a sober appraisal of some of the difficulties.

Long Point. Texas. 1st Jany. 1862

John H. Lewis[1]
Captn Lauderdale's Comp^y
Virginia Point, Tex.
Dear Sir.

Your highly esteemed favor of 26th. ult. came to my table at noon today.

You ask for my views in relation to the present phases and probable ultimates that are to be looked for from the position of the belligerent armies and the British question. To all of which, what I shall write will be nothing more than the simple opinion of an individual, based upon exaggerated newspaper reports.

In regard to the belligerent armies, it is my opinion that the fighting has not fairly commenced, especially if England does not interfere.[2] But that the confederate armies will ultimately triumph over the really barbarians of Lincolndom we need not entertain the slightest doubt. We shall, however, be forced to encounter many privations and hardships and a good deal of hard fighting. Having to commence our preparations from the stump, the movements of our forces have been necessarily tardy; consequently the northern soldier has had more time to whet up his courage and to prepare for systematic fighting. On that account, we shall have to fight harder. On which account also, we shall whip them worse.

In anticipation of a proposition from the north for peace, I see that the Confederate Congress have passed a resolution that they will conclude no peace with them, unless Maryland is left free to become one of the Confederate States.[3] That is right and I think indicated that the C.S. will not jump at the first proposition that may be offered for peace. There are a good many claims to be set up against the North besides the rights of the lukewarm Marylanders.

As for the Trent affair, all the civilized nations have already pronounced it a gross insult to the British flag; and if she submits to it, it will be what she has never been known to do before.[4] If Lincoln backs down, he will have the entire Abolition force upon his back immediately, and if he does not back down, a thing which he has already declared he will not do, and his congress sustains him in his resolution, he will most certainly have to prepare himself in short order for a war with England.

But let that affair go as it may, though it may result somewhat favorably to the southern coast towns, we should have nothing to do with England. We should enter into no alliances with her or any other European power. If England goes to war with the U.S. she will be certain to break up the blockade; and I am decidedly of the opinion that it would damage our cause. Let the blockade remain three years, and the confederate government will have placed herself in a condition to be independent of old England or any other country, in respect to manufacturies and all else that is necessary to sustain a free people. I do not object to anything calculated to devil and harass the incorragiable thieves of the north, but I do not feel any great degree of interest in British interference, nor can I now see how it will ultimate advantageously to the south; especially should we have anything to do with the English quarrel.

As to the attack on Galveston, that will depend on the successes of the Lincoln fleet further east. If they can take and establish themselves permanently, at several of the more conspicuous southern ports, you may then expect them to attack Texas sea ports. What advantage in a military point of view would it be to them, even if they passed Galveston now? And what harm would it do to Texas, except the damage it would inflict on the property of the loyal citizens of the place? They have business elsewhere, sufficient to employ all the force they have means to sustain; business which they cannot leave for such small game as Galveston or any other point on the seashore of Texas.

Except to drink their liquors and spend their money for their little tomfooleries, I can see no reason why the people of Galveston should desire to have the soldiers quartered in the town. Except you had plenty of heavy, long ranged guns, forty thousand men on the island could not prevent two or three first class war vessels from burning the town, from an anc[h]orage out of harm's way on the gulf side. Then, where numbers would only increase the carnage without being of any possible protection to the city, why should they want them there? As a piece of prudent generalship, I should oppose it as futile and altogether improper, should the place really be invaded.

To leave Galveston to join the army in Kentucky, Virginia, or Missouri, at this season of the year would kill more of the Texas troops than all the battles. Of those of the Texas soldiers who are there [Kentucky, Virginia, Missouri] now, great numbers are dead, and the remainder are all sick. Many of them who were in condition to travel have returned; some of them to this county. The letters that have been received from there corroborate the report of the returned soldiers, and it is distressing to contemplate. Of all the Texan volunteers that went to Kentucky there are not 300 able to go on duty, and they all look badly. Nothing but indomitable texas courage could force men to do military duty under such disparaging circumstances.[5]

There is no local news or anything that I could say about the people of this settlement that would be of interest to you. I thank you for your good intentions in regard to the oysters, but if you have not started them I would prefer that you wouldn't do it. There are so many delays and mishaps on the R[ail] Road that they would very probably spoil before they could reach Long Point.
—All's well—

Very Respectfully
Gideon Lincecum

[1] John Hawkins Lewis was mustered in on 25 October 1861 at Virginia Point as a sergeant in Company G of the 10th Regiment of Texas Infantry. He died of dysentery on 17 September 1862 (National Archives, *Compiled Service Records*, roll 340).

[2] For a discussion of the Confederacy's desire for British intervention and its efforts towards that end, see Current, ed., *Encyclopedia of the Confederacy*, 2:479–85, 710–12.

[3] The Confederate Congress resolved that no peace would ever be concluded with the United States that did not give Maryland the right to choose the Confederacy if she wanted it (E. Merton Coulter, *The Confederate States of America*, vol. 7 of *A History of the South*, p. 45).

[4] On 8 November 1861 a Union naval vessel stopped a British mail steamer, the *Trent*, on the high seas and seized the Confederate commissioners, James Mason and John Slidell, who were on their way to England to represent the Confederate government. The seizure evoked outrage by the British government and the threat of British intervention in the war. Contrary to Gideon's expectation, President Lincoln approved the release of the two commissioners on 26 December, which cooled the crisis (Current, ed., *Encyclopedia of the Confederacy*, 2:481–82). For a full treatment, see Norman B. Ferris, *The Trent Affair: A Diplomatic Crisis*.

[5] Fighting in Kentucky at this time were the 8th Texas Cavalry Regiment, better known as "Terry's Texas Rangers," and the 7th

Texas Infantry Regiment, both serving with Maj. Gen. William J. Hardee's Central Army of Kentucky (U.S. War Department, *War of the Rebellion: A Compilation of Official Records of the Union and Confederate Armies*, series 1, 7:76–78, 852–53; Wright, comp., and Simpson, ed., *Texas in the War*, pp. 20, 24, 78, 80, 113–14, 163).

In writing to an acquaintance in Mississippi eight days later, Gideon compared the Federal invasion of the South to "the intrusion of a destructive weed" into a "fine meadow": "I would . . . read you a lecture on the stultifying powers of the Gossypium [cotton] if I didn't know that the Yankees had opened a school on the subject for you. That will all come right again after we whip them sufficiently. And that we shall most certainly do, in the course of two or three years. We'll show them who 'wipes out.'"[1]

Ten days later Gideon extended his prediction of the length of the war to "three or four years"; the longer the better, he thought, for the growth of Southern manufactures and the breakup of the North. He also pointed out how he was saving gunpowder by using the bow and arrow for hunting. To his friend, Colonel Hay, he wrote:

Long Point. Tex. 18th Jany. 1862

Col. S. D. Hay
Huntsville, Texas
My Dear Sir.

Your favor of 13th. instant, enclosing J. H. Banton's circular came to hand day before yesterday.[2] It caught me in the act of compounding gun powder. Not much powder though. I was just putting up a few pounds for home consumption. I don't need much, however, as I do all my shooting for small game with the bow and arrow. It would amuse you to hear the remarks of our highly intelligent, <u>sober</u>, nonextortionate community, when one of them, by chance, comes across me while out shooting with my long bow. They think, I suppose, that what they say to me then is quite smart; and maybe it is, I am a poor judge of elevated thought, when well expressed, and therefore must not complain at them. Neither do I: But I can't avoid replying, when they bawl at me, "Once a man and twice a child." I reply, "In addressing myself to your red nose, I can inform you, that I feel more at ease under the excitement produced by the use of my bow and arrows than I should under the excitement of alcoholic liquors or a plan to speculate on the necessities of the unfortunate." "Oh! pshaw," say they, and they hurry on to liquor and to villainy. . . .

You apologize for your failure to visit me as you promised and ask if I can't come over soon and see you all. Well, I cannot think of anything that would be more agreeable to me than that would. But my folks are all gone to the war, and I am attending to things about home. We must not fail to make a full crop the coming season. The war will, as I most ardently hope, continue three or four years, and it behooves every one to do all he can to increase the quantity of provision supplies. The southern states will remain united; and if the war can be kept up for only three years, Lincolndom will be split into three or four bogus governments, which will run to ruin as fast as the Mexicans have. Some of their softest rogues have suggested the propriety of a recognition of confederate states as a government. They be damned. We have not recognized them as a government yet. The constitution of the U.S. was ruptured by them, and their government is a despotism. Therefore we cannot recognize it as a government. No let us fight them until there is not a man left in the whole south, sooner than acknowledge them as a government, much less make peace with them. Peace indeed. They are the spoilers of our once great nation and now we must spoil them. We'll do that "shore." I didn't want to talk about the war; but when I thought of the cause of my being forced to forego the pleasure of visiting and enjoying the society of my friends, I forgot myself, and have manifested a little ill temper—you will forgive me. . . .

Don't you esteem our legislature an affair of distinction? They passed a good many relief bills, protected the Sabbath, enacted the damnable stay law, and made a desperate effort to drain the last dollar from the treasury.[3] I have a list of their names; and if ever one of them gets elected again, for any office, either for honor or profit in Texas; it won't be by my vote, as sure as the gun's iron. . . . Respects from the old lady and Sarah and from me.

Most Sincerely thine.
Gideon Lincecum

[1] Gideon Lincecum to V. M. Johnson of Tacaleche, Miss., from Long Point, Tex., 9 January 1862, LP, Box 2E366.

[2] Joab H. Banton graduated from Austin College in 1854 as the valedictorian of the first class that earned the A.B. degree in Texas. In 1856 he received with three others the first Bachelor of Laws degrees awarded in Texas. One year later he received one of the first A.M. degrees. He practiced law in Huntsville and was appointed judge of the 33d District. His "circular" referred to here has not been located (George L. Landolt, *Search for the Summit: Austin College through Twelve Decades*, p. 79).

[3] On 7 December 1861 the ninth Texas legislature approved a law described as "An Act suspending all Laws for the collection of debts and liabilities on bonds, promissory notes, bills of exchange and contracts for the payment of money until the first day of January 1864 or until six months after the close of the present war, should it terminate before the date named, or until otherwise provided by law." It was indexed as the "Stay Law" (Hans P. N. Gammel, *The Laws of Texas, 1822–1897*, 5:449–50). Gideon's reference to the legislature draining the last dollar from the treasury referred to a bill that provided for legislators to be paid per diems and transportation expenses from various special funds in the treasury, including

the school fund and the university fund (Francis R. Lubbock, *Six Decades in Texas: Memoirs of Francis Richard Lubbock*, edited by C. W. Raines, pp. 351–54).

Criticism of the Texas legislature was nothing new for Gideon, and his fault finding became stronger, not weaker, as the war went on. To an English visitor in Texas, who shared with Gideon an interest in Spiritualism (as did Colonel Hay), Gideon stated emphatically what he thought the outcome of the war should be.

Long Point. Tex. 19 Jany. 1862

R. B. Hannay[1]
Hempstead, Texas
My Dear Sir.

. . . In relation to our great war, it must continue until we whip them into their senses, or until the north splits up into three or four bogus republics, when they will go to ruin as fast as did the Mexican Republic. The confederate states, remaining united, will progress in grand style to a magnificent power among the nations of the earth. I am opposed to any peace that will put the slightest restriction on our notions of the states rights principles. I would prefer that the war should continue until not a man in the whole south should be left alive, sooner than submit to anything else. The old motto, "Liberty or death" suits my notions very well, just at this juncture.

You said you was coming over soon! All's well.

Thine.
Gideon Lincecum

[1] R. B. Hannay was visiting his brother on the lower Brazos River when the Civil War started and was unable to return to his home in England. From 1861 to 1868 Gideon wrote to him frequently. The

last letter was addressed to Hannay in London, England (Burkhalter, *Gideon Lincecum*, p. 160).

Gideon took a special interest in local soldiers who were fighting in the war, especially those who served with members of his own family. The following letter is an example.

Long Point. Texas. 29 January 1862

Dr. J. Boring, A.A.S.[1]
C. S. A.
San Antonio, Texas
Sir.

What I am about to say to you may not be considered of any weight in your decision on the subject; but it can do no harm for me to state that feeling some interest in the health and soldiership of the young man, F. M. Gaston, [of] Capt. G. W. Campbell's compy., Sibley's Brigade, now on furlough; and whose unflinching patriotism sets him out on foot for San Antonio tomorrow, I noticed his case.[2]

On his return to this place, I examined him carefully. I found that he had been well treated during the active stages of the disease; and that his system had been prepare[d] and left in a condition to recover rapidly. Which he did; gaining flesh and cheerfulness, as speedily as could be desired. But the constitutional defect, which I had many times noticed in him previously to his joining the army, seems to be somewhat deeper seated; manifesting itself in the form of a dry, raspy, husky hacking cough, at every (even moderate) sinking of atmospheric temperature.

I have no desire nor am I attempting to procure his exemption from the service. Neither have I heard him utter a single syllable that would indicate anything but a determined resolution to return to his post. It is my opinion that in a warm climate he is able to perform the duties of an average soldier. But I should not be willing to risk him during the winter and spring months in a higher latitude than he is now in.

Very Respectfully
Gideon Lincecum, M.D.

[1] The only service record we could find for Dr. Boring is a listing in the index to *Compiled Service Records* for "Jessee Boring" as "Gen. and staff surgeon" with no state specified. After the war ended, Dr. Boring practiced medicine in Chappell Hill, Texas (Nath Winfield and Judy Winfield, *All Our Yesterdays: A Brief History of Chappell Hill*, p. 33).

[2] F. M. Gaston is listed as a private in the muster roll (as of 5 September 1861) of 5th Regiment, Texas Mounted Volunteers (Cavalry), Company F, mustered in Washington County (Hall, *Sibley's New Mexico Campaign*, p. 273). Service records also place him at Jordan Saline (March 1863), Hempstead (July 1863), Richmond (September 1863, with Terrell's Regiment), and Mound Prairie (September 1864) (National Archives, *Compiled Service Records*, roll 33).

On the same day, Gideon wrote to another member of Sibley's Brigade and provided an update on the war from his perspective.

Long Point. Texas. 29th Jany. 1862

Lieut. B. B. Seat[1]
Sibley's Brigade, New Mexico
(Cap. Campbell Company F
5th Reg[t] T. M. V.
El Passo, Texas)
My Dear young Friend.

Your welcome letter of 10th. inst. came to hand yesterday—18 days en route—

You desire that I shall give you the latest war news. There has been but two battles of any importance in a long time. That took place in the cherokee nation, between Apothleyoholo the great Creek Warrior, having under his command in the fight 4000 men—and some Texas rangers, an Arkansas regiment also, some chahta [Choctaw] and chikisha [Chickasaw] Indians, amounting altogether to 1200 men, under Genl. McIntosh. McIntosh attacked their camp and routed them in a few minutes; persued them 25 miles, breaking up Apothleyoho's army entirely. They had been armed and equipped by the Lincolnites with an extravigant outfit. It, however, turned out a failure, like all their plans have so far. Our men took possession of Apothleyholo's camp, which was quite rich. The finale of the battle sums up: 300 warriors killed and over 500 of their women and children captured. Also, 20 negroes, 1100 horses, 43 loaded wagons, 90 yoke of oxen, 500 beef cattle, 600 sheep, and a large lot of ammunition and provisions. They had been furnished with the best kind of provisions and other conveniences, even feather beds.[2] It is said that Apothleyoholo's command is completely broken up.

. . . on the 15th Jan. near Prestonsburg in Ky. a severe fight took place between Genl. Marshall with 2500 men, and the Lincolnites, who were 8000 strong—Genl. Marshall retreated before them until he reached a narrow gorge in the mountains.[3] In this position he received the overwhelming forces of the enemy. The enemy fought bravely, but were finally routed, and a Bull run fight was re-enacted. Their loss as near as could be ascertained was about 200 killed and wounded. The confederate loss was 25 killed and 15 wounded.[4] Marshall, finding his men all tired down, fell back upon Prestonsburg. There have been some other cases of skirmishing, but the results are not worth naming. 8 or ten days since, two of the Lincoln vessels made an attack on the little Fort Velasco, at the mouth of the Brazos.[5] They fired 22 guns but the little guns at the fort began to pester them as I suppose, and they made haste to take distance. The citizens evacuated Galveston for a while, but since the arrival of the long range rifle cannon, they have all gone back again. There is, however, a general threatening of a forward movement in the entire army and navy of Lincolndom, and it is, I believe, generally thought that they will give our boys something to do soon.[6] The boys are at every point ready for them. All our important sea port towns have been greatly strengthened recently. New Orleans, it is thought, is prepared to resist successfully the entire Federal force. All the way up the Mi[ssissippi] river, great and very powerful preperations have been made for the reception of the grand army and 13 iron clad gun boats, when they attempt, as they have promised, to descend the river on their way to New Orleans. The Memphis papers say that enough torpedoes and submarine batteries have been made and carried away from their foundries to blow up all the vessels on the river.[7]

Missouri and Kentucky are at this time in the worst condition. Quite a number of the citizens of Mo. and some Kentuckians are here now, who, having made shift to escape with a few of their negroes, have brought them to Texas, hoping thereby to save them. Having left their families behind, they are in great haste to return. Some of them belonging to the army are here on furlough, and they hire [out] their negroes where they can;[8] most, however, are put out for their victuals and clothes. The accounts that these men give of the state of affairs in those divided states are truly distressing. Every thing that spite and malice, and cherished with a natural propensity for thieving, from the midnight assassin with his incendiary box of matches, to the broad daylight robbing and plundering, is performed there daily and hourly; and even more horrible deeds than these are being enacted there between men who had lived [as] neighbors for years.[9] But I will not extend the list of horrors.

The general sentiment of the English people and of Canada is embodied in the little slip from the Manchester Guardian (England) herewith enclosed. But we should not look to England or any other power. We can do the work ourselves. Let England and France remain spectators of the American strife. It will redound more to their credit; and besides, it will afford them an opportunity to witness the results of a game those two nations have never seen fairly plaid out. They will see if they let us alone, that half the number, when contending on the battle field, for the liberty in a just cause, can utterly discomfit and destroy the villainous hosts of the tyrant. If we can steer clear of European interference, and keep up the war for two or three years, we shall see Lincolndom split up into three or four petty dynasties who will rob and prey upon each other as freely as they plunder our borders now. Mind that.

The Texas boys who went to Kentucky and other stations North have not tarnished their ancient fame, but a large portion have fell victims to disease.[10] Poor fellows, they went willingly to the aid of their brethren in the struggle for liberty. They could boldly face the foe to their rights and die freely, but they could not stand so great an odds in climate. They died reluctantly and sullenly. There is a great deal said about the god of battles. Heads of departments on both sides of the line of unholy stripe are constantly directing the attention of the two armies and of the community to his wonderful providences. Well, if there be any such warrior god, and we are to judge of his character, from what we see going on now; it is a "dem" [damn] bad one. For taking "hisn up one side and down 'tother, he is doing as much harm as good."

No changes have taken place in this settlement since you left. In fact there are but few remaining to make a change, should such a thing be desirable. The old lady sends love to Jo and Cash.[11] Tells them to be brave and steady; And to yourself, firmness and discretion—"Le" [Leonora] got a letter from

George yesterday. Sarah is at Brenham, aiding in a concert for the hospital benefit. I, having all confidence in you, have nothing more to say at this sitting.

Gideon Lincecum

[1] B. B. Seat is listed as a second lieutenant in the muster roll (as of 5 September 1861) of 5th Regiment, Texas Mounted Volunteers (Cavalry), Company F, mustered in Washington County (Hall, *Sibley's New Mexico Campaign*, p. 272; National Archives, *Compiled Service Records*, roll 35). Lt. Beck Seat of Brenham (twenty-eight years old in January 1862) is identified as one of Gideon's "Infidel" correspondents in Burkhalter, *Gideon Lincecum*, p. 107n. In May 1859 Gideon subscribed to the *Boston Investigator* for Seat.

[2] The great disparities between Gideon's accounts of these battles (probably based on newspaper reports) and the later analyses of them by Civil War historians (some of whom disagree) are indicative of the remaining uncertainties about many Civil War battles. In contrast to Gideon's version, Stephen Oates says that in the winter of 1861 a bloody uprising was led by the Creek chieftain Opothleyahola (spellings of his name vary), who was violently opposed to Confederate alliances with the Five Nations in the Indian Territory. In October he gathered two thousand of his warriors and "crush[ed] Colonel D. H. Cooper's Confederate Indian cavalry in running battles at Round Mounds (November 19) and Bird Creek (December 9)." Thoroughly beaten and weakened by desertions to the enemy, Cooper requested reinforcements from Col. James McIntosh at Van Buren, Arkansas, who agreed to help and picked sixteen hundred of his best horsemen to ride with him to meet Cooper at Fort Gibson. Once they met, he and Cooper planned a trap for Opothleyahola, with their respective forces approaching his camp from two sides. However, McIntosh arrived first and decided not to wait for Cooper before striking. After his forces had been pinned down for two hours, it was only through a furious assault by a group of Texans under Lt. Col. Walter Lane that the battle of Chustenahlah was won by McIntosh, with Opothleyahola's troops fleeing into Kan-

sas. McIntosh's troops suffered nine fatalities and forty men wounded. The subsequent arrival of Cooper and Col. Stand Watie, in command of three hundred Cherokees, resulted in their planning and carrying out an intense pursuit of the remnants of the Creek forces, most of whom were hunted down and killed. Oates says that the decisive defeat of Opothleyahola meant that by 5 January 1862 all Federal resistance in the Creek nation had been stamped out (Stephen B. Oates, *Confederate Cavalry West of the River*, pp. 31–33). Another source gives a somewhat different account, indicating that on 9 December 1861, in an engagement at Chusto-Talash (Bird Creek), Indian Territory, Confederate forces (mainly Indians) defeated pro-Union Creek Indians led by Opothleyahola, although subsequently the Confederates had to withdraw because of supply shortages. On 26 December 1861 there was another engagement, this time at Chustenahlah, Indian Territory, again with pro-Union Creeks led by Opothleyahola against Confederate Indians and Texans. After severe losses, the Creeks fled, some reaching Kansas after severe privations (Long and Long, *The Civil War Day by Day*, pp. 148, 152). Neither source mentions the extravagant outfitting of Opothleyahola's camp (e.g., feather beds) that Gideon referred to. The exact figures cited here by Gideon appeared in the *Galveston News* of 28 January 1862 under the heading "Plunder," with the *Tyler Reporter* cited as the source.

[3] On 10 January 1862 (not 15 January), a battle was fought to a draw near Prestonburg (Middle Creek) in far eastern Kentucky. The attacking Union troops were led by Col. (later President) James A. Garfield. Each side withdrew but thought it had won (James G. Randall, *The Civil War and Reconstruction*, p. 279; *Official Records of the Rebellion*, series 1, 7:46–50). Brig. Gen. Humphrey Marshall (1812–72) of Kentucky, a veteran of the U.S.-Mexican War and a former congressman and minister to China, led the Confederate forces in the battle at Prestonburg (Warner, *Generals in Gray*, pp. 212–13).

[4] Gideon's figures on casualties at Prestonburg were not far from the mark. The Confederate commander, Gen. Humphrey Marshall,

reported his loss at 11 killed and 15 wounded and estimated the Union loss at more than 250 killed and about 300 wounded (*Official Records of the Rebellion*, series 1, 7:46–50).

[5] Old Velasco, Texas (founded in 1831), was on the east side of the Brazos River, sixteen miles south of Angleton and four miles from the Gulf of Mexico in southeastern Brazoria County. During the Civil War the port of Velasco was fortified by Confederate troops and eight gun batteries. The port played an active role in the exchange of cotton for European guns, ammunition, milled goods, and medicines. In an attempt to stop this vital trade, Federal troops on vessels offshore fired on shore defenses, patrols, and small craft trying to outrun them. In January 1862 several Union vessels engaged the shore batteries at Velasco and Paso Cavallo (the main entrance to Matagorda Bay), testing their strength and range. By February 1862 Col. Joseph Bates's defenses at Velasco were reportedly stronger, improved by cannon originally intended for Aransas Pass. At Velasco there were also reported Confederate attacks on U.S. vessels on 4 July 1862 and 11 August 1862 (Long and Long, *The Civil War Day by Day*, pp. 237, 250; *New Handbook of Texas*, 6:718–19; Alwyn Barr, "Texas Coastal Defense, 1861–65," *Southwestern Historical Quarterly* 65 [July 1961]: 9, 11).

[6] The Union strategists were indeed planning to give the rebels "something to do." The "Anaconda plan" called for tightening the coastal blockade, seizing control of the Mississippi River, advancing up its eastern tributaries (especially the Tennessee and Cumberland Rivers), advancing on Richmond in the east, and tightening the noose on the Confederacy (McPherson, *Ordeal by Fire*, pp. 208–9; Bruce Catton, *This Hallowed Ground: The Story of the Union Side of the Civil War*, p. 53).

[7] Gideon was overly optimistic about the Confederacy's growing capacity to defend the Mississippi River against the expected Union attack. The Union navy was growing rapidly and was more heavily armed. Advancing both downriver and upriver, by April Union forces had gained control of all of the river except the portion between Vicksburg and Baton Rouge (McPherson, *Ordeal by Fire*, pp. 230–32; Catton, *This Hallowed Ground*, pp. 148–51).

[8] For a good treatment of the "hiring out" system in Texas, see Campbell, *An Empire for Slavery*, pp. 82–92, 243–46.

[9] The borderlands, especially Missouri and Kentucky, experienced much random, internecine warfare reflecting the deep divisions and rivalries within their populations (McPherson, *Ordeal by Fire*, pp. 157–59; Foote, *The Civil War*, 1:357–58).

[10] In general, for every soldier killed in battle in the Confederate army, there were three deaths from disease (Long and Long, *The Civil War Day by Day*, p. 712; see also Steiner, *Disease in the Civil War)*.

[11] Joseph and Cassianus Lincecum, Gideon's grandsons.

A few days later Gideon wrote a very different sort of letter to John Lewis, the local soldier he had written to on the first day of the year.

Long Point. Texas. 2nd February 1862

J. Hawkins Lewis
Post, Virginia Point, Tex.
Esteemed Young Friend.

Your very acceptable communication of 28th. ult. came to hand yesterday. It breathes, like all the letters I receive from our boys in the army do, a degree of suspicion, though somewhat smothered, that the heads of departments, both civil and military, are at fault somewhere. Too tardy in their movements is the word they use to express veiled thoughts, and it means a great deal more. It indicates a deep-rooted dissatisfaction at the unnecessary inactivity and useless expenditure of the time and means and strength of the common soldier, while the pets and favorites of the government are luxuriating in speculations and peculations of the deepest, darkest, and most damnable character. And whether this dissatisfaction amongst the common soldiers arises from the fact that their position in the army precludes the possibility of taking a hand in the frauds and downright thievings that is daily practiced in every department of governmental appointments or whether it swells up from the pure patriotic hearts of the true devotees of the spirit of liberty, the ultimates will be the same. If the villainies and multiplicities of flagrant wrongs that are being practiced upon our people, both in and out of the army, be permitted to continue, the results will be, that tired of being held in check, for the purpose of extending the time and widening the field for the opperations of the heartless peculator, the common soldier will become impatient, and signs of demoralization and insubjection will be visible.

To a sharp observer, occupying a position from whence he could overlook the entire scene of our difficulties without knowing the cause of it or what the parties are aiming at, he would be forced to the conclusion that the two governments had concocted and were successfully carrying out a plan to rob and plunder and ruin the peace and happiness of the independent and well-to-do inhabitants on both sides of the Mason's and Dixon's line. And he would say to himself, "If that suffering people did but possess sufficient intellectual decernment to discover the weir [wire] traps and snares by which they are environed and were <u>honest</u> enough themselves, to know how to do right, they would at once stack their arms. Tell those who raised the difficulty to do the fighting, and return to their families and <u>honest</u> vocations."

"Intelligence and honesty." There lies the rub. The masses do not possess it. Neither do the assumed higher classes possess it. It is a rule that seldom varies, that the higher the order of the intellectual developments, the greater the power and the inducements for fraud and deception. To imitate the masters of ceremonies and those characters whose superior cunning have placed them in the highest and safest thieving positions, is the boasted <u>privilege</u> of the toadies and lower grades of intellectuality. You know all this. And you also know that the high handed game of fraud and villainy is daily played off before their faces, in open sun light, and the masses cannot avoid seeing it. But they are nevertheless mum. Shut up as tight as a disturbed oyster. It would be looked upon as a foolish departure from the known rules of plain truth for me to ascribe this silence among the masses to any other cause than the fear of losing the chances of getting a hand in the great and universally acceptable game in the short route to wealth and honor themselves. They know they possess the numerical superiority; and if they entertained no hope of winning a stake at some stage of the game, they would at once cease to aid as performers in it. Upon the knowledge of this proclivity to dishonesty in the great godserving masses of the people, despots stake their fortunes in the game for thrones. They care not how much sorrow and blood and murder, plunderings and destruction of cities and countries and people the toy may cost, so they obtain it. Then all pretensions to freedom of thought or speech amongst the people who played the bloody game and won the position for the despot must be put down or the throne topples. This is the condition of all monarchical governments. They are all violent opposers of any degree of individual rights or claims to freedom by the great mass of the people. They put down the sentiment of liberty everywhere they can. Don't forget that, as we pass along the rugged route.

The southern confederate states hoisted the banner of liberty. Proclaimed to the world the principles of individual state sovereignty; have throttled the foe and are manfully struggling in the bloody contest for the holy principle. It is a hard life and death conflict. Many may become wearied and look around for assistance. Where is it to come from? From a crowned despot? The spirit of liberty never has and never can receive any valuable aid from a crowned head. You will cite me to France, in the time of our first struggle for freedom. But France was approximating, at the time, to a republican form of government—in the transition state; and in her resentment to England, who opposed their plans for a free people, she came to our aid. England is not in the condition now that France was then. She entertains no love for republics. The despot at Washington suits her notions of propriety much better. Her interest, however, inclines her to get a finger in our cotton. If she attempts to render any aid to our cause, she will have herself well paid for it. The Goddess of Liberty will have no joyous triumphs to flap her wings over, after our alliance with any despot. You say, "when we can with proper care and statesmanship form alliances with England, which will enable us to secure credit" &c. I say so too, but I doubt the statesmanship—It would have resulted a great deal more to our credit and the success of our cause, if we had have let Europe alone from the start. The friends of liberty do not reside over there.

Thine in holiness

All's Well Gideon Lincecum

One wonders how much young John Lewis's morale was lifted by Gideon's sweeping criticism of the government and citizenry the soldiers were defending. To his "Infidel" friend Judge Rutherford, who was apprehensive about the course and impact of the war, Gideon wrote more encouragingly.

[February 1862; heading missing]

To J. A. Rutherford

. . . "This war will retard science," &c, you say. It will in the Lincoln despotism, but not in the southern confederacy. The creative spirit that has been so long asleep from the use of northern opiates is now wide awake, and we hear of wheels, looms, cotton, and woolen factories. Iron foundries, gun factories, powder mills, paper mills, shipbuilding, new inventions of many descriptions and character springing up everywhere, over the length and breadth of the confederacy. And I predict that if we can keep the war up for no longer a term than three years, we shall be the most self-sustaining and most independent people on the globe. We must all, therefore, oppose every peace movement that may be offered until the terms shall cut off all commercial intercourse with the northern states. This we can be certain to effectuate, if the enemies to liberty amongst us are not too numerous. Your allusions to the double teachings of the bible is a truism. But that is the very grounds upon which all villainies are sustained. Don't the heads of departments on both sides of the Mason's and Dixon's line issue their proclamations for thanksgivings, and publish the wonderful providential interferences in both armies, and don't ignorance see the shielding hand and shout his praise? But all this only serves to demonstrate what has been many times repeated: "that ignorance is the cause of all our suffering.["] War is among nations as natural as quarrels and combats between individual man or dogs. You speak of the present war as a check upon progress and science. Why, didn't we progress and progress through a long series of years, until we progressed into what is about to turn out one of the bloodiest and most disastrous conflicts the world ever saw? And are we not to view this great "irrepressible conflict" that our rulers and drivers had told us of so long before it came, as the highest ultimate attainable by human ingenuity at the present period of Earth's existence? You speak of the great number of lives that will be lost &c. And I will endeavor to console you, by assuring you that there is no danger of losing the seed of humanity. You say you sleep with your gun "for the sake of the blacks." We have about 6,000 blacks in this county, and a more willing, subordinate set of negroes I have never seen anywhere.[1] We sent hundreds and hundreds of them to throw up breast works at Virginia Point. They conducted themselves so orderly that they received high praise.

I wrote and forwarded a letter to you on the 20th ult. Yours was 39 days en route. Present me respectfully to your family, and believe me, not much frustrated, and that I remain as ever, in righteousness thine.

Gideon Lincecum

[1] In 1860 the slave population of Washington County was 7,941, out of a total population of 15,215. This compares to a total population in 1850 of 5,983, of which 2,817 were slaves (*New Handbook of Texas*, 6:835).

Gideon's fertile mind, which led him to explore so many branches of the sciences, now kept coming up with ideas that might help in the prosecution of the war or relieve the growing shortages on the home front. With sulphur, a vital ingredient in gunpowder, in short supply, Gideon's mind reached back to recall a source he had seen when he was on the Alabama frontier in 1818.

Long Point. Texas. 6 Feb. 1862

To the Mayor
of Tuscaloosa, Ala.
Sir.

In these troublous times, when we are cut off from the manufacturing world with but a small supply of the actual and most necessary material for carrying on the war against our demented invaders; to make the matter work as conveniently as possible, it behooves everyone to think and to labor too as far as in him lies, for the purpose of strengthening our powers of resistance and to sustain our ultimate independence. We must as fast as possible become a manufacturing people. At present, our greatest want is gun powder. This article of defence would be produced almost in every settlement, if people could procure Nitre and Sulphur.[1] The nitre can be extracted with but moderate labor from every horse lot and smoke house in sufficient quantities, to say nothing of several saltpetre caves that can be worked to advantage; and I think that plenty of sulphur can be procured near your city. I will tell you where to find it, and you must get some of your chemists to analyze it for you.

It is forty years since I saw it, and it may be that I am mistaken as to the character of the mineral I am about to refer you to. I feel certain, however, that you will find that I am correct if you make the examination. Projecting from the right bank as you go down and in the bed of the river, 8 miles below Tuscaloosa, is the most extensive deposits of Sulphuret of Iron that I have ever met with in any country.[2] Sulphur enough for the War. Let me hear from you.

Very Respectfully,
Gideon Lincecum

[1] On the supplying of nitre (also known as saltpeter or potassium nitrate) and sulphur, see Current, ed., *Encyclopedia of the Confederacy*, 3:1146–48.

[2] In March 1818 the Lincecum clan, headed by Gideon's father, Hezekiah, and including Gideon, his wife Sarah, and their first two children, began a westward trek from the Ocmulgee River in Georgia. They stopped at Tuscaloosa, Alabama, and remained there until November 1818. Gideon had time to explore the countryside and apparently found a deposit of sulphur eight miles downstream on the Black Warrior River. Sulphur is one of three components in black powder, the other two being saltpeter and charcoal (Lincecum and Phillips, *Adventures of a Frontier Naturalist*, pp. 49–58).

What Gideon heard from the mayor of Tuscaloosa, if anything, we do not know, as little of his incoming mail has been preserved. He did hear from his sister Emily and her hus-

band, D. B. Moore, however, from their home on the Texas frontier, and he hastened to reply.

Long Point. Texas. 18th. Feb. 1862

Dear Brother & Sister,

Your kind favor of 4th, inst. came to hand at noon today, and we read the news it contained with deep interest and sorrow. We are sorry to hear that the weapon of the wily savage has reached and deprived your family of one of its members, and interested in your statement that the balance of the family are well, and doing well as could be expect[ed] in these troublous war times.[1]

It is true that the war is bearing heavily every where now, and promises to be a great deal worse. It is my impression that our troubles are not fairly commenced yet; and we should prepare outselves for any and every species of hardship, aye even death and the destruction of everything we have on earth, sooner than submit to the yoke that is preparing for us by the fanatic vandals of the north. We must defeat their tyranous schemes or be found on the gory battle fields. This sentiment is general in the south.

They have enacted in their congress at Washington, that they will make the rebel states pay the expense of the war; and as we shall have no money wherewith to pay the war debt for the North their Generals are to be instructed to seize our lands, negroes, and other property; destroy the white people, put overseers over our farms and negroes, and make them produce 15 millions of cotton bales per annum, until the war debt is extinguished.[2] For this purpose they are at this moment, straining eve[r]y nerve both by land and sea. Their war preperations are incredibly extensive, and they are determined to wipe us out. So far, however, they have failed almost at every point. They have gained but few victories. None where the battle was an important one.[3] They have by arraying extraordinary force succeeded in capturing some of the small unimportant points along the sea coasts, but they dare not venture out on the mainland. They seem to aim their main effort at Charlestown and Savanah; but as yet they have succeeded only in taking a few of the islands about the mouths of the rivers. In Missouri, Kentucky and east Tennessee, the people being divided, they are having terrible times. Great numbers are gathering up some of their negroes and running them farther south. Several families from Missouri have recently arrived in this vicinity, have hired out their negroes & returned to the Army, to see the balance of the fighting. The accounts these men give of the state of affairs in Missouri are truly distressing. Being pretty equally divided, the people only meet to kill each other, burn houses and plunder and destroy property. The same savage warfare is dayly perpetrated in Kentucky and east Tennessee. Besides the war that is carrying on among the citizens of these disaffected states, there are large armies of Lincolnites from other states, quartered upon the people, who are devouring and otherwise destroying the wealth of those rich countries with a ruthlessness, and diabolical malevolence that the veriest savage would shudder to contemplate. They boast of having already in the field 600,000 of the best equipt soldiers in the world, and that, having the advantage of overwhelming numbers, inexhaustable means, and all the Navy; they are able, and do intend to wipe us out. There is no two ways about it, they say.

The 12th. of the present month was the day they had appointed for a general forward movement;[4] the attacks on all our defences was to be simultaneous and the wiping out process was to commence. The appointed day has passed, and we are not wiped out yet. And that aint the worst of it. Another february will come and pass, and another, before they can wipe us out, and then they may find themselves somewhat wiped. But they will doubtless give us heavy and expensive work to do.

I have now given you a sketch of the most prominent and best looking features on the Lincoln side of the picture. Powerful and well arranged as may appear their numbers and appointments, their extensive naval force, their numerous artillery, and fine small arms with plenty of amunition, they are, nevertheless, the subjects of many fearful (and what will prove to be) disasterious drawbacks. Antagonistic to all the splendor and opulence of their navy preparations, their 600,000 strong, well equipt army and their deep laid plans for robbing and subjecting the rebel states, is, in the first place, facing them at every point of approach an army 400,000 strong, pretty well equipt, possessing an iron will and indomitable courage, and all ready to lay down their lives and fortunes for the cause in which they are engaged.[5]

In the second place their army is made up of foreigners, and the out of business rabble of their crowded cities, who are fighting for pay and the promise [of] plunder, constituting a species of soldier who are never reliable in boldly contested battles.[6] In the third place the northern farmers and mechanics, many of them, are getting tired of the badly conducted government and not only expensive but ruinous war, and are complaining loudly at Lincoln and all his officers, both civil and military. In the fourth place their Banks have refused to lend them any more money and will not agree to take their issues of treasury notes, in consequence of which, they are now, to keep their army in motion, being forced to issue their irredeemable bonds on a scale so extensive that it will preclude all expectation of even the possibility that the government can ever find means to take them in again.[7] Resulting from this extravagant issue of government script is a general panic amongst the merchants and business men of every discription; adding to all this their national debt, which according to their own statements, amounts already to a billion of dollars; and the general derangement and suppression of shell factories, commerce, and their entire labor system; they are confidently looking for a ruinous and universal crash.

In the fifth place, like all robbers, they do not possess the courage to face and fight these bold spirits who are boldly & manfully contending for nothing more than their natural rights.

In the sixth place, their governmental, and military officers do not possess the intellectual capacity, to enable them to cope with the governmental and military officers of the confederacy.

In the seventh place, they have themselves split up into several parties; whereas, except the border states and a few towns in Texas made up of foreigners and yankees, the south is a united brotherhood, asking and contending for nothing but their rights.[8]

Contemplating the very nearly true picture which I have drawn for you, I think that you will find the chances for ultimate success largely preponderating in favor of our loved confederacy, and that we should be encouraged to fight on.

Having given you a statement, as it stands in my mind, from a careful examination of the accounts of both parties, as to the present aspect and probable ultimates of our existing war, I will now proceed to say something in regard to our individual home affairs and family relations.

Well, our entire family, which at this time, counting in the old lady and myself, amounts to 56, are all enjoying vigorous good health. Notwithstanding the fact that our brood are already somewhat large, the prospects for a great many more are quite promising. Our married children are all settled off on good homes, are sober, industrious, and are successful in the accumulation of property, living very comfortably, & creditably. The old lady, as well as myself, are very healthy and have made up our minds to remain here below until we enjoy the luxury of seeing the confounded, blasted, damned, theiving yankees utterly discomfitted and trampled in the sloughs of ignomenious disgrace.

It did not rain a great deal last year, but enough during crop time to enable us to produce abundant crops of corn and sugar cane, which with the heavy mast of acorns has filled our smoke houses with a superabundance of thick bacon, our barrels with 500 gallons of superior syrup,[9] and overflowed our cribbs with large sound corn, which had not been the case during the previous seven years. It looks mighty well to me, for I had been buying and eating foreign bread until my means had just about run out. Its all right now. One full crop set all straight again. Our greatest difficulty at the present is the war tax. Every body are anxious to pay and will sell property to do so, but there is no money to buy it.

We received yesterday a letter from George Campbell, bearing date, 25th of January. They are all well. Campbell is captain of Company F, Sibl[e]y's Brigade, and are for the present stationed in Fort Thorn, New Mexico.[10] They are three or four days march from Fort Craig, the place they set out to battle against.[11] It was garrisoned by 1000 regular Federal troops and about 2000 Mexicans, whom they had enlisted to join the Lincoln Army. General Sibley had issued a very pretty and sensible proclamation to the inhabitants of New Mexico, which had the effect to discredit the tales that had been told them by the Lincolnites, and Sibleys Brigade was received with open arms by the Mexicans. Thus gaining the privilige of marching his troops through their teritory unmolested, he set out for Fort Craig and had progressed to Fort Thorn, 60 or 70 miles from the Federal garrison, and were waiting for all their men to come up, when they received information, as Campbell states, that the Lincoln troops had evacuated Fort Craig and had marched in the direction of Calafornia. Sibleys Brigade, as soon as they establish a government in New Mexico, will continue their march toward Missouri.[12] Cassianus and Jo, Lycurgus' two older boys, are in Capt Campbell's company, and George says they are soldiers of the true Lincecum stock.

The old lady is very anxious to see you all, and thinks of trying to make the trip in may, if every thing goes well. Sarah sends love to all, and will see you if her mother pays you a visit. I shall go too if any does. And in the mean time shall offer up my most holy prayers for your saf[e]ty and success in all things needful.

Your Brother,
Gid

[1] Pete Ketchum, who was married to Sarah Eleanor "Sally" Moore, a daughter of Boone and Emily Moore, was killed by Indians near Hondo (Sowell, *Early Settlers and Indian Fighters of Southwest Texas*, p. 596).

[2] On 6 August 1861 Congress passed a limited "Confiscation Act" and on 17 July 1862 it would pass a much broader, more severe act, but it never went as far as Gideon charged here. However, some Radical Republicans, such as Rep. Thaddeus Stevens, made fiery proposals to turn the South into a wasteland and repopulate it with freedmen (McPherson, *Ordeal by Fire*, pp. 266–67, 269–70; Randall, *Civil War and Reconstruction*, p. 371).

[3] Probably Gideon had not yet heard of the Union capture of the strategically important Confederate strongholds of Fort Henry on the Tennessee River (6 February) and Fort Donelson on the Cumberland River (16 February).

[4] On 27 January 1862 President Lincoln issued "General War Order No. 1," directing a forward movement of all Union armies on 22 February (the anniversary of George Washington's birth). He hoped that this rather clumsy stratagem would counteract public impatience and prod General McClellan into action, but it had no military effect (McPherson, *Ordeal by Fire*, p. 222).

[5] Gideon underestimates the Union advantage in numbers. Although there is no accurate means of determining how many indi-

viduals served at a given time, estimates are that at the start of 1862 the Federals had a two-to-one advantage, which steadily mounted, reaching three-to-one by the end of 1864. The estimated numbers at the beginning of 1862 were 637,126 Union troops and 258,680 Confederate troops. These are total enrollments; both sides suffered from heavy absenteeism (Long and Long, *The Civil War Day by Day*, p. 706).

[6] Probably what Gideon means by "foreigners" is recent immigrants, but records show that three-fourths of the Union army were native-born Americans (McPherson, *Ordeal by Fire*, pp. 356–57; Long and Long, *The Civil War Day by Day*, p. 707).

[7] Estimates of the cost of the war vary. One source argues that in January 1863, with the war not half over and increasing in tempo, the daily cost of war for the North was $2.5 million per day (*Congressional Globe*, 37th Cong., 3d sess., part 1, p. 286). Much of the war expense was financed by paper money issues and loans. However, about 20 percent of the Federal receipts by 1865 came from the nation's first income tax, enacted 2 August 1861 (Davis Rich Dewey, *Financial History of the United States*, 12th ed., pp. 267, 299, 329–30). For a more recent discussion of how the Union financed the war, see McPherson, *Ordeal by Fire*, pp. 203–7. For a modern estimate of the cost of the war, see Phillip Shaw Paludan, *A People's Contest: The Union and Civil War, 1861–1865*, 2d ed. p. 113.

[8] A significant number of Southerners fought for the Union. Generals George Gordon Meade, Winfield Scott, and George Thomas are prominent examples (Warner, *Generals in Blue*, pp. 315–17, 429–30, 500–502; see also Richard N. Current, *Lincoln's Loyalists: Union Soldiers from the Confederacy*, esp. pp. 31–37).

[9] One of the food shortages most complained of was sugar, and of all the substitutes, sorghum (often referred to as "sorgo") was most often used (Massey, *Ersatz in the Confederacy*, pp. 65–66).

[10] The Confederate invasion of New Mexico Territory in 1861–62 was the westernmost campaign of the Civil War. Henry Hopkins Sibley raised three regiments—the 4th, 5th, and 7th Texas Mounted Volunteers—from central and south Texas. Gideon's son-in-law, Capt.

George W. Campbell, was in Company F of the 5th Regiment, as were Cassianus (nicknamed Cass or Cash) Lincecum and Jo Lincecum, two grandsons. On 22 October 1861 Sibley started west with thirty-two hundred men and reached Fort Bliss, on the Rio Grande near Magoffinsville, by late December. During January 1862 he marched to Mesilla, proclaiming his invading force the "Army of New Mexico." Fort Thorn was located on the Rio Grande about forty miles north of Mesilla and ninety miles south of Fort Craig (Hall, *Sibley's New Mexico Campaign*, pp. 49–52; Donald S. Frazier, *Blood and Treasure: Confederate Empire in the Southwest*, pp. 44–47, 75, 117–26, 135–36).

[11] On 7 February 1862 Sibley started the seventy-mile march up the Rio Grande toward Fort Craig, which was defended by thirty-eight hundred Union troops under the command of Colonel Canby. Sibley's forces crossed the Rio Grande below Fort Craig and forced the Battle of Valverde on 21 February 1862, defeating the Union army. However, Canby blocked the supply line south to Mesilla, and Sibley moved north toward Albuquerque and Fort Union. Located one hundred miles northeast of Sante Fe, Fort Union was the principal military depot in the Southwest (Hall, *Sibley's New Mexico Campaign*, pp. 49–52; Frazier, *Blood and Treasure*, pp. 146–47, 157–78).

[12] Gideon was misinformed. Sibley planned to march north from El Paso, occupy New Mexico, seize the rich mines in the Colorado Territory, and then go west through Salt Lake City to take the seaports of Los Angeles and San Diego. But Sibley's campaign was a disaster. Its key battle, at Glorieta Pass, was a significant Union victory and the "waterloo" of the Confederacy in the far west. Of Sibley's thirty-two hundred troops, five hundred were captured and taken to Illinois as prisoners of war. Another five hundred died as a result of either combat or disease. However, the three Lincecum family members who were among Sibley's troops returned to Texas unharmed (Hall, *Sibley's New Mexico Campaign*, pp. 49–52; Frazier, *Blood and Treasure*, pp. 208–30). For an account written by a soldier in Sibley's Brigade (Company C, 4th Regiment of Texas Mounted Volunteers, or the "Victoria Invincibles"), see Don E. Alberts, *Rebels on the Rio*

Grande: The Civil War Journal of A. B. Peticolas. See also Alberts's more recent work, *The Battle of Glorieta: Union Victory in the West*.

Gideon's reports and comments on the war continued to go out in many directions, except, of course, to the North. To his young friend, John Hawkins Lewis, down at the Gulf, he wrote at great length about the root causes of war in general (ignorance and venality) and then expressed some concern about the progress of the present war in view of several recent Union victories in Kentucky and Tennessee.

Long Point. Texas. 25 Feb. 1862

John H. Lewis
(Cap. Lauderdale's Co.
Virginia Point)
Fort Hebert, Tex.[1]

. . . Our neighbors are mightily down in the mouth on account of the news of our late reverses in Kentucky and Tennessee.[2] I look upon it in quite a different light. To me, it is the long looked for signals to our generals for deeds of daring; a great oppertunity to display their long boasted military prowess and valor. If Davis is the man I take him to be, we shall hear of him soon in the bloody strife.[3]

We may look now for a series of bloody conflicts. I have confidence in the fidelity and generalship of many of our military leaders, and notwithstanding the fact that the papers have been constantly filled with the marvelous preperations by the Lincolnites and hardly anything published in regard to preperations by our own government, it cannot be that they have been idle. No, no, certainly no. But they have been actively employed, availing themselves of every possible means to strengthen themselves. They have also been closely watching the movements of the enemy and are fully apprised of the intention of his every motion. It is my opinion that they are getting the yankees about where they want them. Anyhow, if we can't whip them now, we shall have to abandon the field fighting and set at them with the guerilla mode of warfare. I am not sure that it would not have been best at the outset. Everybody's well!

Very sincerely thine
Gideon Lincecum

Before posting this letter, Gideon added as an afterthought an interesting comment about the home front at Long Point:
[P.S.] The people are getting up frequent concerts everywhere, and sending considerable money to the army hospitals. Do you hear anything of it? They are making one at this place, which will come off in two weeks. They intend the proceeds for your company they say.

[1] Fort Hébert, named for Brig. Gen. Paul Octave Hébert (1818–80), who commanded the defenses of Galveston at this time, was situated at Virginia Point on the mainland across from the city of Galveston (Warner, *Generals in Gray*, pp. 131–32; *New Handbook of Texas*, 3:539).

[2] Gideon is referring to the recent fall of Forts Henry and Donelson and perhaps the success of Gen. George Thomas in eastern Kentucky at Mill Springs (Logan's Crossroads) on 19 January 1862.

[3] As commander-in-chief, President Jefferson Davis was, in a large sense, already "in the bloody strife," and with his West Point background, distinguished record in the U.S.-Mexican War, and remarkable service as secretary of war (1853–57), he did not hesitate to make suggestions, if not decisions, regarding military strategy. He probably would have loved the more active role in the field and perhaps toyed with the idea, but he likely felt a higher responsibility to remain where he was (Eaton, *Jefferson Davis*, p. 242).

If Gideon's next letter to young Lewis is any indication, the paper shortage was not yet serious, at least not at the Lincecum household, for Gideon wrote at great length about the home front and the news from the battle fronts as well.

Long Point. Texas. 15 March 1862

John H. Lewis
Fort Hebert, Texas
Dear Sir.

Your communication, freighted with patriotic anxiety, forebodings, and fears for the fate of our badly prepared, distant armies of 9th. inst. reached me Thursday, 3 days ago.

In accordance with my observations on that topic, you have very clearly expressed what seems to be the universal sentiment of the people, young and old, in all quarters of the confederacy that I have been able to hear from. That is, dissatisfaction with official action, heartless speculators, faithless foreigners, and deficiency of Arms and fighting fixtures. There is a general flutter, a universal breaking up of what, before, I had denominated the coagulated confederacy. This clabber has been recently pretty severely stirred, churned up, is now boiling and foaming, promising ultimates. Those ultimates, at this stage of ebullition, can only be guessed at. It may all turn out to be whey or it may culminate in a fine large mass of rich butter. From the marked change in the countenance of community, I feel confident that the latter, though the boiling surges and overwhelming waves to be encountered may oft and deeply try men's souls, will finally be awarded to the brave and daring sons of the South.

This conclusion is based solely upon my observations on the greatly change[d] features and marked determination in the aspect of society. Every face presents a sedate firmness that speaks. Its language is "death in preference to submission to the hated enemies of liberty, the upstart despot and his inhuman, godserving fanatics, and heartless, thieving hordes of the North."

Everybody, as far round as I have so far heard from, are moving or preparing to do so; and the current of their movements sets towards the seat of the war. Companies, squads, and sometimes even single soldiers are daily seen passing through all parts of the country, hurrying to someone or other of our armies. A traveller but a few days from Price's army reports that on his way to the south the road was constantly full of soldiers, and that from every portion of the country he could hear from it was the same thing, not only thousands and tens of thousands, but it was said that even hundreds of thousands were streaming onwards towards Price's position.[1]

All this argues that a grand crisis is at hand, and whether it terminates for or against us at the present, it is encouraging to know that there is so much unanimity and determined courage manifested in the action of the patriotic defenders of southern interests. I entertain the hope, for it should be so, that every man in the South who is a true friend to libert[y] has made a solemn vow to himself, that he will at least destroy one and as many more as he possibly can; that he will fight to the death and that he will neither take prisoners nor suffer himself to be taken. Make that the rule of our warfare, and we shall fear no retaliation by the enemy on our prisoners; for they'll have none. Let us sweep the battlefields or be swept ourselves; for it would be abundantly better for us and it would greatly expedite our sufferings to have a ponderous cylinder of red hot iron rolled over the whole South, parching all life into cinders, than for us to surrender our cause and our homes to the Lincoln government. No situation that humanity could be placed in, could equal in my conception, the horrible degradation they are preparing for us. Let every man who deserves the name throughout the confederacy make the fierce resolve that so long as there is one southern man alive, the war is not ended; that so long as there is a foe to his rights and liberties, he will <u>strike</u> and strike to the death.

We have among us, it is true, a good many dead heads, besides real enemies and some neutral. But let us move onwards with the irresistible tramp of stern resolves, we cannot be conquered. We have a million and a half of strong fighters, besides a large number of lads and sprightly old men who are capable of doing much mischief upon a pinch, and there can be no danger, with a <u>proper</u> management of our resources.

From the purport of our last dispatches, it is quite probable that we have had bloody work at four points, if no more. Heavy fighting was imminent at or near Boston Mountain;[2] New Madrid;[3] Savannah, Geo.;[4] and perhaps Nashville and Manassas.[5] Also, at another point which I had forgot to name in my catalogue. It is Fort Craig. J. E. Shepherd was here today, and said he saw a letter yesterday, dated at Fort Craig, which was written by young Chauncy Shepherd; as late as 18th Feb., Chauncy stated that they approached Fort Craig in considerable force, surprised and made prisoners of one of their advance pickets, 22 in number, who were Mexicans.[6] There is but one pass through which the fort can be approached. Sibley's forces entered that, and when they had advanced to within 800 yards of the fort, a long taw fight commenced, which lasted an hour or two.[7] The fort lost five men killed; our side "nobody hurt." He stated that they intended to storm the place the next day (19th). He also stated the garrison to be 5,000 strong—3,000 Mexicans & 2,000 regulars. The wise ones think there will be but little fighting in taking the fort, but Chauncy thinks differently.[8]

In this county and in Burleson the war excitement is running very high. In Burleson I hear that there is a general uprising. They, the government officers, are trying to enroll and form militia companies of them. They pay no attention to it, but are forming companies and squads of cavalry and going right off now. It is the same in this county. Texans have a horrible idea of the militia service, and to avoid it they are running off in small squads and joining any regiment of cavalry they can get into, even in other counties.[9] J. V. Matson had made up a pretty large company of Cavalry for state service, and understanding that they would not be received, except for the term of the war, they agreed to that; and when he went to the governor to tender the service of his company for that term, the governor would not receive them as cavalry.[10] They were then discouraged and they partially disbanded. Matson, in the meantime—and it has all been done in the last five or six days—went to Hempstead to see Col. Carter.[11] Carter was absent, but Col. Wilks was there,[12] and he agreed that if Matson could succeed in making up a company of forty and return his list of men, sworn in for the war, by tomorrow night (Sunday), that he would receive them as cavalry. Matson had time to give two day's notice, and early this morning, they met at Union Hill. All the officers of the previous company resigned [and] re-enrolled themselves, numbering 45. Elected their officers, were all sworn in for during the war, and Matson is again on his way to Hempstead. I suppose there is no doubt of his getting into service as mounted men now. If the company is received, it will soon fill up, for the people abhor the militia service.

Everyone from this vicinity who is fit for service, and has the means to get a horse and other necessary equipments are doing so and are hurrying off, for they detest the infantry in every form. There are, however, quite a number who will not be able to get into service as cavalry. They hate the idea of being drafted; and Mr. G. W. Taliafero, now present, and who has been daily circulating among the people of both counties,[13] gives it as his opinion that they would, as they will not be able to organize full companies, prefer joining the already organized companies at any of the stations to being drafted. Those companies now in service which are not full he thinks will very certainly be filled up soon. They [the able-bodied men remaining] are too much thinned out to be able to get up new volunteer companies, and they have already commenced straggling off in search of places in the already organized companies at the different encampments, thereby, seeking to avoid the draft.

The universal movement which is rapidly going on in the entire south inspires my old worn-out, battle spirit with full confidence in our powers and capabilities to whip them like hell; and I shall be greatly disappointed if the next dispatches, which will not reach us till Tuesday, fail to bring the news that we have utterly discomfitted the infernal thieves in several quarters.

We have no occurrences of interest. Nothing but war talk and plans for vengeance in every coterie of either males or females. Some of the females talk of equipping themselves anyhow, and I have no doubt that if the enemy should succeed in getting into Texas many of them would be found fighting. Everybody well. And I am thine—

Gideon Lincecum

[1] A former congressman, U.S.-Mexican War veteran, and governor of Missouri (1853–57), Sterling Price rose to the rank of major general in the Civil War, playing a very active role in the Missouri-Arkansas-Louisiana theater of the war. He had been victorious at Wilson's Creek in Missouri (10 August 1861), but by the time Gideon wrote this letter he had already been defeated at the Battle of Pea Ridge (Elkhorn Tavern), 7–8 March 1862 (Warner, *Generals in Gray*, pp. 246–47).

[2] In early March Federal troops under Gen. Samuel Curtis, having driven Confederate troops from Missouri, were threatening to drive them from Arkansas as well, when Maj. Gen. Earl Van Dorn led these troops through the Boston Mountains in a counteroffensive and attacked Curtis's outnumbered forces at Pea Ridge, just

south of the Missouri border, on 7 March 1862. The two-day battle of Pea Ridge (or Elkhorn Tavern) resulted in a Confederate defeat and solidified Union control of Missouri (William L. Shea and Earl J. Hess, *Pea Ridge: Civil War Campaign in the West*, pp. 45–46, 52, 62–63, 110–12; Foote, *The Civil War*, 1:279–93).

[3] On 14 March the Confederate army had to abandon its strong position at New Madrid, which is situated on a big bend of the Mississippi River in southeastern Missouri. The Confederates were in danger of being cut off by a much larger Union force, which cut a channel across the bend. Island no. 10 nearby, which was more stoutly defended, fell to the Union on 8 April (McPherson, *Ordeal by Fire*, p. 230).

[4] Although Savannah itself was not attacked at this time, the Union managed to seize Fort Pulaski at the mouth of the Savannah River on 11 April 1862, after isolating it and subjecting it to intense bombardment from guns placed on nearby Big Tybee Island in a combined army-navy operation. The seizure of Fort Pulaski gave the Union control of the mouth of the Savannah River, thus strengthening the Union blockade of the Confederate coast (Long and Long, *The Civil War Day by Day*, p. 198).

[5] With his thinning forces widely dispersed, Gen. Albert Sidney Johnston withdrew his Confederate troops from Nashville on 23 February 1862, and Union troops of Gen. Don Carlos Buell took over the city on 25 February. Johnston would make his stand (and give his life) six weeks later at Shiloh (*Official Records of the Rebellion*, series 1, 7:424; McPherson, *Ordeal by Fire*, p. 226). Manassas was abandoned by the Confederate army on 10 March 1862, but Union general George B. McClellan (1826–85) had not planned to use it as a stepping stone to assault Richmond anyway. He planned to use "the side door," coming up the peninsula between the James and York Rivers, precipitating a series of battles called the "Peninsula Campaign," which was set in motion 17 March (McPherson, *Battle Cry of Freedom*, pp. 424–27; Current, ed., *Encyclopedia of the Confederacy*, 3:1191–94). For a full account, see Stephen W. Sears, *To the Gates of Richmond: The Peninsula Campaign*.

[6] If the letter referred to was in fact dated 18 February or earlier, it must have been written prior to the Battle of Valverde, which resulted from Sibley's attack on Fort Craig. See notes 8–10 above for letter to Boone and Emily Moore, 18 February 1862. To position the forces near Valverde, the army would move to the east bank of the Rio Grande, bypass Fort Craig, and then recross at Valverde ford, some six miles from the fort. As for the "one pass" through which the fort could be approached, from Paraji (eight miles south of Fort Craig) northward to a point almost opposite the post, the valley was bounded on the east by a basaltic mesa some forty to eighty feet in height. Parallel to the river valley were ridges of drifting sand, and the ravines between the ridges concealed the movement of Sibley's troops until they were close to the fort (Hall, *Sibley's New Mexico Campaign*, pp. 78–79; Frazier, *Blood and Treasure*, pp. 157–78). For a thorough treatment of the battle, see John M. Taylor, *Bloody Valverde: A Civil War Battle on the Rio Grande, February 21, 1862*.

[7] "Taw" refers to "at long taw, at a distance" (William A. Craigie, ed., *A Dictionary of American English on Historical Principles*, 4:2297.

[8] Gideon's numbers are somewhat exaggerated here. Although Sibley reported that there were 6,000 men at Fort Craig, records show that in February 1862 Colonel Canby was in command of 3,800 men, of which 1,200 were seasonal soldiers. During the Battle of Valverde (21 February), 1,750 of Sibley's troops were engaged; 36 were killed, 150 wounded (38 died later), with 1 missing. The Union forces had 68 killed, 160 wounded (17 died later), and 35 missing. In George Campbell's company (F), 4 were killed and 7 wounded (Hall, *Sibley's New Mexico Campaign*, pp. 272–74).

[9] As a comment on this problem, an item in the *Galveston News*, 20 March 1862, states, "The numerous independent squads of Texians now leaving this state without organization to join certain regiments from other states will operate to the prejudice of Texas, as the number left from which to raise the 15 regiments will thereby be diminished while our state will have no credit for those who join other regiments. . . . [Moreover,] we fear that the 15 regiments will require nearly all the men left able to bear arms, without having any

adequate force for the protection of our seaboard and frontier."

[10] J. V. Matson was Gideon's son-in-law. No official record of his company of state cavalry has been found.

[11] A native of Virginia, George Washington Carter, D.D. (c. 1828–1901) served as president of Soule University at Chappell Hill, Texas, from 1860 to 1861. He was authorized by the Confederate secretary of war to recruit a regiment for the CSA in Texas. In 1862 he raised three regiments: the 21st Texas Cavalry (his own), Franklin C. Wilkes's 24th Texas Cavalry, and Clayton C. Gillespie's 25th Texas Cavalry. Carter's regiments took part in the Red River Campaign (*New Handbook of Texas*, 1:999; Winfield and Winfield, *All Our Yesterdays*, pp. 8, 22).

[12] On 24 April 1862, Franklin Collett Wilkes (1822–81), commander of the 2d Texas Lancers, was elected colonel of the 24th Texas Cavalry, which marched to Arkansas that summer. Wilkes and most of his troops were captured at Arkansas Post on 11 January 1863. They were exchanged at City Point, Virginia, in April 1863 and returned to active duty with the Army of Tennessee. In July 1864 Wilkes was assigned to the District of Texas and had the misfortune to be captured again in Tensas Parish, Louisiana. He was exchanged a second time in March 1865 (*New Handbook of Texas*, 6:973; Anne J. Bailey, *Between the Enemy and Texas: Parsons's Texas Cavalry in the Civil War*, pp. 23–24, 31, 104–5).

[13] Although G. W. Taliafero was not listed in the 1860 Census for Washington County, a George W. Taliafero witnessed a transfer of property in the village of Long Point, from Gideon Lincecum to John Wilson, on 5 August 1857 (Deed Records, Washington County, Tex., vol. P, p. 603). No service record for G. W. Taliafero was found.

If paper was not yet in very short supply, cloth was, despite the abundance of cotton and wool.[1] *In some desperation in this regard, Gideon wrote to General Besser in Huntsville, who was using the labor of prisoners in the state penitentiary to make cloth.*

Long Point. Texas. 31st March 1862

Gen. John S. Besser[2]
Huntsville, Texas
Dr. Sr.

Please be so kind as to inform me as early as convenient if there is any possible chance to obtain a supply of goods for negro clothing, for summer. Our negroes will be naked in spite of all we can do, if you cannot assist us. And as the good fellows are so obedient and orderly these troublous war times, we are grieved to see it.

Notwithstanding the fact that we have plenty of the raw material laid up in store—cotton and wool—and could, and would help ourselves by spinning and weaving it if we could procure cards. Cards, however, are out of the question—

In our family there are about 100 who will need and must have summer clothing. If you can exchange the suitable manufactured article for our raw material, be so good as to write to us what kind you will take and the price it will command, as well as the price of your goods, so that we may know how much to carry over; and the time for us to have it there, and you will see by our promptness, how bad we need it and how much you will oblige us.

If you cannot furnish the woven fabric, could you not supply us with cotton yarns and wool rolls? This would enable us, with a great deal of labor and trouble in manufacturing looms and wheels, to make cloth, if we can procure slaies— [A "slay" is "a reed used in weaving to beat the weft."]

I hope, however, that you have it in your power to furnish the woven article. Please write—

Very Respectfully
Gideon Lincecum

[1] The South had been accustomed to receiving most of its clothing material from Europe and the North, and as the war dragged on

the shortage of textiles became a major problem. The cotton mills of the South had produced a coarse grade of material used most often for slaves' clothing, but even if the Southern mills had produced a better quality of cloth, there were not enough of them to supply the needs of soldiers and civilians. Many clothing factories were taken over by the Confederate and state governments and used to produce clothing for the armed forces. Civilians had to produce their own cloth or renovate old garments (Massey, *Ersatz in the Confederacy*, pp. 79–80; Kerby, *Kirby Smith's Confederacy*, pp. 65–67).

[2] John Slater Besser was financial agent for the Texas State Penitentiary at Huntsville from 1852 to 1863. As much as six thousand yards of cloth were produced daily at the penitentiary during the war (*New Handbook of Texas*, 1:507; Ralph Wooster, "Life in Civil War East Texas," *East Texas Historical Journal* 3 (1965): 93–102).

Desperation faced Gideon in another regard. He was out of money to pay his taxes and sought help.

Long Point. Texas. 25 April 1862

W. E. Allcorn[1]
Brenham, Texas
My Dear Friend.

With the hope that I could work along some way without troubling you, I have made every shift that I am capable of to raise money to pay my War and state taxes, to but very little effect. I still lack $125—of being able to meet the demands of my country in carrying on the war; and this, as you know, must be paid in twenty days from the first of May. Can you help me? Don't promise me if you can't; for if I am forced to make sacrifices, I want time to make sale of my property myself. Let me know by the 1st of May.

In righteousness,
I am thine ever.
Gideon Lincecum

[1] W. E. Allcorn is listed as residing in Brenham in the 1860 Census (Eighth Census, 1860, Washington County, Tex., p. 154). According to the 1850 Census, W.E. Allcorn lived near Gideon on a farm and his property was valued at $30,000 (Gideon's was valued at only $9,000). Both men had been born in Georgia (Seventh Census, 1850, Washington County, Tex., p. 292). It seems reasonable that Gideon would be asking Mr. Allcorn for a loan.

In spite of his difficulty in paying his taxes, Gideon went on record favoring an additional tax to be levied by the county for the relief of families of the local volunteers. As secretary of the local relief committee, he wrote the following:

Long Point. Texas. 24 April 1862

To the Chief Justice and members
of the Hon. County Court for Washington County
Gentlemen.

At a meeting of the relief committee, held this day at Long Point, said committee having been appointed by the citizens of this and the adjoining precinct of Gay Hill to take charge of and distribute to the outfit of the volunteers of the said precincts, and to the necessities of the needy wives and families of the absent volunteers, ample donations of corn, cotton, beeves, cows & calves, &c &c., subscribed by a portion of the patriotic citizens of the aforesaid precincts; which liberal donations have so far been carefully and prudently distributed by the said relief committee for the purposes intended; and there is a large amount still available on the subscription list; and the committee have no objection to the continuation of their duties as distributing agents of the donations thus supplied. Yet, taking into consideration the unequal bearing of this method of supplying the needy families of our patriotic volunteers, who are absent in the service of their country, the said committee passed a resolution to address a letter to your

Honorable body, recommending the propriety of equalizing the burthens of supporting the families who need such aid, by levying a sufficient tax upon the county for that purpose.

Gideon Lincecum, Secty.
Respectfully
S. D. Lauderdale, Presdt.

Although cloth and money were hard to come by, production from the area's farms was bountiful, as Gideon reported to the Galveston News.

Long Point. Texas. 5 May 1862

Editors News.

Having returned last evening from a considerable tour through the magnificent farms of this and the adjoining county of Austin, I concluded that a paragraph or two on what I saw of the encouraging promise of the growing crops would not, in these times of disaster and sacrifices, be amiss.

I passed a great number of large farms in which the people and their negroes were busily engaged ploughing the ground, which was in nice order and clothed for miles and miles in the most luxuriant growth of corn I have seen in ten years. With but few exceptions, the entire crop is corn, which is generally from waist to shoulder high. Two or three large fields had not been planted, and these, to my mind, as I thoughtfully rode along the extended strings of high fencing, spoke louder for the patriotism, honor and good sense of the owners, than did the four or five large plantations that occurred, which were planted in cotton. The cotton also looked healthy and thriving, but to me, it was but a flagrant manifestation of a contracted spirit and weakness in the planters of it; and I could not avoid the impression that those widely extended plantations of thrifty growing cotton plants were but the flourishing curses of a glorious but highly offended principle.[1]

From what I have myself seen in Washington and Austin counties, added to the equally favorable reports from many other counties, with good indications for plenty of rain, I may safely predict that there is no danger of a failure in the corn crop; and as there is perhaps nearly or quite double as much as ever before planted, there will be an immense surplus.

I also saw great numbers of hogs everywhere. The acorn crop is heavy, grass is very fine, cattle plenty and many of them fat now. Community manfully sustaining the needy families of the absent soldiers, paying the war tax freely, and rejoicing at the equalizing influence of the conscript law.

Thine
Gideon Lincecum

[1] In hopes of inducing France and England to assist the Confederacy and break the Union blockade, the Davis government had discouraged the planting of cotton in order to intensify a shortage in foreign markets (Current, ed., *Encyclopedia of the Confederacy*, 2:479–85; see also Frank Lawrence Owsley, *King Cotton Diplomacy: Foreign Relations of the Confederate States of America*, 2d ed., revised by Harriet Chappell Owsley, pp. 24–26, 43–45, 50).

In contrast to those farmers who seemed to be displaying less than full patriotism by planting cotton, Gideon was very hesitant to let his own interests take precedence over the needs of the Confederacy. He did make a trip to Huntsville to try to get some cloth, but he was reluctant to press his case ahead of the general need.

Long Point. Texas. 10 June 1862

Genl. John S. Besser
Huntsville, Texas
Dr. Sir.

For the purpose of ascertaining truth in regard to procuring supplies from your establishment, I visited Huntsville; saw you and the press by which you are daily and hourly subjected to; and from your replies to other men, learned the answers to my questions. I really had not the affrontery to pester you, and so left without asking you anything in favor of self. Nor do I now, except it may happen to be convenient for you.

My Son L[achaon] J. Lincecum and Mr. G. W. Gentry[1] will go over to your place, carrying some wool, &c. They will, if it is necessary, remain there till they can obtain some goods for family use. If by remaining they can obtain supplies in turn, and if this letter be considered as an application, with the date of their arrival, it will relieve me very much and lay me under lasting obligations, for you to deliver to my son, for the use of my family 2 ps. Osnaburgs[2]—1 ps twilled woolens, and ten or twelve hanks of thread. If it is not convenient for you to do so, I shall not complain, as when I was there, I saw and know that you are doing all you can.

Very Respectfully
Gideon Lincecum

[1] George W. Gentry is listed as residing in Long Point in the 1860 Census (Eighth Census, 1860, Washington County, Tex., p. 152).

[2] "Osnaburg" is a heavy, coarse cotton in a plain weave, for grain sacks and sportswear.

Apparently his son returned empty-handed, for six weeks later Gideon made another request, in person, without success. Despite a number of Confederate military victories, material shortages were becoming more severe, and the Texas farmer's traditional foe, drought, had returned. In late July Gideon described the overall situation to the Boone Moores in South Texas and lambasted the Yankees as usual.

Long Point. Texas. 25th July 1862

Dear Brother & Sister

Hondo, Medina County, Texas

Your very interesting letter reached us yesterday; it reached us in eleven days.

We were glad to hear from you. It had been some time since we had news from that god-forsaken region.

We are sorry to hear that your corn crops have turned out a failure. The drought has also pressed heavily upon our crops. We shall nevertheless be able to cribb plenty for home consumption and a small surplus for the army.

Our family and all the connection are healthy; indeed there is no sickness in this vicinity. I might mention, however, that there are but few people in the country for disease to prey upon: the women and children, a few old men and soldiers that have been refused a place in the army are all that are remaining for the hydra-headed monster to sting at this time. There went from this precinct 221 volunteers. The conscript law caught a few Dutchmen who resided in the background towards the Yegua bottom, and that was all it could find in this precinct. It is rather a lonely looking country about this time. Portions of Sibley's brigade began to drop in yesterday, and as they have a 60 day's furlough, and two companies of them went from here, our society will be filled up a little during that period. This settlement have already commenced preparations for giving them a fat barbecue and a ball as soon as they all get home, which will transpire in the course of ten or twelve days. The old lady is in for it, but she, as you know, is always in ecstasies at the thought of a big frolic of any kind. Well, let her rip, she shall not have her requirements stinted.

I returned two days ago from Huntsville, whence I had been trying to procure cloth to clothe our nakedness but failed. Notwithstanding the fact that they weave and finish off six thousand yards . . . per day, there were so many people in

[line] ahead of me that the superintendent told me that it would be five weeks before my turn could be supplied. The time set was so long that I preferred nakedness to such extraordinary detention, and so returned empty as I went. People in this country are complaining mightily, and indeed some of them are really frightened at the thought of approaching nakedness. They seem to have no inventive force and are folding their arms in utter helplessness. Others who were provided with a pair or two of old half-worn cotton cards are spinning and weaving long pieces of elegant janes, with which they are clothing their families quite stilish. If cards could be had, they would all be at it, but the cards lie outside of the region of probability even.[1] Quite a number of people are tanning their hides and will be able to shoe themselves the insuing winter. Numbers again have made no provisions to meet the approaching contingencies. Your humble servant belongs to the latter class. It affords a most excellent opportunity for it, and if the lord wants to get me on his side, now is the time for it. He can hook me in now by sending me a few sides of good shoe leather, <u>shore</u> [sure].

My crop of sugar cane was light and pretty dry this year. We are just done grinding and boiling it. We produced but 250 gallons of syrup. We made a thousand gallons last year. Quite a falling off. It is, however, fully sufficient for our own consumption.

From all directions the war news is encouraging. We are driving the accursed robbers on every battlefield, and we shall continue to drive them if our officers can keep sober. The late dispatches gives us successes everywhere, and the Yankees are becoming mighty tired of the war.[2] Let us, as we did not begin the war, never ask for peace. With the prospect of rich plunder and rapine, they sought the strife with us, and now let us all die in the conflict, sooner than even hint to them a proposition for peace in any form. The Yankees, if hostilities were to be suspended now, would find themselves utterly ruined; and if we can make out to keep up the war even two years longer, they will be driven to such abject poverty and degradation that they will accept of the condition of bondage to obtain peace. Let us all labor for that one object. Let every man in the confederacy make it his study and assiduously labor to produce all the provisions and munitions of war as possible; let the war cry resound from every hamlet and village throughout the south. Let the little boys who are left at home be taught by their patriotic mothers to hate, aye, detest the infernal hook-nosed yankees, and to think and study out mischief and plans of devastation on the battlefield and swear eternal enmity to the entire race. Serving as we have for forty years, the villainous demands and thieving notions of the damned creatures, it would be sin in us; it would be an unpardonable violation of the laws of decency and self-respect to treat or come to terms with them on any subject; as to peace, there is no possible ground for it at this time that would not disgrace us, short of abject submission by them. Nothing else could remunerate us for the damages they have wantonly inflicted upon us. No, no, let us hoist the black banner, and neither ask, nor give quarters until we thoroughly chastise and obtain all our rights from them, or destroy and devastate the whole South in the attempt. As long as there is one man left, let him make battle.

As for making a trip out to your country this year, though it would afford us more pleasure than anything else I can think of, we shall be compelled to forego that satisfaction. The protracted drought and the heavy bearing of the war has rendered us too poor to take or think of taking pleasure now. But we submit cheerfully to the privation, and more, we are laboring daily to scrape up something to render comfortable the hundreds of worn-down soldiers who are every day stopping with us.

There has been nothing new or exciting occurring in the

connection now or for a long time past. The old lady is in better health than usual and is quite cheerful on every subject, except the war; when that topic is brought up, she curses the yankees and wishes she was a man. Sarah and Lysander are still with us. Lysander went and tried to be a soldier two or three times, but his asthma was so bad none of them would let him stay; and the poor fellow does his wheezing at home. There is no sickness in this portion of Texas, but the few that are left are sulky and quarrelsome.

The old lady, who is sitting near while I write, sends her love to both of you and all the children, and says she will pay you a visit sure, as soon as the war is over. For myself, I am quite robust and healthy, would be glad to see you; can do nothing now but subscribe myself your affectionate brother.

Gid

[1] Of all the tools needed to produce cloth, cards were the most needed and the scarcest. Before the war was half over they had increased in price from forty cents to over thirty dollars a pair, and they continued in great demand throughout the conflict (Massey, *Ersatz in the Confederacy*, p. 87).

[2] Again, Gideon is exaggerating. By 25 July 1862 the Confederate army had suffered a number of setbacks in the West, from West Virginia to New Mexico but had gained important victories in the East. Especially important were Stonewall Jackson's triumphs in the Shenandoah Valley and Robert E. Lee's brilliant defense of Richmond against McClellan's Army of the Potomac (McPherson, *Battle Cry of Freedom*, pp. 454–60, 463–69).

Little of Gideon's correspondence for the rest of 1862 has been preserved, but two letters written in November have survived. The first notes the loss of a good young soldier and the increased strain of the war.

Long Point. Texas. 10 Novr 1862

Jos. C. Sniveley
My Dear Sir.

Yours of 27th. ult. did not come to hand till today. Your previous letter was received last week.

And you had no one but me to whom you could tell your sorrows. Well, you could not have selected one who can sympathise more deeply with you or that feels the loss of him for whom you mourn more seriously than I do.

"Dan" was not only my friend, but he was one amongst my few favorites.[1] He was a substantialy firm man and a brave patriot, who would have done himself and his adopted state credit if he had lived to go into battle. Our cause has most certainly lost a co[u]rageous warrior. He is gone, and we must give our sympathies to the many mourning families who are suffering from the same cause that occasioned his untimely death.

The war bears hard on our people, and from the recent proclamations eminating from the demented federal government, it will bear harder still.[2] There is but one course left for the confederacy, and that is death, or success. The idea of submitting to such a dinasty as they are fixing up is far more horrible, in my estimation, than death in any form. . . .

We all feel the loss of your Brother deeply—Alls well.—

Your Friend.
Gideon Lincecum.

[1] Daniel Sniveley was the brother of Joseph. He was mustered into Wood's Regiment of the 32d Texas Cavalry, Company A, as a private on 22 March 1862 and "died in hospital of disease" at Camp Bee on 26 October 1862 (National Archives, *Compiled Service Records*, roll 176).

[2] The "proclamations" Gideon referred to probably included President Lincoln's preliminary Emancipation Proclamation, dated 22 September 1862, and his suspension of the Writ of Habeas Cor-

pus for action endangering the Union cause on 24 September (McPherson, *Ordeal by Fire*, p. 293). He might also have had in mind the orders proclaimed by Gen. Benjamin F. Butler (who became known as "Beast Butler"), the occupation commander of New Orleans (McPherson, *Ordeal by Fire*, pp. 382–83; Randall, *Civil War and Reconstruction*, pp. 665–67).

The second letter, to his British friend Hannay, who was still stranded in Texas, tells of Gideon's response to the need for clothing and shoes.

Long Point. Texas. 16 Nov[r] 1862

R. B. Hannay
Navasota, Texas
My Dear Friend.

Your pencil note of 12th. inst. came to hand yesterday; and I must say that I was glad to hear from you, and that you were "fat" and well. I was thinking that by this time you had landed safe and sound in your native country, and that you would have the good sense to remain there until our villianous war should be settled. You have, however, been defeated in your intentions and will now, very probably, have to remain until the unnatural conflict ceases. I have, from mere habit, termed our war "unnatural conflict." That, however, is not my true sentiment on the subject. Far from it. I know that from misdirection in the genus homo, the prevailing sentiments are desire of power, plunder, theiving, lying and all manner of dissimulation and misrepresentation; and that on this plane of human action war is as natural, and I may say as necessary as the thunder storms and rain. . . .

I shall wait impatiently for your plan for the establishment of manufactures. Something in that way might be done in aid of the peoples effort to clothe themselves. But if they could procure cotton and wool cards, the whole country would instantly be transformed into one grand, efficient, manufacturing establishment. A card manufactury would produce the greatest benifit, and the profits to the owners would be very great. . . .

I went round among the mechanics, trying to get them to make for me the necessary machinery for making cloth. At their prices, I found that it would cost me $125—I thought it was too much. To prove whether I was correct, I went to work myself and completed the entire outfit for making cloth in one month. One good loom, two spinning wheels, 1 clock Reel, 1 warping Mill, 1 pr. winding blades, 40 spools, and spool rack, 2 fine reeds, or sleys, 3 shuttles and several other things of smaller note, besides the temples, which I had like to have forgotten. People who have seen these things assure me that they are better made than any they have seen in the country. I am now busy making wooden shoes.[1]

All's well!

Thine as ever.
Gideon Lincecum

[1] The problem of shoes was very serious throughout the Confederacy, among soldiers and civilians alike. With a severe shortage of tanned leather, all kinds of skins were substituted, from horsehide to the skins of dogs, deer, sheep and goats, squirrels, and pigs. Shoes were also made from old leather articles, including trunks and saddles, and wooden bottoms were often substituted for leather soles. Some were even made entirely of wood (usually ash, poplar, or willow), hollowed out in the manner of Dutch footwear. Various kinds of cloth were also substituted for leather (Massey, *Ersatz in the Confederacy*, pp. 80–85; Kerby, *Kirby Smith's Confederacy*, pp. 64–67, 261).

"Wooden shoes" and yet "all's well"! Those two comments speak volumes. While the shortage of leather may have im-

pelled Gideon to make wooden shoes, elsewhere in the state tanneries were springing up to meet the need for leather, as Gideon described in an undated letter in late 1862 to the Galveston News.

Editor of the News—In your issue of the 10th instant, I notice a call by you, for "information in relation to tanneries in Texas and what efforts are being made for supply of leather—also in regard to domestic manufactories, such as shoemaking, spinning and weaving by the old fashioned spinning wheels and hand looms."

I can answer for Washington and a considerable portion of the adjoining counties. There are very many efforts on a small scale to tan leather; most of which experiments were made too late in the season to procure sufficient bark; hence they have not succeeded in producing leather to any extent worth naming. They have got their bristles up, however, and they will come it next year. Most of the leather from which shoes are made in this section is brought from the quite numerous tanneries [in] eastern and northeastern counties. There are also three or four tanneries in Fayette county, turning off considerable supplies of leather for the neighborhoods in which they are situated. We have plenty of shoemakers amongst us to meet the demand if we had the material to work upon.

[Gideon]

Ever since October, Federal naval forces had besieged and controlled Galveston Island, but not until Christmas morning did they land troops at the wharves. At dawn that same morning, Gideon, according to his annual ritual, stood at his open doorway barefooted (not in wooden shoes!), with his old black violin in hand, and played three times over the Scottish ballad "Killiecrankie." Although the tune celebrated a Scottish victory over the English in 1689, it could have served on this occasion as a harbinger of the victory Confederate forces would achieve at Galveston at the dawn of the New Year, one week later.

CHAPTER 5

1863

The new year began with the remarkable victory of a rag-tag force of Texans over the Union soldiers and sailors at Galveston. Ably directed by Maj. Gen. John Bankhead Magruder, the Texans not only drove the Union force off the island but also sank one Union vessel, captured two others, and sent the rest in flight out of the harbor and the bay.[1]

Gideon rejoiced at the news, even though one of his grandsons, Cassianus, was wounded in the battle.[2] *To his friend, Judge Rutherford, Gideon wrote,*

Long Point. Texas. 21st January 1862 [1863]

John A. Rutherford
Lamar, Texas
Dear Sir.

. . . I suppose you have long ere this had the particulars of our brilliant affair at Galveston on the morning of the first of Jan. One of my gang got his scull cracked there by the explosion of a shell;[3] he will get over it I suppose, tho' I have not heard from him since it happened. San Antonio has not been captured, nor was any portion of the soil of Texas in possession of the Yankees at the latest accounts. There were 4 large vessels anchored in the Gulf, off Galveston a week ago, and they commenced bombarding the city; but three or four shots from a small breach loading rifle cannon, invented by Col. Nichols,[4] of that place, forced them to draw further off, since which time they have been more civil. For some reason General McGruder has forbid all communication with the city, in consequence of which we have had no news from there in the last ten days. We shall hear something soon. . . .

Before mentioning the Battle of Galveston in this letter, Gideon had given the judge a long lecture on how to cope with the shortages caused by the Union blockade and chided him for being so pessimistic:

. . . Your letter of 28th Decr. 1862 came in yesterday. . . . In all that well written penciled letter, you have not recorded a single cheerful thought. You are diseased, my friend, and I would advise you to take less animal food. Live principally on hominy and sand. Don't laugh, nor growl, for I am in earnest; nor must you consider me in a growling humour, I only tell truth. I am indeed in fine health and highly exhilarated spirit and temper. The war works well, and we shall finally overwhelm the infernal thieving northmen with utter ruin. They have sought it long. It is near at hand now. You say you are ruined already, having nothing left you but fine looking wheat fields, stock to feed, and something for Jackson to feed them with, a good farm upon which you reside, your companion still living, old black Mary to cook for you, and one brave son in the army, who will no doubt fight courageously to protect you, even in your ruined condition. Ruined! Well, well. I have no intention to make light of your case, for I have no doubt it looks to you as you have stated, and it will continue to look so, and even more dreadfully ruinous if you do not get yourself in better health. If you don't get better this year, I shall have to go up and prescribe more sand for you. What think [you] of this page, and do you feel any better?

You "write with Pencil, because of the Blockade." And if you had learned to help yourself in place of acknowledging your dependence on the infernal yankees, by paying them ten prices to make ink and other equally cheap and simple things, you would have suffered no inconvenience from the blockade. I have not bought a single foreign article since that event occurred. I never did use their ink, and now I am determined never to make use of anything they may hereafter produce. Ink? why that's one of the most simple things to make in the chemical world. I am acquainted with forty formulae for making good ink.[5] . . .

For pens, sharpen up your knife, get the goose quills and

make your pens. I have never written half a dozen lines with a yankee pen in my life. I could never get my consent to submit to such consummate, helpless laziness. I am not attempting to dictate a course for you or anyone else to pursue, I merely tell what I do myself. I get along very well.

There's another page, such as it is, do you feel better now? I do!

"The blockade" you say.—Glorious blockade for us, for it will be the making of the confederacy.[6] It has operated as a permanent insult to the entire people of the south, in such manner as to inspire them all with eternal, irreconcilable resentment, so strong, that with every man and woman in the Southern states who have souls and sufficient self-respect to claim a place amongst the decent nations of the earth, resolves of perpetual enmity and eternal separation will be made and sworn to before high heaven. So mote it be.

"The blockade" you say. Well, we, like many other short sighted secessionists, had not laid in sufficient clothing to do us two years even. To remedy this piece of negligence, I made, during the summer, three trips to Huntsville, hoping to procure cloth to clothe my negroes for the coming winter. It turned out an entire failure. I then went round among the mechanics, intending to get them to make the necessary machinery & outfit for manufacturing cloth at home. I needed 2 good spinning wheels, a clock reel, 40 spools, warping mill and spool rack, 3 sleys, 3 or 4 shuttles and a good loom. At the prices asked for this set of machinery, by our mechanics it would cost $125. I thought it too much, and to ascertain whether I was right or not, I went to work and with my own hands, produced the entire outfit in one month; and the people who have seen them flatter me by declaring them—the whole set, sleys and all—to be the best they have seen in the country. Now we all know that a man of my age, who never done such work before, could not earn $125 in a month. You will say this is the effects of the blockade. So say I, and have presented you with the remedy. How do you like it?

After completing the machinery for spinning and weaving, I thought of the scarcity of colouring material in market. Coperas,[7] $2.50 cts. per pound, every other article to aid in the dy[e]ing processes equally scarce and high priced. Our women were all discouraged, and the spinning and weaving of anything but plain coarse cloth was about to be given over; and all this they said was clearly attributable to the cruel blockade. People don't think for themselves. Of their own accord, they can do nothing but grumble & complain. Hence the most of them require leaders and instructors. These defects are inherited from their progenitors. It is a regular congenital conformation for which nobody is to blame. But for the sake of our reputation for veracity we should be careful not to overrate them. I was speaking of coperas as a necessary mordant in dying black and various shades of brown. Well, when our women were told that to put into some old pot or other vessel that would hold it a gallon or two of weak vinegar or sour beer, and pitch into it a quantity of the old rusty pieces of stove pipe, scraps of hoop iron, horse shoes, any rusty scrap of old iron, that it would produce a fountain of the acetite of iron—a much better article for dying cotton than sulphate of iron (coperas) because it will not rot the thread—from which they might at pleasure draw any desirable amount for dying black or brown, and the longer it was kept up, the better and richer it would become; they all very readily complied and the cry for coperas has ceased. The black signs of the beneficial effects of the vinegar of iron upon the woven fabrics of both cotton and wool are to be seen in many families. It's all very simple now, and coperas is not in demand.

What is stated on the previous page is not all. I have been earnestly at work, making a chemical analysis of the colouring material found in the barks and roots of our forests and prairies. The results of my experiments, having brought out many brilliant colours, has delighted and very much encouraged the ladies of this vicinity. These colours are, some of them, not only cheap but really bright and pretty. I have not yet completed my experiments, but when I do get through with them, if I can procure the paper, I will publish it in pamphlet form and send one to each P. O. for the benefit of the neighborhood. See what the blockade is doing! Horrible? Oh! Horrible as these progressive steps, and thousands of others of greater importance which I might name here, are to some minds, they are nevertheless irrefragably true, and safely resting on an indestructible basis. War is an event in the action of our little globe that must, despite all our little interests, timid fears, and selfish prayers, roll thundering onwards to its ultimates. Be these ultimates what they may, we, the mere lice, crawling and fighting for supremacy among the brushy coating on the earth's back, have to put up with it, take it as it comes, good or bad. And he that can take it with the best grace will, of course, see the most fun. . . .

Guerrilla warfare is very useful to us in the present war. I should like for the South to utterly exterminate the north, but the infernal thieves will cry out enough, long before that happens.

If they succeed in subjugating us, they will most certainly disarm us, establish a king, and force us to pay the expense of the war. But they can't subjugate us by a long gap; and more than that, if the European powers do not interfere in their behalf, we will subjugate them. They are about to go to war among themselves. Our late successes are rapidly hurrying forward that crisis;[8] we of the confederacy will have the satisfaction of seeing them gut and ruin one another, when we will give them a government but never unite with them. They are too hateful. For one, I will never submit to them, but will shoot the first one I see, and I will not cease to shoot at them while

I have life to do so. Submit? Never. And the same spirit pervades our whole people, with but few exceptions.

I am 125 miles from the coasts, and like yourself, dependent on the papers for the news of what is going on there. I sometimes meet with a soldier from the coast. In such cases I can report what he tells me, by letter to you. . . .

We are all well, and none of our gang dead since my last letter. Compliments to your good lady and for yourself, thine as ever

Gideon Lincecum

[1] Maj. Gen. John Bankhead Magruder (1807–71), a soldier for the Confederate States in the Civil War, assumed command of the District of Texas, New Mexico, and Arizona on 29 November 1862. His greatest success was the recapture of Galveston, 1 January 1863, and the consequent, if temporary, dispersal of the Union blockading fleet (Warner, *Generals in Gray*, pp. 207–8; *New Handbook of Texas*, 4:464–65).

[2] For a detailed account of the Battle of Galveston, see Charles C. Cumberland, "The Confederate Loss and Recapture of Galveston, 1862–1863," *Southwestern Historical Quarterly* 51 (1947): 109–30. See also Donald S. Frazier, "Sibley's Texans and the Battle of Galveston," *Southwestern Historical Quarterly* 99 (1995): 175–98. For a fuller account, see Edward T. Cotham Jr., *Battle on the Bay: The Civil War Struggle for Galveston*.

[3] Apparently any wound suffered by Cassianus must have turned out to be minor, as within a month Gideon refers to the boys as unhurt and a few months later says they have come home "without a scratch." See letter to "Brother and Sister," 15 August 1863, below. Perhaps initial reports confused Cassianus with K. Lincecum, a distant relative, who was wounded in this battle. See Gideon Lincecum to Joseph Lincecum, Long Point, Tex., 24 February 1863, LP, Box 2E366.

[4] Col. (or General, as some sources refer to him) Ebenezer B. Nichols (1815–72), though born and raised in New York, came to

Texas in 1838 and became a leading merchant and civic leader, first in Houston and, after 1850, in Galveston. There he became a leader in the secession movement and was active in the defense of Galveston during the war (*New Handbook of Texas*, 4:1010; see also Fornell, *The Galveston Era*, pp. 291–93).

[5] Gideon gives Rutherford his recipe for cheap ink, which the editors can attest did not prove to be of a quality that made it remain readable for a hundred years. According to Mary Elizabeth Massey, "every family had its favorite recipe for ink," and most recipes did not yield a high-quality product (Massey, *Ersatz in the Confederacy*, pp. 146–47).

[6] The Union was seeking to strangle the Confederacy by using its dominant naval power to choke off Southern exports of cotton and other commodities and prevent the import of scarce supplies. The blockade was never complete, but far from being "the making of the Confederacy," as Gideon believed, it was, instead, a major factor in the Union's ultimate triumph (Current, ed., *Encyclopedia of the Confederacy*, 1:176–86).

[7] "Coperas" is ferrous sulfate, which can be used in the manufacture of pigments, inks, and tanning. It is also called green vitriol, iron vitriol, and iron sulfate.

[8] By 21 January 1863 spirits in the Confederacy had been raised by a number of recent successes. In December 1862 Lee's Army of Northern Virginia had badly defeated Burnside's Army of the Potomac at Fredericksburg, Generals Nathan Bedford Forrest, John Hunt Morgan, and Earl Van Dorn had crippled the Union supply lines in Tennessee and Mississippi with their raids, and Gen. Braxton Bragg had inflicted heavy losses on the Union forces at Murfreesboro, though at considerable cost to his own army, leading to his withdrawal that drew subsequent criticism (McPherson, *Ordeal by Fire*, pp. 302–9; Catton, *This Hallowed Ground*, pp. 228–38, 245).

Earlier, in writing to the Galveston News, *Gideon boasted of the remarkable increase in spinning and weaving that was taking place in Texas. In that undated letter, written in late*

1862, part of which was quoted at the end of the previous chapter, Gideon wrote:

. . . As to "spinning and weaving by the old fashioned spinning wheel and hand loom," there is a general movement in that direction everywhere. Looms and wheels are being made by the thousand, and every family who have been so fortunate as to procure cards are manufacturing quant[it]ies of most excellent cloth. But the scarcity and ruinous high prices of the cards operates, with many poor families, as a sufficient barrier to prevent them from doing anything at all towards clothing themselves even. Certainly the card speculators are striving to force community back into the use of the primitive fig leaf apron again.

It is not worthwhile to say anything about what the managers of the state government might have done to aid the people in procuring cards. They be ——— [damned]; but if the people had the cards, I am sure I tell truth when I assert that the whole country would be instantly converted into one grand efficient manufacturing establishment. And from the thousands of buzzing wheels and clattering looms, propelled by willing hands and loving hearts, the ready made clothing and substantial blankets would flow to our armies, as free as water. There are few soldiers in the service who have not a female relative or friend at home, who would not take delight in having the oppertunity to clothe him during the war.[1] I know of what I speak, and the drawback to all this is intentionally produced by a black hearted set of enemies to our cause.

Thine.
Gid

[1] For the role of Confederate women in making clothing for the soldiers, see Drew Gilpin Faust, *Mothers of Invention: Women of the Slaveholding South in the American Civil War*, pp. 45–52.

As good as Gideon's spinning machine may have been, he was looking for a better one and especially needed cards, as he indicated in the next letter:

Long Point. Texas. 14 Jan. 1863

Maj. Green Wood[1]
Danville, Texas
My Dear Sir.

I was, a few days since, at the house of Chas. Abercrumbe.[2] He informed me, but did not know for certain, that some person was manufacturing at Danville, good spinning machines. If so, will you be so kind as to make inquiry about them, and if they are making good machines, engage one for me; let me know the time to go for it and what it will cost me.

If it is true that they are making spinning machines there, they must be in great demand, and I speak thus timely, though we need it badly now hoping to procure one sometime. If we could procure cards, we could make out very well, as we have everything else that is required for the production of various kinds of cloth.

I have pestered you with this matter because I have greater confidence in your judgment of such things. You will therefore please excuse me.

We are all well; that is, the old Lady, Sarah, and myself. The balance of our household having gone to the war, from whence they may never return. But that's nothing, if we can sustain our freedom—our Government against the infernal, thieving yankees. The chances for which are quite encouraging so far.

Present my best regards to your good lady, and believe me

as ever, thine
Gideon Lincecum

[1] Lois Wood Burkhalter identifies Green Wood as someone whom Gideon considered a fellow Infidel (Burkhalter, *Gideon Lincecum*, p. 107n).

[2] Charles Abercrombie was also a fellow Infidel (Burkhalter, *Gideon Lincecum*, p. 107n).

A month later Gideon wrote again to Major Wood, and although he was disappointed that the major could not supply him with a machine, what really bothered him was the behavior of all too many unpatriotic, speculating merchants, traders, and farmers.[1]

Long Point. Texas. 15th Feb. 1863

Maj. Green Wood
Danville, Texas
My Dear Sir.

Your kind letter of 23rd ult. for which I very much thank you—did not reach me until three or four days ago. It had been so long en route, that I at first concluded a reply would be unnecessary. On reflection, however, I feel that a portion of your letter demands that I should return an answer, for I hold that it is the duty of everyone who can say or do anything that has a tendency to forward the cause of freedom or lighten the cords of grief in our hard pressed confederacy should be saying and doing. Also [I hold] that all those brave spirits, those lovers of liberty, men who can control their avarice long enough to permit them to see their duty to themselves and to their devoted country, should freely communicate, expressing their true sentiments on any and all occasions without any kind of reserve or prevarication whatever.

We are environed on every side by a most powerful, most destructive, and certainly the meanest foe that any nation of people ever had to contend with. But mean and accursed as they are in the eyes and under the rules and regulations of all civilized life, they nevertheless fall far short of being our worst enemies! There are those amongst us—and I am sorry to say that they are not few—who under the garb of friendship and a great flourish of patriotism are actually damaging our cause vastly more than the outspoken enemy.

At the commencement they were the greatest encouragers of the war, since which they have made shift to crawfish out of every position they took; and now their every action clearly demonstrates to every thinking mind that they are proud of the results of the war and are pressing every point and circumstance to amass to themselves immense wealth, crush whomsoever it may. I consider the actions and desires of these characters, these bloodsuckers in our midst, far more damaging to our cause in their ultimates than anything that will or can be affected against us by the machinations of the evil hearted and accursed Lincolnites. Unfortunately for the reputation of our planting community, this spirit of extortion and of passive speculation does not confine itself to the merchants and traders alone. They too, the farmers, a great number of them are disgracefully involved and eagerly streching forth their clawy hands, plan[n]ing the processes that must, in their results, inevitably grind down to ultimate starvation or to helpless poverty the widows and orphans, the wives and children of the brave men who are so manfully and courageously sacrificing everything for the cause that sustains and will finally establish these heartless speculators and vile extortioners in the ownership of their ill-gotten gain. The curses of the bereaved widow and the fatherless will fall upon them of course; but they expect that. They seem to be electioneering for that unenviable reputation. What harm will the feeble anathema of the downtrodden widow and neglected orphan do to them? Not a bit. Don't I know that they are the very men that will become the most prominent, first office seekers? That will mount the stump when the war is over, and with the impudence of the devil declare and swear in the name of the Lord, demonstrating to the crippled up and impoverished remnant of the people as clear as mud, that all our military successes, with the final happy termination of the war in honorable peace, is attributable to them. That to their immense sacrifices of time and money, their losses, labour and untiring vigilance, the people, and the government are indebted for the good condition they enjoy and many other glorious advantages resulting from the well conducted revolution. And now that the storm of war is passed, and gentle peace diffusing its balmy influence in the families, cheering the hearts of the exultant and triumphant masses, they are claiming no more than they are justly entitled to, in calling on the people for the suffrages—and the people will elect them!!!

It was of one class of the eternal enemies to our cause that you, in your letter of 23rd ult. desired me to speak, and to urge the representatives of Washington county to tax them so as to amount even to prohibition. They were gone to Austin a week or ten days previous to the arrival of your letter. But what would it avail the people to instruct the members of their legislature? Are they not—a large majority of them—the very selfsame, said speculators. Do look back to the last session of our legislature, and remember if you can, what it was they did there that would benefit the people, or afford protection to our invaded state? They be d—d.

I agree fully with you, in relation to taxing the cotton planters heavily. I think also that the principle should be run further among the speculators; even to the prohibition of every species of trade. The people can make shift without the interference of such heartless thieves.

I thought after the perusal of your letter that I would write to our county members on the subject, but before I had time to do so, I received the governor's message,[2] and as it covered the whole ground, I did not think it necessary.

Taking the man and all the circumstances into consideration, I esteem that message quite a decent state paper.

We are having continuous rains, and that one fact is good for a deeply saturated ground, in which case our lands never fail to produce good crops of corn, even in the absence of summer showers. We should like very well to visit you, but the war has made us too poor for enjoyment of any kind. All's well.

Most respectfully thine
Gideon Lincecum

P.S. Failing to get a machine at your place, I have gone to work, and am making one myself, also, a machine to clean and break wool.

Gid

[1] Mary Elizabeth Massey indicates that "the twin evils of speculation and hoarding were important contributors to shortages" during the Civil War and that "people complained about speculation more than about any other of the war evils." She also notes that Texans, and especially Germans living there, profited greatly from blockade running across the Rio Grande (Massey, *Ersatz in the Confederacy*, pp. 13, 17).

[2] It is not surprising that Gideon approved of the governor's message, since it closely followed his own views. In February 1863 Gov. Francis R. Lubbock (1815–1905) called the Texas legislature into special session and exhorted them to support the Jefferson Davis administration in its determination to resist Lincoln's plan "to Africanize the Southern Confederacy." Lubbock described efforts in his office to provide troops and supplies for the military and urged the legislature to take bold measures to support the war effort, including defending the frontier, providing greater support for the families of soldiers, enforcing limitations on planting of cotton, encouraging planting of grain crops, and raising new tax dollars. As a further demonstration of his support for the war effort, the governor announced that he would not seek reelection; instead he went on to join the staff of Gen. John B. Magruder, and in August 1864 he

became an aide-de-camp to President Jefferson Davis (Ralph Wooster, "Texas," in *The Confederate Governors*, ed. W. Buck Yearns, p. 205; see also Lubbock, *Six Decades in Texas*).

Labeling these Texans as worse than the "accursed Lincolnites" was about as harsh a judgment Gideon could possibly give, considering his extreme contempt for the Northern enemy.

Now truly nearing seventy, Gideon was too old and too busy *to enter the army, as Lubbock did. He took advantage of a rainy day to rest his weary bones and tend to neglected correspondence:*

Long Point. Tex. 22nd Mar. 1863

F. M. Gaston
Jordon Saline,[1] Tex.
My Dear Sir.

Your interesting favor of 10th inst. came to hand yesterday evening, and as it is Sunday and raining I avail myself of so favorable an oppertunity to reply.

I am too busy during fair weather to write letters, and besides, my old semitorpid nerves and flattened and almost exhausted muscles render it quite difficult and irksome for me to write at all. I am, however, striving to steady and strengthen my nerves and increase the volume of my muscular system by the application of daily labour. Necessity for wearing apparel has some hand in impelling me to labour. I have succeeded in making a spinning machine, having 30 spindles to it. It is thought by the "Muggins" around here to be a grand machine. To save the few cards we are fortunate enough to get hold of, I have commenced a machine for cleaning and breaking wool. This, I can already see, will turn out to be a valuable acquisition to our manufacturing department.

When this machine is completed, the greatest drawback to our spinning and weaving establishment will be the scarcity of cards. I have not the wire, or it should not be long till I would have cards plenty.

Everything about this vicinity is moving on in about the same stile it was when you left. No deaths or marriages nor any recent babes that I have heard of. The war seems to have put a check upon everything. I did not expect, however, it would force a blockade upon the baby ports.

In respect to your furnace, I would suggest that you increase your fire bed, that is, make it deeper by adding a foot or so to that end of your furnace, widening it a little as you draw it back or outwards, and raise your stack higher. A small fire bed attached to the side of your furnace opposite the first sluggish kettle, arranging it so that the draft will strike its bottom fully, will increase the heat greatly, with but a very small additional supply of fuel.

You can facilitate the evaporating process to nearly one half the time by suspending a wheel over each kettle, having arms and many thin slats attached to them, the more the better—so constructed and shaped that when the wheel is made to revolve, the arms with their numerous slats will dip as deep as possible into your boiling brine. Then turn the wheel slowly through the boiling water. The wheel must revolve vertically, and you will soon perceive from the increased quantity of steam escaping from the wet slats as they revolve that evaporation is at least doubled. The philosophy consists in the fact that by your slatted, revolving wheel you have largely extended the evaporating surface. Hence, the more dipping slats you can crowd on to your wheel, the better, because you thereby increase the amount of surface to be exposed while wet and heated to the open air, as your slats are momentarily emerging from the boiling kettles. Try one of these wheels. I think you will be pleased with it. It may be constructed entirely of wood on a cheap plan. Anybody can make it. It will save wood and increase the quantity of salt per day.

We are all well. Nothing new or strange occurring in Long Point.

Thine as ever
Gideon Lincecum

[1] Jordan Saline, Van Zandt County, in northeastern Texas, was named for John Jordan, who acquired title to the land over a large salt dome in 1845 and developed the saline prairie. Prior to the war the Southern states had bought much of their salt from the North or imported it from Europe. Since salt was vital to civilians as well as the military during the Civil War, the Confederate government took over the salt works and operated it until after the war. The salt works produced enough for the army, but civilians could not get sufficient salt due to the blockade, speculation and corruption, and inadequate transportation (*New Handbook of Texas*, 3:1003; Current, ed., *Encyclopedia of the Confederacy*, 3:1362; Kerby, *Kirby Smith's Confederacy*, pp. 68–70).

Somehow Gideon found the time four days later to write a very long letter giving a Texas lady extensive advice on preparing dyes for clothing.[1]

Long Point. Texas. 26 Mar. 1863

Mrs. Mary H. Taylor[2]
Navarro County, Texas

Most respectfully, I reply to your application on the subject of the cheap coloring material of Texas, and the processes as far as my experience goes. The gentleman who reported my experiments to you was incorrect in respect to the alum. I cannot produce that very useful mordant on terms that would pay, nor have I as yet been able to produce the Turky red or indigo blue from any plant I have tried so far.

Coperas, or acetite of iron, which in coloring cotton is superior to the sulphat of iron (coperas) because it never damages the goods—and it is fully as good in coloring wool—may be had to any desirable quantity by the following process. Throw into some vessel that will hold it, all the old waste iron about your place: scraps of tin, old hoop iron, old stove pipe, any iron scrap. Then fill the vessel with weak vinegar or sour beer, set it in some safe place. It soon becomes a fountain, from whence you may draw at any time, and the longer it stands the better and richer it gets. It should be kept filled up all the time with the weak vinegar or sour beer, and the liquor that is left, after dipping your goods, should be poured back into your coperas fountain. It is not proper to put this coperas liquor in with your bark, but saturate your cloth by steeping it in the liquor (I'll call it vinegar of iron)—for black dye, two days, stirring and wringing often. Then place the goods in your coloring decoction and turn it, lifting it often, until you have the desired shade. For lighter shades, keep it in the vinegar of iron a shorter time.

The vinegar of iron is applicable in all cases where you would use the coperas, and it is equal to it in dying wool, superior for cotton or silk, and much more convenient. The ladies are all familiar with the process of coloring black, brown, and the various shades of these two colors—I need not say more on that subject.

To color drab and light reds, the ley [lye] of some strong ashes is the proper mordant and it is applied after the goods have been boiled sufficiently in the coloring matter. The ladies all know how that is done. The brightest red I have produced on cotton was done with the red elm bark, the wild peach bark next; the goods being washed in ley after thoroughly boiling them in a strong decoction of the bark.

The bright yellow cannot be produced without alum and the acetite of lead. The alum you will have to procure from the druggists; the acetite of lead you can make at home. Put a pound or so of lead into a glass jar (shot or finely chopped up lead)—an old pickle bottle will answer—fill it up with good vinegar; let it stand in a warm place five, six days, shaking it often, when it will be fit for use. The proces for dyeing yellow, a specimen of which you will find herewith enclosed, is not difficult, but it requires that you be exact as to quantity in the proportions of your mordants.

For wool: let the wool be boiled for an hour, or longer, with about one sixth of its weight of alum, dissolved in sufficient water to keep the goods wet while boiling. Then, right from the alum bath, without rinsing, plunge it into a strong preparation of black oak (*Quercus tin[c]toria*) bark. That is, pretty finely bruised black oak bark, in quantity half the weight of your goods, put into sufficient warm water to cover all fully; into this preparation the wool is to be placed, and turned and pressed in the liquor; at the same time raising the heat gradually, to the boiling point, which must be continued until the desired degree of color is brought out. Then sprinkle into the liquor a quantity equal to one hundredth part of the weight of the cloth, of clean, finely powdered chalk, and continue the stirring and turning and boiling 8 or 10 minutes longer. By this time, a pretty, bright, lively yellow will be produced. Wring it out and dry it, after which wash it with soap; wring it well, and spread it out to dry again.

The process for dyeing cotton or linen yellow is a little different. Make a saturated solution of alum, and to three parts of this solution add one part of the acetite of lead. This solution must be heated a little above blood heat, and kept at that temperature; the cloth or hanks should be soaked in two hours, then wrung out and dried. The soaking may be repeated and the cloth or hanks again dried as before. It is then to be barely wetted with lime water and dried again. The soaking in the alum and vinegar of lead may be again repeated, and if the shade of yellow is required to be very bright and durable, the alternate wetting in the lime water, and soaking in the alum and lead may be repeated three or four times. Then the dying liquor is prepared by putting twice the weight of your goods, of finely bruised black oak bark, tied up in a bag, into a sufficient quantity of cold river or rain water. I mean any soft water. Into this water with the bag of bark, the cloth or hanks are to be put and turned in it for an hour, while its temperature is gradually to be raised till you can't hold your hand in it. It is then to be raised to the boiling heat, which must be continued but 3 or 4 minutes; if boiled too long, it will aquire a shade of brown.

The pecan (*Carya olivaeformis*) bark, treated in the same manner, as directed for the black oak bark, will produce equally fine yellow colors. The bark of the Spanish buckeye (*Daubentia*), by boiling the goods with the bark in water two hours, and then washing in ley produces a very pretty drab color. Red Elm (*Ulmus americana*) treated in the same way colors cotton the reddest of anything I have yet experimented with; next best to it is the bark of the wild peach (*Cerassus cardinaensis*). This article colors wool a most beautiful bright brown, almost a red color. It will also color cotton from a very fair Nankin, through many shades to a good arnetto; this dye is treated with ley also. The best black dye material is the heartwood of the mesquite (*Algarobia glandulosa*).[3] Chip the wood very fine, and treat it with the vinegar of iron, just as you would logwood. The mesquite wood is equal, perhaps superior, for coloring dead black, to the logwood itself. We have a small weed in our prairies, the perennial roots of which are red, capable of producing many shades of color on cotton goods, from a pretty bright red, through the various phases of brown, to a dead black. I have experimented with many other barks and roots, many of which produce bright and useful colors for stripes &c. But the prettiest, the cheapest, and most abundant of all the coloring material for coloring wool is found in the poor land green [Spanish] moss, which so profusely drapes the scrubby post oaks, elms, and other trees growing on poor glades and stony knobs, almost in every climate. It can be had in any desirable quantity.

You cannot produce a clear yellow in an iron vessel. Acquire copper or brass boilers, and they should be bright and clean. You should not be satisfied with dingy or dull shades of yellow. The black oak and pecan barks are capable with the proper manifestation of producing the brightest and richest yellows. I think I have discribed it so that you will understand the process. A small quantity of yellow, striped in with the beautiful moss dyes, and black, produces quite pretty linseys for little girls' dresses.

The process for dying with the green moss is so simple that I had thought to omit the discription of it, besides it is pretty extensively resorted to by the ladies in many parts of the country. However, I will discribe my method, as it can do no hurt.

An iron pot will do. Fill it with clean water, put in a layer of moss, then a portion of your cloth or hanks or wool; then another layer of moss; then a layer of your goods, and so on, alternating the moss and the goods until your pot is nearly full. Now put your fire under it, and after you have raised it to a boiling heat, commence stirring and turning and pressing it down, and continue boiling for the space of an hour and a half. Then wring it out, wash it, and when it is dry, you will have a very pretty and very durable bright, but rather light brown. If you are not satisfied with it, cary it through the same manipulations with a new lot of moss, and the process may be repeated even four times. It will receive a deeper shade every time. I admire the deepest shade above any color. Enclosed you will find a lock of wool, dyed the third time.

I have given you the processes with those articles which I think most likely to be of use to you. You will find the vinegar of iron to answer all the purposes for which you would employ the coperas, and that is really a better article. The acetate or vinegar of lead will supply fully the place of the sugar of lead, which is a costly article these heartless times. The alum you will have to procure from the drug stores. You may, however, supply yourself with many good colors without the alum. Are the people of your region not growing the indigo? It will flourish finely in any portion of Texas.

I am quite an old man, 70! and the war is bearing heavily on me. Until the war came, myself and my old lady were spending the evening of our protracted existence quite pleasantly. Our children settled all around us on good homes, and doing well. We had nothing to do but to go about among them, receive their visits, and hear their accounts of their successes in their battles for subsistence. But the war came, and our children and grandchildren are scattered—the efficient male members—on a more hazzardous field and are battling for liberty. Those that are left behind are the helpless women and children, who need clothing. Their tattered raiment sent me to work, a thing I was not skilled in, never having worked before. Yet I have succeeded in making with my own hands, wheels, reels, sleys, shuttles, a fine loom, spools, warping mill, and a spinning machine, having thirty spindles. And am now making a wool breaking machine.

Respectfully
Gideon Lincecum

[1] Throughout the South, the shortage of commercial dyestuffs during the Civil War forced people into the woods to search for plants that would color homespun and home-knit articles (Massey, *Ersatz in the Confederacy*, p. 97).

[2] The only Taylor we have identified in Navarro County is J. W. Taylor, listed as residing in Corsicana in the 1870 Census (U.S. Bureau of the Census, Ninth Census, 1870, Navarro County, Tex., p. 012).

[3] The pecan, *Carya olivaeformis*, is now *C. illinoensis*. Gideon's "Spanish buckeye" might be the genus *Ungnadia* Endl., also known as the Texas buckeye or the Mexican buckeye. The family is the Sapindaceae or soap-berry family. The seeds are spherical, one to one and one-half centimeters in diameter, dark brown to blackish, and poisonous. Another possibility would be the genus *Aesculus* L., the buckeye or horse-chestnut, which is in the family Hippocastanaceae or buckeye family. The elms are in the genus *Ulmus*, and *U. americana* L. is the American elm; the red elm is *U. rubra* Muhl (Donovan S. Correll and Marshall C. Johnston, *Manual of the Vascular Plants of Texas*, pp. 460, 494–95, 1004–6). The wild peach or laurel cherry was known to Gideon as *Cerasus caroliniana*; however, today we call it *Prunus caroliniana*. *Algarobia* is now called *Prosopis*. *P. glandulosa* is the honey mesquite tree (J. C. Willis, *A Dictionary of the Flowering Plants and Ferns*, 8th ed., revised by H. K. Airy Shaw, pp. 40, 225).

One has to marvel at the time, energy, ink, and paper Gideon was willing to expend on such a very long, painstaking letter to a correspondent he barely knew and from whom he expected no reward other than *what she might be able to contribute to a home front at war. Three months later Gideon was finished, for a time at least, inventing and making new machines, and for a change had little advice to pass along to the readers of the* Galveston News:

Long Point. Tex. 26 June 1863

Editor of the Galveston News
Houston, Texas

Our people, with the exception of a few inefficients and old men, having all gone to the war, meteorology dried up, for want of room; Entomology and Botany, dryer still, with the readers of the present <u>times</u>; crops are pretty good everywhere and everybody <u>knows</u> it; there is nothing for me to write about that would be of any advantage to you or interest to your warrior subscribers; and as I am not satisfied, under all the circumstances, to use and enjoy your labor when there is no chance for me to reciprocate in kind, please enter the enclosed $10 to my credit, and when the time comes for me to pay more notify me, if it should be tomorrow even.

I have finished all my spinning and weaving machines; they are operating satisfactorily, and not being able to think of anything else to make that would be of use, I have laid away my tools and am floating down the time-stream like an old watersobbed log—slowly, but surely, and am a long way past island no. 70. I desire to keep afloat until I see the Yankees ruined.

Thine truly
Gideon Lincecum

In writing a lady in Independence, Gideon excoriated the folks in Millican and then, of course, the Yankees.

Long Point. Texas. 13 July 1863

Mrs. S. B. Baker[1]
Independence, Texas

I made the trip home to dinner, sure enough, but 8 miles of the distance was through the rain. I did not, however, sustain any serious injury from it, and finding all well at home, I was soon restored to as good condition as I was before my visit to that unholy place—that scab on the back of mother earth called Millican.[2]

I was also cheered up considerably on ascertaining the fact that Capt. James S. Lauderdale had returned home safe and sound from his long and perilous imprisonment amongst the infernal thieving, hooked nosed yankees;[3] and I was still more highly elated and gratified at the amount of glorious news from our victorious armies. May our forces never cease to kill and slay the God dishonoring, hell deserving rascals, so long as one of them can be found within the bounds of the confederacy. This is by no means a pious prayer, but I should belie my feelings if I was to alter it. So let it go as it is.

The Lauderdale connection are all well, so is Mrs. Malone and her family.[4] The old man Lauderdale is well, but lays pretty close at home this hot weather.

We are going on making syrup, but on account of the small cane, which in consequence of the sore drought is dry, and we cannot produce exceeding 125 gallons a week, which is a very poor turn out. However, we must hang on to it, for it is perhaps our only chance for sweetening; the yankees having destroyed the cane crops of Louisiana almost entirely, we shall get no sugar from that quarter. . . .

Accept assurances of my sincere esteem and respect from

Your most obt servnt
Gideon Lincecum

[1] Mrs. Sophia Baker is listed as residing in Independence in the 1860 Census (Eighth Census, 1860, Washington County, Tex., p. 218).

[2] Millican was situated fifteen miles southeast of Bryan in southern Brazos County. Settled by two men named Millican in the 1820s, it served as the terminus for the Houston and Texas Central Railroad from 1860 to 1867. During the Civil War it was the site of a training camp for five thousand Confederate troops (*New Handbook of Texas*, 4:747). Gideon probably found Millican "unholy" because it was a boomtown with such things as gambling, saloons, and prostitutes.

[3] James Lauderdale, age forty-five, is listed as residing in Long Point in the 1860 Census (Eighth Census, 1860, Washington County, Tex., p. 152). He came to Texas from Columbus, Mississippi, with his father, Sam D. Lauderdale, in 1858 (Burkhalter, *Gideon Lincecum*, p. 141n). A captain in the Confederate army, he was cap-

tured at Arkansas Post, Arkansas, 11 January 1863 and transported to Camp Chase, Ohio, and then to Fort Delaware, Delaware. He was exchanged on 29 April 1863. On 8 May 1863 he was in Chattanooga, Tennessee, but was sent to General Hospital #4 in Richmond, Virginia, on 14 May 1863, where he was diagnosed with chronic diarrhea and sent to Galveston (National Archives, *Compiled Service Records*, roll 340).

[4] A Mrs. M. R. Malone is listed as residing in Brenham in the 1860 Census (Eighth Census, 1860, Washington County, Tex., p. 223).

Evidently, when Gideon wrote to Mrs. Baker he had not yet heard of the crushing Confederate defeats at Vicksburg and Gettysburg, but even after he had received that news he put an optimistic interpretation on the situation, as the next letter shows.

Long Point. Tex. 27th July 1863

F. M. Gaston
Hempstead, Texas
My Dear Sir.

Your very polite, and highly acceptable communication of today reached me about 8 p.m. I was gratified and truly interested with its contents. It seems strange, however, that you and your officers still entertain doubts as to the fall of Vicksburg! Vicksburg and Port Hudson are both in possession of the Yankees, and as I conceive, greatly to our advantage.[1] If the 40,000 men who have been pent up at those two places for the last 18 months had been properly officered and distributed along the banks of the river, with all that parade of cannon and small arms, they would have damaged the Federal preparations a great deal more than they have done at Port Hudson and Vicksburg; though they have hurt them some as it is and will hurt them more before they all get away from there.

All our late news is very encouraging, and from the positions of our forces, we may venture, I think, the prediction that our summer and fall campaign will be crowned with success generally.[2]

We have superior commanders, braver and better trained, and hardier soldiers, who value as they do their lives the cause they are fighting for. The Yanky cause is disgusting to themselves, mean as they are, and we shall soon be in a condition to increase their disgust most damnably. We are able to keep the war up for an indefinite period, and we should not think of a cessation of hostilities so long as a single principle of Southern rights are impinged on by the infernal, humanity dishonoring, damned Yankees.

There is nothing right or honorable in that villainous people. They are begot, bred and borne by and under the immediate instruction of their fanatic priests, raised and trained by disappointed and badly soured old maids, in their truth destroying Sunday schools—no thinking man would expect them to be good people. And it would be a great piece of weakness in our government to listen to any overture that may come from them for a suspension of hostilities at any time, even to bury their dead. They care nothing for the dead, nor further than their expectation of gain goes, for the living—They be damned.

Except a very large assembly of gentlemen and ladies, negroes, children and dogs that took place at the big lake last Saturday, there has been nothing to disturb the ordinary monotony of this section of country.[3] I was with them at the lake. There were perhaps 150 individuals there, all fine and bright, and having plenty of fish, which were, by management of Mr. T. Affleck, well prepared, they seemed to enjoy themselves exceedingly.[4] The thing was well got up, executed in good style, having the greatest abundance of fat fish—is terminated satisfactorily. Nothing occurring on the ground to mar the good feeling that seemed to cheer up every countenance.

We are all well, but little fun nowadays—

Respectfully thine
Gideon Lincecum

[1] After six weeks' siege, Grant's army forced the surrender of Vicksburg and its thirty thousand Confederate defenders on 4 July 1863, one of the greatest turning points of the war. Gideon was perhaps unaware that at the very same time, at Gettysburg, Robert E. Lee was withdrawing his army after an even more crucial defeat (McPherson, *Ordeal by Fire*, pp. 312–15, 330–32). Port Hudson in Louisiana represented the last hold of the Confederate army on the Mississippi River. Its surrender on 9 July allowed the "Father of Waters" to again go "unvexed to the sea" (Abraham Lincoln to James C. Conkling, 26 August 1863, in Don E. Fehrenbacher, ed., *Abraham Lincoln: Speeches and Writings, 1859–1865*, 2:498). For discussion of the siege of Port Hudson, see McPherson, *Battle Cry of Freedom*, pp. 637–38. See also Lawrence Lee Hewitt, *Port Hudson, Confederate Bastion on the Mississippi*.

[2] About the only encouraging news Gideon might have received at this time was, perhaps, the deadly draft riots in New York City, 13–16 July, and Lee's success in withdrawing his army safely to Virginia after his major defeat at Gettysburg. Gideon's prediction of general success in the summer and fall campaign fell far short of the mark, especially after Grant's team took over at Chattanooga and trumped the Confederate success at Chickamauga (19–20 September) with even greater victories at Lookout Mountain and Missionary Ridge (24–25 November) (McPherson, *Ordeal by Fire*, pp. 334–40; Catton, *This Hallowed Ground*, pp. 339–68).

[3] The "big lake" near Long Point could be Lake Lange near Mill Creek, west of Brenham, or perhaps a lake on the Affleck property, Glenblythe Plantation near Gay Hill.

[4] A native of Scotland, Thomas Affleck (1812–68) established Glenblythe Plantation near Gay Hill in Washington County in 1858. During the Civil War he served as chief purchasing commissioner for Texas, and many army supplies came from his shops at Glenblythe

(*New Handbook of Texas*, 1:43; Burkhalter, *Gideon Lincecum*, p. 156n).

In early August Gideon wrote to his son-in-law in Austin and once again showed greater hostility to profiteering Texans than to the hated Yankees.

Long Point. Tex. 4 Aug. 1863

Mr. G. J. Durham
Austin, Texas
My Dear Sir.

. . . We are all well, with a growing antipathy towards the yankees and their southern friends.

Let Anarchy come. Who will it damage? Nobody but the southern arm of the Lincoln forces! They are here all amongst us, collecting and sending off our cotton daily. Our state government winks at their action. Let this thing roll on. It has already got up the signs of a revolution. After which, will come anarchy, and then some fine fun, particularly for those fellows who have been doing business with counterfeit notes and government funds in the name of the confederacy.

Thine as ever
Gideon Lincecum

Gideon was in far better spirits the next day when he wrote to the Boone Moores.

Long Point. Texas. 5 Augst. 1863

D. Boone Moore
Hondo Valley
Castroville,[1] Texas
Dear Brother & Sister.

Your kind letter of 12th July did not reach me until yesterday. We were all truly glad to hear from you all, for it had been so long since we had received a letter from or heard from you in any other way, that we began to conclude that the Indians had got you sure enough. We are all proud, however, to hear that you are all safe and prospects pretty good.

You desire me to give you the war news. For a long time—ever since the fall of Vicksburg—we have had no dispatches from East of the Mississippi River.[2] Madam rumour has been very busy since that disastrous event, but there is so much and such flagrant contradictions in those reports and rumours that we place no reliance in any of them. By these rumours and slack twisted reports, Washington City has been captured half a dozen times. As also Baltimore and Philadelphia. There is no truth in any of it.

Our forces this side of the great river are doing very well. They are fighting more or less every day. We get letters from Jo and Cash almost every week;[3] they say the fighting is fine—good as could be desired; but the privations and hardships are heavy and fatiguing. They have so far, though they have participated in many battle[s], come out without a scratch, and are all the time healthy. We heard from them by a returned soldier today. They are both enjoying vigorous health, and in good spirits.

Leonidas and Leander are both over 40 years of age, but they are too in the service. Lon is War tax collector for this county, and Leander was detailed to attend to the sick in the absent soldiers' families. Lucullus was detailed for the same service in another settlement. Lachaon is beef contractor, buying up beef cattle and driving them to the army. The last drove, he took across the river at Natches, but a few days previous to the fall of Vicksburg. He crossed 956, swam them over. Lysander has tried the camps three or four times, but the diseased condition of his lungs incapacitates him for the life and duty of a soldier, and he was twice ejected.

George Campbell, after returning from the Arizona campaign, drank himself to death. He dropped dead in a dogery [saloon] at Brenham, leaving his wife and seven children poorly provided for. Matson, Mary's husband, is here, fat and doing well. He has been superintending the negroes on his own and his brothers farms. His brother has been in the army all the time since the war.[4] Durham is War tax collector for the state. Cassandra lost her two pretty little girls last year; they died of putrid sore throat, and she grieved herself half to death about it.[5] Mary and Leonora have all their children, alive and healthy. The connection at this time are all healthy, and was it not for this infernal war, are all well to do.

My family has increased considerably since I saw you. When we are all together, counting the old lady and myself, there is 61 of us, with a prospect for considerable increase. There has been no change in our household since I saw you. Sarah and Lysander constitute our white family, and from appearances now our family will be apt to remain at that number.

The old lady and I were enjoying the evening of life in good stile and should have past off the life stage quite pleasantly, but for the interruption provided by the damned yankee invasion. We were spending our summers in the mountains and a portion of our winters on the delightful sea coasts. In both situations the sources of enjoyment was very great and we appreciated it finely. We can't go now, our horses have all been used up in the army as well as our money and other appliances. And so we shall be compelled to rust and rot where we are, which to me is by no means an agreable reflection. However, when I get through the rotting process, it is likely that I shall not care what the yankees does then. But until I do rot, they must keep out of my way.

. . . Remember me to all the family and receive for yourselves my best wishes and affectionate prayer

Gideon Lincecum

[1] The Moores had recently moved from Hondo to Castroville. The two towns are eighteen miles apart in Medina County.

[2] The fall of Vicksburg had indeed been "disastrous," increasing the isolation of the Trans-Mississippi and forcing Texans to rely even more on their own resources (Kerby, *Kirby Smith's Confederacy*, pp. 253–81).

[3] All persons mentioned in this letter are Lincecum family members identified in the appendix.

[4] Richard Matson is the brother of Gideon's son-in-law James Matson. He was a private in Company F of the 21st Regiment of Texas Cavalry (National Archives, *Compiled Service Records*, roll 111).

[5] The Durhams lost two young daughters (Sarah and Mary Leonora) to diphtheria in April 1862 (Burkhalter, *Gideon Lincecum*, p. 83).

That there was unrest on the home front as well as disillusionment among some of the troops was evident in Gideon's letter to a Texas soldier in September.

Long Point. Tex. Sep. 2nd 1863

F. M. Gaston
Terrell's Regnt.[1]
Richmond, Tex.
Dear Friend.

Your kind favor of 23rd ult. came to hand last Thursday. You have been marching about pretty smartly.—Well, "that is the way they used for to do, when I was along with the carolina crew."[2] I hope, however, that they have sense enough to have you at the right place at the right time. The action of our leading officers in the trans-Mississippi department may be all right, and they [are] clever fellows and will soon begin to manifest signs of improvement. At all events, the people are expecting something from them. We, sometime ago, were all complaining at Genl. Sibley, for his mismanagement and drunkenness. Now it seems to turn out that they are all Sibleys. Be that as it may, the war is an existing fact, pressing heavily upon us; will have ultimates, and these ultimates will be in exact accordance with the intellectual force of those who are entrusted with its direction. No more, nor any less. Take that for consolation.

You complain at the infernal speculator, depreciation of the currency &c. That is awfully out of joint, and the no souled, damned speculators—who are nothing more nor less than the southern arm of the Lincoln forces, are the sole cause of it. These vile rascals should be all put to death. They are damaging the Confederacy more than the open enemy are. The people everywhere are becoming highly incensed at the conduct of these faithless men, and are moving, in many of the counties, in a manner that shows they are greatly exasperated.

We had a large and exceedingly unanimous meeting at Brenham day before yesterday, and they passed some very strong and very pointed resolutions—They will soon be published, and I will not repeat them here.[3]

I also find that the returning soldiers from every point are complaining, not at the service and its hardships, but at the depreciation of our currency, the speculators, and the dissipation of the officers generally.[4] They swear vengeance generally against the speculators. Large numbers of soldiers are returning, some with, and some without furloughs. They are all mad and threatening. From the general movement of the people and the ceaseless murmur that is heard everywhere, I judge that a great and significant revolution is about to take place. People are everywhere tired of the old fogyism and consumate recklessness of our official corps, from the highest to the lowest. The history of the abuses of all government demonstrate very clearly that reform never has occurred in such abuses until the masses of the people themselves took the case in hand. Then the speculators, peculators and the perpetrators of the wrong cry loudly against the injustice of the people for interfering, and brand and stigmatize them with every evil epithet they can think of. They always try to frighten the people by their dreadful accounts of the anarchy and confusion that must follow the unlawful interruption of their nice little speculations.

Anarchy! is a species of government that is dreadful to the villianous usurpers, plunderers and wrong doers generally, but to the masses it is good and proper. It is a declaration of individual rights, with a determination to maintain those rights. Theives call it mobocracy, anarchy, riots, &c &c.

We shall soon know how, up this way, who are our friends and who our enemies. Officers have been appointed to take the resolutions that were passed at Brenham last Monday to every man in the county and offer it to him for his signature. All friends to our cause will sign it, for there is nothing in the resolutions contrary to justice or to individual rights. Those who do not place their names to it are to be considered enemies and will be dealt with as such.

The people have been bearing this thing very patiently a long time. This patient forbearance amongst the people has no doubt been an encouraging thing to the extortioners and theiving speculators. The people, however, can stand it no longer. Forbearance is no longer a virtue. They are about to recoil, and this recoil will be frightful to villiany.

So mote it be. I for one would be glad to see those heartless, liberty-hating scoundrells overtaken by the sword of justice everywhere, and utterly blotted out. They are already beginning to fly, and now is the time for people to commence the action of retributive justice with them. I hope ere long that I shall see the people hunting, chasing and capturing them by the hundred. There will be more real sport in it than in a wolf hunt, and surely the people will save their scalps, which ought to be made a legal tender to pay tax with. In the case of these enemies to the southern cause, there should be no court trials; that he has been speculating in staple articles is sufficient to know; the sentence has been passed in the peoples convention already; there is nothing to do but to execute it, which I sincerely hope they will do without hesitation.

The people will begin first with the men who said they were government agents, and whether they turn out to be government agents or not, we all know that they have been practicing a fraud, both on the people and the government, and the people will deal with them accordingly. Their sub agents will come next, will be considered equally guilty—and if any of them who have been acting as mere dupes to the government agents should suffer the penalty, they must console themselves by the reflection that like the poor dog tray, they were found in bad company.

I can't say now how this thing will terminate. The censure seems to be universal and is lying at the door of many of the highest official names in the trans-Mississippi service. Be them who they may, however, I hope that the people, when they find the truth, will make no difference among rascals, be their station what it may.

If this movement amongst the people progresses as it should do, it will produce a good change in the entire aspect of our affairs and will hasten the war to a favorable termination.

Nothing strange has transpired in this vicinity since you were here. We are all well.

I remain as ever, Thine
Gideon Lincecum

[1] The 34th Texas Regiment was commanded by Col. (later General) Alexander W. Terrell of Austin, who led it in the 1864 Red River Campaign in Louisiana, discussed below (*New Handbook of Texas*, 6:258–59).

[2] Probably this little ditty had its origin in the adventures of the U.S.S. *Carolina*, a schooner of the U.S. Navy in the War of 1812, which played a heroic role in the Battle of New Orleans in December 1814.

Launched in 1812 at Charleston, South Carolina, the two-masted vessel was armed with fourteen guns. On 23 December 1814, manned by a crew that included a number of Jean Laffite's Baratarians, the *Carolina* began Andrew Jackson's battle against the invading British army with a deadly cannonade of its camp. Four days later the ship lay becalmed in the Mississippi within reach of British artillery; some red-hot shot set the ship ablaze and the vessel exploded. However, most of its crew escaped and later got revenge by manning two guns on Jackson's defense line that helped to win the decisive battle (Robert V. Remini, *Andrew Jackson and the Course of American Empire, 1767–1821*, pp. 251–53; William S. Dudley, ed., *The Naval War of 1812: A Documentary History*, 1:583–86).

[3] We were not able to discover what "the very strong and pointed resolutions passed at Brenham Aug. 4, 1863" were. However, the *Galveston News* did publish resolutions from several other communities. For instance, the resolutions of the citizens of Goliad were published in the *News* on 20 October 1863.

[4] There were growing incidents of desertion and even mutiny in Terrell's Texas Regiment. See correspondence in *Official Records of the Rebellion*, series 1, 26:278–80, 469–71.

Six days later the situation in Texas brightened, as young Dick Dowling and his handful of Texans beat off a large Union invading force at Sabine Pass and sent them packing.[1] *It was the greatest victory of the war in Texas, but the blockade continued, the fighting outside of Texas intensified, and the Confederacy's need for funds grew more acute. Gideon addressed this financial plight with a remarkable proposal he made in October in another of his letters to the editor of the* Galveston News*:*

Long Point. Texas. 9 Octr. 1863

Editor News.

From the great number of suggestions, seen in the papers, on the subject of sustaining our currency, it is fair, I think, to conclude that the honest patriotic citizens of the confederacy, entertain the warmest solicitude for its speedy restoration to a specie valuation. Many are trying to devise some acceptable plan for that purpose; and was it not for the opposition that is thrown in the way by the soulless speculators almost any of the propositions that have been offered, would answer the purpose.

One gentleman of good standing, who owns a large amount of lands as well as plenty of other property, proposes that every man in the confederacy shall sell one fourth of his property, land and all, for confederate bonds, and immediately on receiving payment for the property so sold, commit the money to the flames and destroy it.

At the first blush this plan sounded pretty well, but when we reflect that where every man is selling, there can be but few purchasers—that as confederate bonds are not rated as property, they would not be sold, and on that account, if no other, this plan could not be made to bear equally on community. It is therefore impracticable.

I propose for the consideration of the Confederacy, as an amendment to all the plans that have been offered, that as soon as the war tax now under assessment shall be collected, that immediately thereafter, a day shall be set apart on which every man in the confederate states shall go to the nearest or most convenient Election precinct to him at the time, and then and there, under his most solemn oath, diliver into the hands of the president magistrate the one fourth part of the amount of all the confederate notes, bonds, &c which he may, on that day, possess, hold or claim, either in his own right or in the right of any other person or persons whatever. And it shall be the duty of the presiding Magistrate there to destroy, on the same day, all the monies so placed in his hands by publicly burning it to ashes.

Here now occurs an oppertunity for the manifestation of the most exalted patriotism the world ever saw. A manifestation at which vandal yankeedom, and plodding Europe would stand aghast. It would appease the ire of all the gods and excite the admiration of every intelligent, thinking man on the globe. And is not this glorious, this courageous people, who have already astonish[ed] the world with so many patriotic sacrafices, capable of performing this last and greatest of all achievements? We shall see who will come to the ring and register his name on the Nation's Escutcheon, from whence it can never be erased.

I will for one, and I own <u>some</u> of the money.

Gideon Lincecum

[1] See "Victory at Sabine Pass," in Gallaway, ed., *Texas, the Dark Corner of the Confederacy*, pp. 145–49. Not only did Dowling's small force thwart the Union invasion, they also sank two Federal vessels, killed 19 men, and took 315 prisoners without any loss to themselves.

While Gideon's proposal was commendable, it must have fallen on deaf ears. Had he and his fellow Southerners followed his advice and burned a fourth of their Confederate notes at this time, they would at least have gained some satisfaction for a patriotic act. Instead, the notes proved worthless at the war's end.

Gideon appeared to be in a mellow mood when he resumed correspondence with Joseph Sniveley in October.

Long Point. Texas. 13 Octr. 1863

Jos. C. Snively
Wood's Regnt, C.S.A.[1]
My Dear Sir.

Your quite welcome letter of 1st inst. did not come to hand until this morning.

Until I received it I did not know where you were. I received a letter from you some time ago [in] June. You were then near Brownsville. Now at Liberty; well, that's better than laying up at the same place all the time.

I was at Liberty 28 years ago, I noted it in my journal, the which, as you ascertain little attachment for the place I will try to raise your love for it by copying the notes from my journal into this letter.[2] "Feb. 28th 1835. Reached the town of Liberty; it is situated in a sandy prairie, some distance (2 or 3 miles) from the Trinity river, at the head of tide water. . . ."

The news during the last four days is quite cheering. The great battle, so long reported, at Chattanooga has at last come off.[3] Victory, though very costly, has perched with her bloody wings, on our banners. I hope our army may find itself in a condition to pursue the advantages won, to the utter discomfiture of the old Dutch man, for he was or is the best general they have to their name.[4] The boys in Louisiana are performing fairly, though we have a rumor, which we hope is not true, that Genl. Tom Green is being hard pressed by the Yankees.[5] The rumor was dated Shreveport 6th inst.; dispatch said nothing about it; it was of the same date.

Almost everybody has gone to the war now. I stay here by myself having no associates, until I have almost forgotten the language. I spend my time altogether in the investigation of the natural sciences. . . . Some of the old fellows around here have been stepping off to the "good hunting ground" recently, leaving me almost alone. Old Dr. Morriss, and Col. A. M. Lewis, both took their departure a few weeks ago, leaving me no playmate now but Judge Baylor.[6] He, to be sure, does very well, visiting me pretty often. He performs on the violin, and we spend our time quite pleasantly, so long as we keep from thinking of our kindred and friends who are participants in the hateful, bloody strife. The judge is a preacher, if you recollect; I can very well stand his fiddling, for he performs pretty well and knows some good pieces; but when he undertakes, as he sometimes does, to approach me on the subject of religion, I can't stand it. That is, I can't maintain my gravity. For it looks to me that a man of his oppertunities and his middling good sense ought not to talk about such foolishness, particularly when there is no one present but a single friend who is in earnest on all serious subjects.

People here are struggling hard, trying to clothe themselves. Having so few cotton cards increases the difficulty very much. Yet I find community pretty well enveloped in homespun. Paper nearly all gone—all's well.

Very Respectfully, as ever
Gideon Lincecum

[1] Woods' Regiment, the 36th Texas Cavalry Regiment, was commanded by Col. Peter C. Woods (Wright, comp., and Simpson, ed., *Texas in the War*, pp. 29–122, n. 221).

[2] Gideon's 1835 journal of his trip to Texas has been published. See A. L. Bradford and T. N. Campbell, "Journal of Lincecum's Travels in Texas, 1835," *Southwestern Historical Quarterly* 53, no. 2 (1949): 180–201. However, the notes quoted in this letter are entered for 14 February, not 28 February.

[3] Gideon is referring to the big but short-lived Confederate victory at Chickamauga on 19–20 September, which forced the Union troops to fall back to Chattanooga, where they were penned in until U. S. Grant came to the rescue (McPherson, *Ordeal by Fire*, pp. 334–40; Warner, *Generals in Blue*, pp. 410–11; Catton, *U. S. Grant and the American Military Tradition*, pp. 111–14).

[4] The "old Dutchman" must be a reference to Gen. William Rosecrans, who, contrary to Gideon's opinion, was deemed inadequate by Lincoln and Grant and was replaced on 19 October by Gen. George Thomas as commander of the Army of the Cumberland (Warner, *Generals in Blue*, pp. 410–11; Catton, *U. S. Grant and the American Military Tradition*, pp. 113–14).

[5] Brig. Gen. Thomas Green (1814–64) was one of the most admired Texas officers in the Civil War. A veteran of the Battle of San Jacinto and of the U.S.-Mexican War, he served with distinction in New Mexico and at the Battle of Galveston. Gallantly and effectively he would lead Texas troops in the Battles of Mansfield and Pleasant Hill, only to be killed three days later at Blair's Landing by a shot from a Federal gunboat (Warner, *Generals in Gray*, pp. 117–18). Green was called "a warrior of warriors" by his superior, Gen. Richard Taylor (Brown, ed., *Journey to Pleasant Hill*, p. 458). For a full portrait of Green, see Odie B. Faulk, *General Tom Green, Fightin' Texan*. At this time, in early October 1863, Tom Green's Texans were being rather "hard pressed" by a much larger Union force near Opelousas in south-central Louisiana, but before October was over it was Green's men who were doing the pressing and forcing a Union retreat (Winters, *The Civil War in Louisiana*, pp. 279–99). Green would play a major role in Louisiana the following spring.

[6] No record of the death of Dr. Thomas W. Morriss has been found. Apparently Gideon had gotten over the anger he felt toward the Morrisses when they failed to join the Long Point Minute Men in 1861. Asa M. Lewis was in Texas by 1839 and settled in Columbus, in Colorado County. He served as a Colorado County delegate in the Texas House of Representatives for the Seventh Congress of the Republic of Texas (1843–44). In 1844 he was elected a town commissioner of Brenham, Washington County, where he was a prominent attorney. In the 1850s he urged the Texas legislature to encourage railroad construction, and in 1856, when the Washington County Railroad Company was granted a charter, he was one of its commissioners (*New Handbook of Texas*, 4:179; Winfield and Winfield, *All Our Yesterdays*, p. 25). Robert Emmett Bledsoe Baylor (1793–1873) was a prominent Baptist minister and educator living at Gay Hill. His name was given to Baylor University because he played a key role in its founding. He was the judge of the state's Third Judicial District from 1846 to 1863 (*New Handbook of Texas*, 1:424–25).

With his "paper nearly all gone," Gideon wrote fewer letters the next two months, but he found enough paper to write a long letter to his English friend Hannay and raised again the prospect of disloyalty and vigilantism in Texas:

Long Point. Texas. 22. Octr. 1863

R. B. Hannay
Millican's, Texas
My Dear Sir.

Your highly esteemed and very agreeable communication of 18th. inst. came to hand at sunup this morning. At the same time came the Galveston News and the Houston Tri. Wy. Tel.[1] We consider the news all very favorable, yet feeling deep concern and solicitud for the position of our army; they are fighting so long. We can but hope for the best ultimates. It is true that our successes recently have been very great, even if one half of what has been reported be reliable.

I was really taken by surprise when I heard that the Tories had been arrested. There are a great many more implicated in the plot. Dr. Lewis and nine other traitors were arrested in La Grange day before yesterday, and on their way to Houston passed through Brenham yesterday evening.[2] I hope our authorities may be in possession of all their names and that the guards, or somebody else, may hang every one of them. I can make no excuse for them. If they were unfriendly to our cause, they had plenty of time to have passed beyond the Mason's and Dixon's line, and no true patriotic Sou[t]herner would have molested them. But to remain here, entering into the War speculations, many of them amassing fortunes and at the same time craking and disparaging all confederate efforts, besides organizing themselves into a regular system of traitors, whose fortunes were to be made with the downfall of the republic: I can feel no pity for them.

I understood a day or two ago that both the Tafts were

missing from Houston, and the supposition is that they had been hung.[3] Mrs. Mesner also stated the same thing to Sarah, on a visit to Brenham last week, last Munday.[4] Have you heard of anything wrong with the Tafts? I hope the report is not true, but if they are guilty, I hope they may not make good their escape. I didn't like it when I heard that the old man had sent his son Jo off just at the time that the war was opening.

I have been listening for some grand implications and developements from Austin. I have heard more complaint from that quarter than any other portion of the state.[5] However much I may hope that it was unfounded, there was too much of it, for it to be all false. Headed as they were, by such great leaders, they have perhaps managed their treasonable plots in better stile than the Houston and Brazos traitors. There is ex Gov. P. —[6] The great H—[7] and P—[8] and R—[9] and S—[10] and S—[11] and other Hamilton men[12] in Austin who should, if reports are true, have been sent, not out of the country but up a tree, long ago. Southerners are a great deal to[o] tender in their notions on the subject of political offenders. I should be glad to see them, under present circumstances, more vigilent and as gnarly as a pine knot. Every suspicious action should be noted and promptly dealt with. There is no time for parl[e]ying now. Men all have a chance now to clear themselves of all suspicions. Those who do not think enough of our cause to put themselves to that much trouble, to relieve the minds of those by whom they are suspected, may suffer the penalty of their foolish obstinacy without any sympathy from my tender heart, I can assure you. . . .

Recently I hear a good deal said in reference to the great number of "fellers" who have obtained licence to preach. Not having flocks for such a number of shepherds, the poor lascivious, avaricious creatures have entered into the plane of the speculators and peculators. A goodly number of the Godly Saints, if you recollect, had been sometime ago, for their opposition to the cause of liberty, transported ——— up a tree; and now, those who were fortunate enough to escap[e] justice have become emboldened from the blind lenity [lenience] that our intellectual cowards have manifested in letting them run at large; they are perpetrating villainies of many types.

It would please me to hear that a company of saint catchers had been organized, armed with the lasso, and sent out with strict orders to rope and haul up a tree every one of the Lord's Shepherds they could find who have no flocks and claim exemption from military service on account of having license to preach. Damn them, why then don't they go to the army and preach, where there are the most and the wickedest people.

The enclosed article you sent me is a good thing. There are many plans and suggestions being developed on the subject of our depreciated currency, in all portions of the confederacy recently. Many of our southern men are honest. They abhor the idea of repudiation, and they cannot keep silent on the subject. I know one man[13] who has proposed for a day to be set apart, not for thanksgiving and prayer, but for every man in the Southern Confederacy to go to the most convenient Election precinct to him at the time and there under his most solemn oath, deliver into the hands of the presiding magistrate, the one fourth of all the Confederate notes, bonds, &c he may possess, hold or claim either in his own right, or the right of any other person or persons whatsoever; and the magistrate shall then & there, on the same day, publickly burn the money so placed in his hands, to ashes. Let the people do that and there will not be much room [left] for doubting their patriotism. . . .

We have no news hereabouts to write you that would give the least pleasure.

Very respectfully Thine
Gideon Lincecum.

[1] Begun in 1835 by two brothers named Borden, the *Houston Tri-Weekly Telegraph* was acquired by Yankee-born E. H. Cushing (1829–79) in 1855. As its editor, Cushing made it one of the more important newspapers in the state. It never stopped publishing during the Civil War, despite having on occasion to print on butcher paper and wallpaper. According to Mary Elizabeth Massey, "The files of the Houston *Tri-Weekly Telegraph* resemble a rainbow," as seven different colors and shades were used between October 1862 and November 1863 (Massey, *Ersatz in the Confederacy*, p. 141). In 1864 it became the *Houston Daily Telegraph* (Marilyn McAdams Sibley, *Lone Stars and State Gazettes: Texas Newspapers before the Civil War*, pp. 262–63; *New Handbook of Texas*, 2:458; see also Emory M. Thomas, "Rebel Nationalism: E. H. Cushing and the Confederate Experience," *Southwestern Historical Quarterly* 73 [1970]: 343–55).

[2] No record of the fate of Dr. Lewis and "the nine other traitors" arrested in La Grange 20 October 1863 has been found.

[3] Gideon's address book lists a Joseph S. Taft, bookseller, in Houston (Burkhalter, *Gideon Lincecum*, p. 161n). He also corresponded with a P. B. Taft in Houston (see Gideon Lincecum to P. B. Taft, Long Point, Tex., 20 May 1858, LP, Box 2E364). No record of the arrest or hanging of anyone named Taft in Houston was located, nor did we find any published reference to a "Jo Taft" being sent to Europe just before the war started.

[4] Marietta Mesner is listed as residing in Brenham in the 1860 Census (Eighth Census, 1860, Washington County, Tex., p. 140).

[5] Austin was indeed a hotbed of Unionists. One historian reports, "As the state capital and the home of many conservative lawyers and merchants, the city provided the Union cause with more leaders than any other place in Texas." Travis County was one of only eighteen counties to vote against secession (Marten, *Texas Divided*, p. 64).

[6] In referring to the six individuals he designated with initials, apparently Gideon was referring back to 1860, when a "Union Club" was formed in Austin. Those who attended its first meeting drafted and signed a letter which was published in newspapers across the

state, proposing a "Union of Union Men." Most prominent among this group was "Ex Gov. P," Elisha Marshall Pease (1812–83), governor of Texas from 1853 to 1857. Although a native of Connecticut, he had fought in the Texas revolution. He attended the first meeting of the Union Club of Travis County, and his refusal to support the Confederacy persisted after the Civil War began, resulting in a tax collector confiscating his horse and buggy in lieu of payment of the war tax in 1862. During Reconstruction, Pease was appointed governor by Gen. Philip Sheridan in 1867; he resigned the office in 1869 (Buenger, *Secession and the Union in Texas*, p. 53; *New Handbook of Texas*, 5:112–13; Marten, *Texas Divided*, p. 72).

[7] "The great H—" refers to Andrew Jackson Hamilton, a leader in the "Opposition Clique" in Texas, a faction of the regular Democratic Party that opposed secession, reopening the slave trade, and other Southern extremist demands. He attended the first meeting of the Union Club of Travis County and signed the letter circulated by its members. His outspoken opposition earned him notoriety, and late in 1862, alleged plots against Hamilton's life forced him to flee to Mexico. He became a hero in the North, and after visiting with Abraham Lincoln he accepted a commission as brigadier general of volunteers and military governor of Texas. During Reconstruction he served as provisional governor from the summer of 1865 to the summer of 1866 (*New Handbook of Texas*, 3:427).

[8] "P—" probably refers to George Washington Paschal (1812–78), one of the organizers of the Union Club of Travis County. He was born in Georgia, served as chief justice in Arkansas during his twenties, and moved to Texas in 1847. In 1848 he was practicing law in Austin. During the late 1850s he edited the *Southern Intelligencer*, a pro-Union journal financed by Swante M. Swenson, another Unionist. Reports of Paschal's Unionist sympathies led to his being jailed and held for trial by a court-martial early in 1864, although he was never tried (*New Handbook of Texas*, 5:80; Marten, *Texas Divided*, pp. 72–73).

[9] "R—" probably refers to John H. Robson of Colorado County, who was also involved in the founding of the Travis County Union Club. Along with George W. Paschal, he represented the Constitu-

tional Unionists as an elector from the western portion of Texas for the 1860 presidential election. Both he and Paschal were pledged to support whichever candidate had the best chance of defeating Lincoln (Buenger, *Secession and the Union in Texas*, pp. 53–54).

[10] "S—" undoubtedly refers to Swante M. Swenson (1816–96), a native of Sweden who migrated to Texas in 1838 and eventually settled in Austin. Despite his being one of the largest landowners in Texas, his Unionist sympathies forced him to leave the state in 1863 in fear of his life. He lived in Mexico and New Orleans for the duration of the Civil War, moving permanently to New York City in 1865 (*New Handbook of Texas*, 6:192; Marten, *Texas Divided*, p. 79).

[11] "The second S—" probably refers to Gustav Schleicher (1823–79) of Bexar County, who attended the first meeting of the Travis County Union Club in September 1860 and signed the letter that its members published in newspapers across the state. An engineer, entrepreneur, and politician, he was born in Germany, migrated to Texas in 1847, and settled in San Antonio in 1850. He served in the state legislature's House of Representatives in 1853–54 and in its Senate in 1859–61. Despite his initial opposition to secession, when the war began he became a captain in the Confederate army, commanding Gen. John B. Magruder's corps of engineers (*New Handbook of Texas*, 5:919).

[12] "Other Hamilton men" refers to Unionists. Notable Travis County Unionists, in addition to the men identified above, included John and George Hancock, Thomas H. Duval, Morgan Hamilton, John T. Allan, and William P. DeNormandie. Only Pease, George Hancock, Morgan Hamilton, and Paschal stayed in Austin throughout the Civil War (Marten, *Texas Divided*, p. 65). Although their politics differed at this point, it is noteworthy that in 1859 Gideon had initiated a friendly correspondence with Morgan Hamilton, after seeing a letter from Hamilton published in the *Boston Investigator* (see chapter 1 above).

[13] Gideon himself made this proposal. See letter above to the editor of *Galveston News*, 9 October 1863.

Neither the sacrifices nor the profits of the war were being distributed equally or equitably among the population, and Gideon felt that state legislators were partly to blame:

Long Point. Texas. 17 Novr. 1863

F. W. McGuire[1]
House of Repvs.
Austin, Texas
My Dear Sir.

Your very kind, and highly esteemed favor—political sentiments and all—with the State Gazette, came to my table at 9 p.m. yesterday.[2] For all of which you have my sincere thanks. I read your letter with feelings of pride and deepest interest. Proud of the sensible view you have taken of the underhanded machinations of the concealed enemies to liberty, and the unmistakable manifestations of firmness, visible throughout the entire letter. Of all this, I repeat, that I am proud. It is a thing of such rare occurrence in Legislative bodies, to find a man who possesses a soul of his own, with sufficient courage to name it. Go on your own way, I shall not even offer a single suggestion. The start you have made inspires full confidence, and I shall not disturb your course by the expression of a solitary though[t] on any subject.

The bills already presented have made their impressions on your mind; you have formed your conclusions, and with these conclusions I agree thoroughly, and most ardently hope that you may succeed in defending and sustaining them triumphantly. Is the rule to oppose, but never succeed with our desires and efforts to overthrow iniquity, to be our lot always? We talk of distributive justice! Pshaw!

The designs of the speculators, members of the Legislature, to monopolize the trade in alcohol by legislative enactments, with the secret workings of the Abolition element in that body, all going on under the high sounding and oft reiterated title of patriotism, sacred rights of the dear people, &c &c is enough, almost, to disgust and turn me to a misanthrope. You say that infernal impressment bill will be brought forward again.[3] Let that bill pass; it will never be put into action. If that is attempted, the gauze that covers the villainy in it is so transparent that everybody will see it, and they will not put up with it. Revolution would most certainly be the result. I tell you my friend, and it is true as gospel, that already there is a deep seated under current, with strong revolutionary symptoms, working in the minds of the masses at this very moment. It is smoldering in the embers of discontent and suspicion of the leading authorities of our state, and will require but very slight, additional reasons for dissatisfaction to fan it into a flame that will fill our country with terror & will not cease to burn until the instigators of it are destroyed utterly. Let them—If they will persist in sowing the wind, let the hurricane come. I shall be mad too and shall seek satisfaction by throwing my force, regardless of consequences, on the side of right. This confusion is not created by the masses. They know nothing about its origin. They feel oppressed from all directions, and when they strike, it will be at the nearest object found in their way. Then comes the reign of terror, in which the innocent as well as the guilty must suffer.

I hope, however, but with little faith, that in the present Legislature a sufficient number of honest, intelligent men may be found to ward off the intended evil, and to place the enemies of equal rights so conspicuously before the people that there can be no mistake as to who they are.

Is it because all are guilty that no man can be brought to account for his villinous actions?

I am pretty well satisfied, many discontented men are calmly waiting to see what will be the action of the present session. They have been in hard service at low wages, whilst those who have seen no service at all have accumulated immense fortunes.

They are not waiting for the legislature to pass impressment bills or anything of that kind for their benefit. But they are waiting for them—as they very well know honest men could do it—to pass enactments that will equalize the service and burthens brought upon them by this unholy war.

That is all that is the matter with them. It is the prime cause of all the straggling and skulking, & soon it will produce a great deal more. This session of the legislature, if they could lay aside self, might restore confidence and thereby harmonize the demoralized condition of community. If they fail to do a good deal, to that effect, we shall see the devil before another session convenes, if there ever is another.

The friends of freedom must stand firm everywhere. I have said in another portion of this letter that under certain circumstances I shall be mad, too, and regardless of consequences shall throw my force on the side of right. That would be a meaningless declaration, if the sentiment was not a pretty gene[r]al one. I hear it from all the returned soldiers, officers as well as privates, and accounts of the black and white lists, kept by our soldiers in our armies, proves that they are apprised of the action of the "stay-at-home gentry," and that they will, when they return, hold them to account.

I have been drawing staves all day, which has pretty well unfitted me for writing. Your kind letter did not require a reply, and there was no actual necessity for my writing tonight. But I felt like saying a few words to you. I have done so, and after reading it over, I find that it contains but little that can do more than amuse you—

I have heard nothing amiss from your settlement.[4] We are all well here.

With much esteem,
I remain dear sir,
Your most obt. servt.
Gideon Lincecum

[1] F. W. McGuire was a member of the tenth Texas legislature (1863–65), representing the 51st district from Yegua, Washington County (Charles F. Schmidt, *History of Washington County, Texas*, p. 38).

[2] Under the editorship of John F. Marshall the Austin *State Gazette* became the leading forum for expression of extreme states' rights views and a mouthpiece for the state Democratic Party. A native of Virginia, Marshall moved to Austin in 1852 and purchased a half interest in the *State Gazette*. In 1854 he bought the remaining half interest in the newspaper and became its best-known editor, staunchly supporting sectionalism and slavery. When the Civil War began, Marshall joined the Confederate army as a private but quickly became a lieutenant colonel in the 4th Texas Regiment. He had risen to the rank of colonel of the regiment before he was killed in his first battle, that of Gaines Mill, Virginia (27 June 1862). David Richardson bought an interest in the *State Gazette* after Marshall's death and became its editor. The newspaper continued to be published, though in a smaller version, during most of the war, and it served as the voice of the Southern cause and the state government (*New Handbook of Texas*, 1:313–14; 4:519–20; 5:567).

[3] The Confederate Congress passed an "Impressment Act" 26 March 1863, providing for the seizure of agricultural products and military supplies at a fair price. It also established a system of arbitration whereby a former owner might negotiate a better price. Impressment, whether of supplies, livestock, or slaves, was a divisive issue in the Confederacy. Many, like Gideon, voiced strong opposition to the invasion of either states' rights, when advanced by the Confederate government, or personal rights, when proposed or implemented by the state government, as it seemed to violate one of the principles behind secession (Current, ed., *Encyclopedia of the Confederacy*, 1:393; George C. Rable, *The Confederate Republic: A Revolution against Politics*, p. 193).

[4] McGuire's settlement is Yegua in Washington County.

Before this year of unrest closed, Gideon wrote again to Hannay.

Long Point. Texas. 20 Decr 1863

R. B. Hannay
Millican's, Texas
My Dear Sir.

Your quite entertaining communication, of 14th ult. came to hand in due time. . . .

We have as yet had no outrages in this vicinity. We had plenty of the proper material for misrule, but by some happy coincidence, it was hurried off to the war early, where they have had full cause for the exercise of their rough natures. What would be crime here is esteemed as virtue there—But let us cease to complain. They say God made man in his own image, and as that was all the pattern he had, he done pretty well, "considering."

At this time of pork and grease, everything in this quarter is exceedingly quiet. They have filled their bellies to their liking, and the controlling animal that dwells within them is content. Bad colds and pleurisies have already commenced, typhoid fevers will follow, and a few of them must die. It is to be hoped that all those who have died from the disease brought on by gormandising in grease and fresh meat may have the privilege of going to hog heaven.

I made a tub[1] today, and writing does not go well with me; and if it did, I have nothing that would interest you to write about. There are no men in this vicinity, and the women won't do anything worth talking about. True, they are all busy spinning and weaving and knitting and so forth, but that's becoming so common that everybody knows all about it; so I shan't say anything on that topic. It looks very well, however, to see them all dressed in garments of their own manufacture. I see some linseys and stripes that are very neat indeed. . . .

We are all well. Receive my blessing, and

Believe me as ever,
most truly Thine,
Gideon Lincecum

[1] Gideon had probably made a wooden tub, since in the previous letter to McGuire he said he had been "drawing staves" all day.

When next Gideon wrote to Hannay it was a new year but not a better one for Texas or the Confederacy.

Chapter 6

1864

Although the Federal forces had been driven out of Galveston and repulsed at Sabine Pass in 1863, the Federal naval blockade of the Gulf Coast continued into the new year. Federal troops also occupied the southern tip of Texas at Brownsville, cutting off some of the trade across the Rio Grande. Material shortages, therefore, continued to be a critical problem for the Texas population, although Gideon, because of his ingenuity, fared better than most. In January he wrote a letter to the stranded R. B. Hannay:

Long Point. Texas. 24th Jany. 1864

R. B. Hannay
Millicans, Texas
My Dear Sir.

Your two letters, one bearing date 7th and the other 20th inst., came together to my table day before yesterday. They were quite refreshing, though not quite so rich in their accounts of the hanging, shooting, throat cutting and thieving performances of some of your former communications. The poetry is excellent. It is a well expressed illustration of the suppressed feelings of only one among the thousands of the truly good and great who are born in to the world and, as soon as the indications of their superior nature begins to be made manifest, they are trampled to death by the great seven headed and ten horned beast. Your noble souled factory girl, rather than connect her destiny with the beast,

"Resolved alone to live—alone to die,
Nor swell the tide of human misery."

She, in my estimation, was a proper object for adoration. She understood the philosophy and use of existence, as well as the cause and preventive of human misery. She knew where lies the great, propagating root of evil, and she had the wisdom and the courage to resolve not to aid it in the work of mischief. If all females possessed the power to judge of and to refuse to propagate the species with none but the intellectual, there would be no more thieving and war. It is the animal—not the intellectual—portions of our organism that consents to fight and steal. Do you hear? . . .

We have no thieving or hanging about here yet, but as such action is daily getting nigher and nigher, we may count on being blessed with a few cases before long—

Before this reaches you, you will have gone to visit your sister-in-law. I should like to know what she has got in her head now. You will find something you didn't expect. I hope it will all go well with you.

I should like it very well that you could get off to Europe with that lot of cotton. But don't undertake to carry it through Mexico. If you can't make a successful run through the blockade on our own coasts, the enterprise won't pay. Anyhow let us hear of your plan if you undertake it, and also how you come out at Mrs. Hannay's.

We are all well and working along through the inconveniences thrown around us by the war. We are done buying goods; we are all clothed in our own manufactures, and we are able now to continue to do so.

Very Respectfully
Thine
Gideon Lincecum

Since money was even scarcer than commodities, the government accepted payment of taxes in kind, and Gideon gave some advice on storing the local collection.

Long Point. Texas. 27 Jan. 1864

Dr. Rippetoe[1]
Brenham, Tex.
Sir.

Mr. C. B. Shepard informs me that you made arrangements with him for the use of the basement story of the large old store house in this place to store the tax in kind in. It will not answer the purpose. It being entirely unsafe, I have not nor can I issue notices to the people until there is a safe place to deposit their produce. Shepard owns two other houses here. One of which (the blacksmith's shop) by two or three daý's labor could be made to answer the purpose pretty well. There will, perhaps, be delivered at this depot as much as 2000 barrels, if a safe store can be prepared soon.

Let me hear from you soon
Very Respectfully,
Gideon Lincecum

[1] A. H. Rippetoe is listed as residing in Brenham in the 1860 Census (Eighth Census, 1860, Washington County, Tex., p. 143). In Schmidt, *History of Washington County* (p. 73), he is identified as Dr. A. H. Rippetoe, who was living in Brenham as early as 1850. In 1861 he was a representative of District 51 (Brenham) in the Texas legislature (p. 38).

While taxes in kind were being gathered, Texas' soldiers were being scattered in many directions, and Gideon had lost touch with young Joseph Sniveley until he received a letter from him on 10 March 1864. He replied at once.

Long Point. Texas. 10th March 1864

J. C. Snively
Cedar Bayou, Tex.

Your communication of 22nd ult. did not come to hand till noon today. I was glad to receive it, for I had lost your whereabouts and would not risk the mailing of a letter that had been sent to my care for you, two months ago; i.e., I received it 2 mos. ago. I did, however, entrust it in the hands of a soldier who stated that he knew you personally, your occupation, position &c. The letter returned by mail a week or so since, from which I concluded that he could not find you or had himself been ordered in some other direction. I shall enclose the letter herewith and hope it may reach you this time. . . .

The dissatisfaction and insubordination of your troops is a sad thing at this period of our struggle. There is wrong somewhere. I hope it may all come right in good time. Our troops are everywhere restless, which, as I am induced to think, originates from the want of confidence in their leaders. I may be wrong, however. . . .

Except that we are all regularly becoming poorer, there has been but little change in this vicinity. Dick Matson was shot through the heart, in a little skirmish at pine bluff, Ark.[1] It was awkwardly done on his part. The Matson families are all well, and so are the people generally, except my "sore arm"—as well as the kindred of your most obedient servant.

Write— Gideon Lincecum

[1] Richard Matson, the brother of Gideon's son-in-law, James Matson, was a private in Company F of the 21st Regiment of Texas Cavalry when he was killed in action at Pine Bluff, Arkansas, on 25 October 1863 (National Archives, *Compiled Service Records*, roll 111).

During the month of March, Gen. Nathaniel Banks and his Union troops were making another move on Texas, but this time he was attempting to come in from the east, ascending the Red River through Louisiana as far as Shreveport. Texas troops, as well as those from other Confederate units west of the Mississippi, were there to greet him and turn him back.[1] Among the Texas soldiers stopping Banks in early April were two of Gideon's grandsons, while two of his sons and two other grandsons were in a Texas force moving southwest. He described the recent developments to his sis-

ter and brother-in-law, who were still on the edge of settlement.

Long Point. Texas. 13 April 1864

Dear Brother and Sister,
[Boone and Emily Moore
Castroville, Texas]

Your very interesting communication of the 3rd instant came to hand in 11 days. We had not heard from you in a long [time]. We had sent a letter of inquiry last winter, but received no answer to it, and we thought it probable that your mail had been interrupted or some other bad thing had occurred. We were very glad to hear that you are still flourishing and hope the good fortune may continue. The damned inhuman yankees are threatening us on all sides, but two or three more such disastrous drubbings as Genl. Kirby Smith bestowed on them 8 or 10 days ago, at Mansfield and at Pleasant Hill in Louisiana will, I think, break them from sucking eggs for some time.[2] You will see the report of the fight long before this reaches you, but I will nevertheless state a few of the principle facts that occurred. We took from them 20 pieces of artillery, a train of wagons, ambulances &c, five miles long, and 2000 prisoners, besides a great amount of small arms and other munitions of war and were at the last accounts still persuing and butchering them.[3] Our loss in officers was heavy. Genl. Mouton and two captains killed, a colonel and several other officers wounded.[4] Loss of privates not stated. The yankee loss was said to be very large.[5] So far this year we have whipped them at every point they have attacked us, amounting to 8 or 10 pretty heavy battles.[6] My opinion is, and is based upon a careful examination of the war movements generally, that we shall break up the robber clans this year.

My family consists now of the old lady Sarah and myself, all the rest having gone to the army. Captn. Onan's Company, who are by this time perhaps as far on their way to Eagle Pass as your place, was made up right here, and took all the men that was left in the vicinity that was worth counting.[7] A portion of that company are Lincecum's. Lachaon, Lysander, Lascassas and Leander, are in that Company, and are assigned to Eagle Pass.[8] Cassianus and Josephus Lincecum are still in Tom Green's army in Louisiana where the fighting is now going on. Captn. Onan's Company were ordered to proceed to Eagle Pass in as short a time as possible, but if any of the boys can know when they are passing your region, they will call and see you. By the above statement you discover that my house is sparsely populated. Our whole brood, when they are all together amounts, if you count in the old lady and myself, to 61. Of this number, nine are in the confederate service: two detailed as physicians and the rest are all women and children. There were but 12 grown men in the family when the war commenced. One, Capt. Campbell, <u>dead</u>. The balance, except the detailed physicians, Leander and Lucullus, in the Service. So you may imagine that we have a lonesome time of it. We should doubtless feel lonesome were it not for the fact that we live where the two great thoroughfares of Middle Texas cross. Few nights pass without company. They are generally soldiers, and to them our house and cribbs are always open free of charge. We have fed away to them three heavy crops, and though it has reduced our means to a pretty low ebb, we are nevertheless sorry that we are not able to do more. All I have shall go free as water to sustain our cause. What would a life in the South under Negro equality and Yankee rule be worth? Oh! Let all I have go, and life too, rather than see that state of affairs. Death is a funny condition, to what that would be. Let the whole South <u>die</u> in preference to submission to that state of damnable degradation. I do hope that the entire people, both male and female, feel as I do upon this subject. That they have, like me, all made before their gods, solemn vows, that so long as life lasts, they will never be at peace with the accursed yankee people; that they will teach their own and all other children with whom they may come into contact, to bear eternal enmity to and also to hate and kill yankees throughout the period of their existence. Let our posterity never forget that the annals of the history of man furnishes no account of such a race of brutalized humanity as the damned yanky, and that he is not nor will he be entitled to anything but death from the coming families of our posterity to the tenth generation. This is the lesson that I teach to the rising generation whenever I am in their company, and I endeavor to impress them with the idea of the necessity and the propriety of such action, so long as they can find one of the hateful tribe to kill. Never again permit one of them to pass with his peddling cart, his lying books, and false maps, but slay him as the enemy of mankind.

We are all healthy, and struggling to clothe ourselves by manufacturing the cloth at home. I saw the old lady, who is in better health than she has been in ten years, yesterday warping a long piece of cloth. She bids me say to you that she would not only be proud of an opportunity to pay you a long visit but that she would rejoice at the prospect of moving out there to live. But the war has, however, spoiled all small things; it has taken our horses till we are not able to make up a team that would enable us to pay you a visit even, and by the time the war is ended we shall be in a condition to care but little for mundane things. We do not repine, however, for our lot has not been an unpleasant one, neither has it been a short one. Come 25th of next October, we have lived together fifty years in the matrimonial tether, which circumstance should of itself satisfy and prevent us from asking more, even were there any power that could give it to us.

We are making a very bad start for a crop in this country. We had to plow up and plant our entire crop a second time, and it is still cold and the ground very dry. Our cattle nearly all perished to death last winter. It was heart sickening to see the starved creatures, suffering for both food and water. In this settlement there are no Union men, and very few of any other sort of men; I don't know of any whole one. Neither is there anything in this vicinity, except what Lysander did three or four days before he left, that could be considered strange.[9]

Most affectionately your Brother
Gideon Lincecum

[1] For thorough coverage of the Red River Campaign of 1864, see *Official Records of the Rebellion*, series 1, 34, pt. 1:162–638. For a careful chronicle, see Ludwell H. Johnson, *Red River Campaign: Politics and Cotton in the Civil War*, pp. 89–169, 206–79, and for a splendid narrative see Foote, *The Civil War*, 3:25–92.

[2] Gen. Edmund Kirby Smith (1824–93), a West Point graduate, U.S.-Mexican War hero, and career officer, had distinguished himself in eastern battles before being given command of Confederate forces in the Trans-Mississippi West (Warner, *Generals in Gray*, pp. 279–80). The Battle of Mansfield (Sabine Crossroads) took place 8 April 1864, thirty-five miles south of the vital Confederate supply center of Shreveport, Louisiana. Confederate troops, including many Texans, directed by Lt. Gen. Richard Taylor (1826–1901), former president Zachary Taylor's son, stopped the advance here of Brig. Gen. Nathaniel Banks's Union troops and forced their retreat. For a fine treatment see Brown, ed., *Journey to Pleasant Hill*, pp. 371–433. See also Foote, *The Civil War*, 3:39–46, and Johnson, *Red River Campaign*, pp. 88–89. For Taylor, see Warner, *Generals in Gray*, pp. 299–300. The Battle of Pleasant Hill occurred 9 April, the day after the Battle of Mansfield, as Taylor's pursuing troops overtook the retreating Union soldiers and inflicted another beating, only to be surprised with a strong counterattack that ended the fight in a draw, although the Federals resumed their retreat the next day (McPherson, *Ordeal by Fire*, p. 413; Winters, *The Civil War in Louisiana*, pp. 348–55; Foote, *The Civil War*, 3:47–50). One authority

has aptly observed, "Tactically the battle of Pleasant Hill was distinctly a Northern victory, although the [Confederate] retreat to Grand Ecore turned it into a strategic defeat" (Johnson, *Red River Campaign*, pp. 165–66).

[3] Gideon's figures, which apparently referred only to the Battle of Mansfield, were not exaggerated, except that the number of prisoners he gives is somewhat high. See Johnson, *Red River Campaign*, pp. 140–41, 166–68.

[4] Brig. Gen Jean Jacques Alfred Alexander Mouton (1829–64), a Louisiana native and West Point graduate, had distinguished himself at the Battle of Shiloh. He led the Confederate charge at Mansfield and was killed in that charge (Warner, *Generals in Gray*, pp. 222–23).

[5] Union losses at Mansfield numbered almost twenty-nine hundred, while Confederate casualties totaled one thousand. In contrast, Union losses at Pleasant Hill numbered almost fourteen hundred, Confederate losses nearly fifteen hundred. One-third of Mouton's division was lost (Current, ed., *Encyclopedia of the Confederacy*, 3:1005, 1317).

[6] Gideon was engaging in exaggeration and wishful thinking. "So far this year" the Confederates had won only a few "pretty heavy battles," Mansfield being the biggest; and they failed to whip Sherman's army, which laid waste the key supply base of Meridian, Mississippi, in February. They did win the battles of Olustee (Florida) and Buzzard Roost Gap (Georgia) in February and turned back the Kilpatrick-Dahlgren cavalry raid in Virginia in March (Long and Long, *The Civil War Day by Day*, pp. 464, 466, 468–69, 471, 482; Catton, *This Hallowed Ground*, pp. 305–6; Foote, *The Civil War*, 2:924–26).

[7] According to one source, the Lincecums were a part of J. M. Onin's company, the Giddings Cavalry Battalion (Janet B. Hewett, ed., *Texas Confederate Soldiers, 1861–65*, 1:396, 2:273). Another source reported that "Captain Owin's [*sic*] Company" was a part of the battalion of Lt. Col. George H. Giddings that joined Col. John S. Ford's "Cavalry of the West" on the Rio Grande (John Salmon Ford, *Rip Ford's Texas*, ed. Stephen B. Oates, pp. 349, 374; Wright, comp., and Simpson, ed., *Texas in the War*, pp. 33, 126–27).

[8] Lachaon and Lysander Lincecum are Gideon's sons; Lascassas,

Leander, Cassianus, and Joseph are his grandsons.

[9] Lysander married Mollie (Maggie) Wood at Long Point just before leaving for the army.

Not all of the Lincecums had distinguished themselves in the recent action. Brazos Lincecum, the son of Gideon's deceased brother, Garland, was even charged with desertion when he and some of the other volunteers became disgusted with their leader and went home without leave. Gideon had a first-hand report of the affair, which he passed on to his sister-in-law, Emaline Lincecum,[1] the mother of Brazos, who had heard rumors that her son might be executed.

Long Point. Texas. 14th April 1864

Dear Emaline

I this moment received a letter from J. C. Snively, Hospital steward for Col. Wood's regiment, in relation to Brazos Lincecum's Case—Snively wrote to me from Moscow [Texas], on the march to Louisiana, and after he had left Hempstead. The following is the exact words of his letter on that subject, which I copy from it.

"Poor Bras Lincecum is one of the number that went home, and is now under charge of the detail left at Hempstead, where a court martial met to try their cause. Out of 35, but 2 plead guilty of desertion, and they did it through ignorance. They were all found about home, and many of them hunted up for detail sent after them, and gave themselves up to the guard.

"I hope they may not be punished with severity, as the object of punishment is only the prevention of crime. I feel certain that they have already been taught a good lesson, without any punishment being added. The two pleading guilty of desertion was sent to Houston, doubtless to wear a ball and chain for a period. The others will be with the Regiment soon."

The above is the exact words of the letter, and it shows

that there was no punishment, except for the two who confessed that they had deserted. Nobody shot, as you was told by our lying, disaffected informants.

All's well.

Affectionately,
your brother,
Gideon Lincecum

[1] See the appendix for information on Emaline Lincecum.

Brazos was not shot. He survived the war and became a trail driver in the aftermath.

Shortages continued to pinch Texas, and Gideon's reputation as a resourceful inventor spread. He was called upon to make machines for others but had to decline because of other shortages, as he wrote one inquirer.

Long Point. Texas. 21st April 1864

Mr. Ephraim Moore[1]
Brazos Bottom, Texas
My Dear Sir.

Your note of 8th instant came to hand last night, and I hasten to reply by return post.

It is true that I did make a machine that shaved the seeds for making sleys very nicely. It finished the seeds so that they needed no further polish after being put in the sley, and I made for my old lady four very good sleys. At least, that is the character they bear among the weavers. I then lent the machine to the neighbor women and it has passed from one to another till I dont know where it is now. I could not procure the material to construct another.

Very Respectfully thine.
Gideon Lincecum.
Sley maker.

[1] Ephraim Moore is listed as residing in Scott Station, Harrison County, Texas, with his wife and three children in the 1870 Census (Ninth Census, 1870, Harrison County, Tex., p. 086). However, he is not listed in the Eighth Census, 1860, for Brazos Bottom, Texas.

The shortages of cash and material led to bartering as well as innovation, and Gideon offered to send some copper to a Confederate munitions factory in exchange for some caps for his gun.

Long Point. Texas. 23 May 1864

Wm. De Ryee, S.[upply?] C.[orps][1]
Austin, Texas
Dear Sir.

Some weeks ago, I sent to your department, by Col. Holland, a bundle of copper.[2] On his return he informed me that he had delivered it to yourself, but that it was at an unfavorable time, and he was unable to state anything to me in regard to what would be the fate of the copper. He told me that he had left the matter in charge of Mr. [G. J.] Durham, who would inform me what went with the little bundle.[3] Mr. Durham, however, had his hands full already, & it is but little trouble for me to attend to it myself.

If the copper is worth anything to the department, please to place in the hands of Mr. Durham, its equivalent amount [in] percussion caps. He will find an opportunity to forward them to me. The birds are eating up my bees, and for want of the caps on my part, they will be able to continue their destructive work. The <u>Merops</u> claim it as their natural rights,[4] but I dispute it on what I conceive to be just grounds, and therefore need the caps. Let me hear from you.

Most Respectfully
Gideon Lincecum

[1] A Bavarian who came to New Braunfels, Texas, in 1856, William DeRyee developed his own system of photography and was known for having produced an album of photographs of the eighth Texas legislature and two celebrated photographs of Gov. Sam Houston. He was in business as a photographer in San Antonio when the Civil War began. He was then appointed state chemist and put in charge of the Texas Percussion Cap Manufactory in Austin. Toward the end of the war he was with the Confederate Nitre and Mining Bureau and developed several important sources of nitrates from the bat caves of central Texas. He also devised a procedure for producing guncotton and using it as an explosive in marine torpedoes (*New Handbook of Texas*, 2:604–5).

[2] Colonel Holland has not been identified for certain. He may have been Lt. Col. D. D. Holland, commander of the 1st Cavalry Battalion, Texas State Troops (Wright, comp., and Simpson, ed., *Texas in the War*, p. 35).

[3] G. J. Durham, Gideon's son-in-law, served as the chief war tax collector for Texas during this time (*Galveston News*, 4 September 1863, p. 1).

[4] *Merops* is a genus of birds found in Europe but not in North America. Perhaps Gideon had read about the genus in a scientific publication. The bird destroying his bees could have been the eastern kingbird (*Tyrannus tyrannus*), which used to carry the moniker "bee martin" (Karl Haller, personal communication, 29 November 1999).

One cannot help but wonder what prevented Gideon from taking care of these birds with his boasted skills as an archer. The birds must have been very clever, or perhaps he was losing his touch.

By late May very heavy fighting was taking place in Virginia and Georgia, as Grant and Sherman were pressing the Confederates hard in both sectors. Gideon reported on the situation there and on the home front to his son Lysander, who was serving on the relatively safe Mexican border.

Long Point. 24th May 1864

Lysander Lincecum
Eagle Pass, Texas
My Dear Son.

Your favour of 15th instant reached us yesterday morning! 8 days from date. It found us all well except the children who are suffering with the whooping cough, some of them pretty badly just now.

We have had no rain during the last four weeks; our crops are beginning to suffer and water is becoming scarce. We had too much crop anyhow for our force, and the backset that we encountered in having to rotate the entire crop, with the damage done by the grubworms, prevented us from having the crop in as good order as it should be. It will soon be clean now, however, and if we an get a good season in 8 or 10 days, our crop will be pretty good yet. Dock's crop is in pretty good order and is looking well, all it wants is rain.[1] They have not been visited with the whooping cough yet at Dock's, and they are staying pretty close at home.

Everything in this vicinity is moving on very quietly, which is, as I suppose, mainly attributable to the fact that there are but very few people, except women and children, left in the country. The women circulate a little scandal occasionally, but as the men are all absent, and the women of course knowing from whence the slander came do not believe it, and the slander has to die in the slimy hole where it originated. If the men were home, they could, and would doubtless, fan up the flame of discord some.

The war news from every section of our army is cheering. Recently, however, Banks has made shift to make good his escape from our boys in Louisiana, and it would not surprise me in the least, to hear of him soon on the coasts of Texas.[2] If he is not ordered to reinforce Grant,[3] which I think quite probable, he will be certain to make an effort to mend his broken reputation by an attempted raid on Texas. Well, the war is bearing heavily upon us everywhere, and our only alternative and the only one we should desire is to maintain our ground or die upon it, struggling to the last for our rights. Life would be a very poor boon under yankee regulations. The papers were not brought up on the cars last night, consequently we failed to get the latest news this morning. There was, however, a rumor that Burnsides has formed a junction with Rosecranse, and that they had attacked and pretty nigh anihilated Longstreets corps, having captured 4000 prisoners and 59 pieces of artillery.[4] This report is said to have come from Marmaduke of Ark.[5] It is not believed here, though we are all suffering great anxiety just now for the fate of our army at Richmond. A few more days will develop all, relieving our anxieties.[6]

We get letters from Jo and several of the boys from beyond the Mississippi. They are all healthy, expressing full confidence in their power to conquer the infernal yankees. Jo is still healthy and unscratched. He sent a lot of pictures of the yankee gals in his last letter; he got them on a boat they took. I have written this for Dock as well as yourself—Cash is still mending.

Your father——Gideon Lincecum

[1] "Dock" is Lachaon, Gideon's son.

[2] Nathaniel Banks's Red River Campaign came to an end on 19 May, when his army crossed the Atchafalaya River near Simmesport (*Official Records of the Rebellion*, series 1, 46:163). Contrary to Gideon's prediction, Banks did not reappear on the Texas coast. Having lost the confidence of the administration, he was relegated to administrative duties in New Orleans (Kenneth P. Williams, *Lincoln Finds a General*, 5:309–10).

[3] By this time in May, Grant and the Army of the Potomac were on the move south from Spotsylvania to Cold Harbor and Petersburg. He would need many reinforcements in the months ahead,

but Banks was not among those so assigned (McPherson, *Ordeal by Fire*, pp. 420–23).

[4] Gen. Ambrose E. Burnside (1824–81), a West Point graduate and brave, dependable officer, had been a failure as commander of the Army of the Potomac at the costly Battle of Fredericksburg in December 1862. However, he had performed better as commander of the Department of the Ohio, successfully withstanding a long siege of Knoxville in late 1863 (Warner, *Generals in Blue*, pp. 57–58; McPherson, *Ordeal by Fire*, pp. 302–4, 317, 333). The rumor about Burnside and Rosecrans was false, and Gideon was badly confused here. No such junction had taken place; in fact, Rosecrans had been removed as commander of the Army of the Cumberland in October. Longstreet had failed to take Knoxville in December and suffered heavy casualties, but by May he was back in northern Virginia with his men, as was Burnside, both ready to participate in the great battle between Grant and Lee that soon began (Current, ed., *Encyclopedia of the Confederacy*, 2:895–97; McPherson, *Ordeal by Fire*, p. 337; Catton, *This Hallowed Ground*, pp. 288, 290–91, 301).

[5] Brig. Gen. (later Major General) John Sappington Marmaduke (1833–87) of Missouri, a West Point graduate and veteran of Shiloh and many engagements in Arkansas and Missouri, was at this time far from the action in eastern Tennessee (Warner, *Generals in Gray*, pp. 211–12).

[6] Far from "developing all, relieving our anxieties," the next few days and weeks and months brought no relief to either side, as the great battle for Richmond would slowly grind toward its fateful end (McPherson, *Ordeal by Fire*, pp. 424–26; Bruce Catton, *A Stillness at Appomattox*, pp. 55–164).

Earlier in May Gideon had made a trip to San Antonio on some business and was poorly impressed with what he saw there. He reported his impressions to his friend Hannay.

Long Point. Texas. 2nd June 1864

R. B. Hannay
Millican, Texas
My Dear Sir.

Yours of 31st ult. reached me this afternoon, and having got through with the Newspapers, [I] find time this evening to reply to you. Your letter asks but one question. To that question I can reply frankly that I never saw a more unlovely, unholy place than San Antonio. The character of men I observed there with few exceptions, and the exceptions appeared to be straggling, were all of the same cast. All with money in their hands and begging for a chance to get more. I saw many heads possessing sharp intellectual force, but do not recollect a single one that was supported by developements of honesty and fairness. The similarity of physiognomy[1] and occupation I found there—and its all bad, and opposed to the true interests of good society—suggested to my mind the fearful thought that it is the last stand on the broad road to perdition, and that the sooner I could make my escape from the hateful place—that filthy cancer on the posteriors of Texas—the better it would be for me. And so, at 9 p.m. of the same day I reached the place, I was ensconced in blankets 10 miles on the road towards home. A feeling of safety rested with me at my camp, for I was perfectly enveloped in a vast ocean of Mezquit bushes, which have taken the place of the grass and placed the once boundless prairie out of sight.

That is the way San Antonio appeared to my mind. You must recollect, however, who it is that gives you this description. To you, whose spirit is formed of different material, the trading talk and the perpetual jingle of the almighty dollar, both of gold and silver, might be full of soothing music: Soul quieting tones, and heavenly harmony that would wake up all your vigelence, and do away the necessity for recuperative sleep. It might be a lovely looking place to a man of your proclivities. To pass through a large town and see piles and piles of Mexican dollars setting on the shelfs and desks in every house, hear the continual jingle of it in the hands of everybody who seem to know of no other thing or business or place in this terene [earthly] abode, might tickle the fancy of some developments very agreeably. Therefore, I pray you not to let what I have said in regard to the foul scab have any influence on your arrangements at all. I saw Illingworth there.[2] He appeared in a fine glee, but he was there only for a few days and left for Laredo the same day I saw him. He has the appointment from the Governor, of Chief superintendent of the state cotton at all the frontier ports. He has a chance now to make a pile. But like yourself, he wont do it. He is always too generous to every body that can make a friendly face.

Dont trouble yourself about books until the war is over. But little satisfactory reading can be done under the war strain.

Thine as ever
Gideon Lincecum

[1] The term "physiognomy" used here reflects Gideon's interest in the pseudoscience of phrenology, which began when he was practicing medicine in Mississippi (Burkhalter, *Gideon Lincecum*, pp. 125–26).

[2] J. O. Illingsworth, an Englishman who was in Milam County, Texas, as early as 1850, was an assistant to the publisher for the *Texas Almanac* in 1860 and during the Civil War served as an agent for the Texas government to supervise cotton trade to England on the Mexican border (Burkhalter, *Gideon Lincecum*, pp. 160n, 170; see also Census data: Seventh Census, 1850, Milam County, Tex., p. 006, and Eighth Census, 1860, Travis County, Tex., p. 267).

The month of June brought news of a number of defensive victories by the Confederate Army of Northern Virginia, as Robert E. Lee consistently outwitted but was unable to shake his dogged adversary, U. S. Grant.[1] *Gideon was greatly encouraged by Lee's successes, as he told his son Lysander, still on the Mexican border.*

Long Point. Texas. 5th July 1864

Lysander Lincecum
Army of the Rio Grande, Texas
Dear Lysander.

Your favor of 16th ult. came in yesterday in company with several others, one to your mother, three or four to Maggy, one to Leonora and one to Leander.[2] Dock got home four or five days ahead of your letters. He found that his family had increased a day or two prior to his arrival. He seemed to be highly pleased and greatly gratified at it. I suppose, however, that to be rejoiced at the birth of a young one is nothing more than natural. That, I believe, is a sentiment manifested in the action of all animals.

The news from our armies every where is favorable and truly encouraging. When we reflect on the immense numbers that have been arrayed against our comparatively small forces, badly equipt, and poorly fed and clothed, while our ruthless invaders were furnished with the most extraordinary arms, fixtures and preparations the world ever saw, aided and sympathised with as they are by all the European nations; for us to hold our own against such odds is more than any one, either friend or foe could have counted on. But thanks to the bravery, prowess and patient patriotism of untiring soldiers, we have not only held our own, but we have scurged our hated foe—our dishonorable, theiving enemy most awfully. Aye more. Besides killing and disabling five or six hundred thousand of hireling soldiers with a great number of the poorer classes of the hell deserving yankees themselves, we have destroyed an extensive portion of their iron and steel clad navy and armed our entire army, almost, with rifles and canon that we have taken from them in regular field fights. We have just grounds to felicitate ourselves on our successes and to inspire hope and courage to fight on furiously. Better would it be that we all die fighting for our rights and liberties than to live under the government they are preparing for us. It would be a gratifying thing to my feelings, to be certified that every man woman and child in the bounds of the confederacy had taken a solemn oath that to die fighting is far preferable to submission, and that so long as they have life and strength to damage a yankee in any manner or form that they will continue to do so. And also to swear eternal hatred to the infernal heartless race, and that they will teach their children, to the tenth generation, to hate and kill the damned yankees on all favorable occasions and never to trade with them to the amount of one cent.

If you can get hold of those fellows who are running off to the enemy and to Mexico, there can be no impropriety in hanging them right up. To be certain that a man has deserted his home and his country and gone to or is going towards the enemy is sufficient grounds upon which to take his life, and it is doing our cause an injustice under such cases to hesitate or delay the execution of such men a single minute.

I am informed by people who have received letters from the Rio Grande, that Babe Irvin, Dutch Anderson, Ingle and some others from this vicinity have crossed the river and gone into Mexico or to the Yankees;[3] Anderson sold his wagon and team and a load of government cotton and took the money and went across the river. These men are not only traitors to our cause but they are damned theives and should be <u>stopped</u> where ever found.

Our corn crop is good; the sugar cane is the tallest we ever had and I think will be very juicy. Everybody wants us to make syrup for them this year. But I have not sufficient force to do it for them, and I cant consent to let them send hands to help.

They are never satisfied with their pay, and their hands wont work.

We are all healthy now, though we have had more sickness in our family this year than we ever had before. Your mother had a right bad spell, but she is now over it and is enjoying good health again. Things are jogging on about as usual. No changes worth naming. I sent herewith, our last Telegraph [Houston newspaper]; the news is good.

Your father,
Gideon Lincecum.

[1] At the beginning of June, Grant was whipped by Lee at Cold Harbor and in the middle of June he was whipped again at Petersburg—whipped but not conquered. Grant now began a long siege at Petersburg that would end nine months later with decisive victory (McPherson, *Ordeal by Fire*, pp. 420–26; Catton, *U. S. Grant and the American Military Tradition*, pp. 119–27).

[2] "Maggy" is Margaret "Maggie" Wood Lincecum, Gideon's daughter-in-law. The other names in this paragraph refer to Lincecum family members.

[3] "Babe Irvin" may be James Irvin, listed as residing in Doddville in the 1860 Census. In 1864 he would have been eighteen years old. The Irvin family lived near Leander W. C. Lincecum. A possible match for "Dutch Anderson" is Peter Anderson, age twenty, listed as residing in Independence in the 1860 Census (Eighth Census, 1860, Washington County, Tex., pp. 191, 218). "Ingle" has not been identified.

Several days later Gideon unleashed the most sweeping defense of slavery, the most extreme characterization of the African race, and the most vicious condemnation of the leaders and the people of the North that he had yet written. This bile spilled out in a letter to Hannay.

Long Point. Texas. 7th July 1864

R. M. Hannay
Hempstead, Texas
My dear Sir.

Your favor of 1st inst came to hand on the 4th. Your being at Hempstead rather took me on surprise. You are, however, a restless bird, which kind of fowl do not roost many nights on the same tree. I write now, with but slight hopes that my letter will find you.

You are engaged in writing an article on slavery. The spirits have hinted to you that they will ere long propose a plan for the gradual abolition of slavery. They must be yankee spirits. No intelligent spirits from the South would think of any plan or scheme that would bear so heavily on the poor negro [as] to propose emancipation in any form. All Southern spirits, and any other honest spirit who have sought information on the subject know, that in the animal kingdom, all inferior races and types fare the best, and are most happy and healthy—enjoy life the best while occupying the subordinate condition to the superior type. All sensible spirits know that the negro is the lowest and the blackest—the filthiest and the coarsest type among the various races and types of the human genus, and that every attempt to place him above his sphere has not only greatly damaged him, but has invariably turned out signal failures. His happiest position is <u>Chattel Slavery</u>, where he is directed and compelled to labor in health, cared for in sickness and decrepitude, and protected and shielded from unmerciful punishment by his owner when he has been guilty of violation of the laws or customs of the country where he is held to service. Any spirit that would propose a change in this <u>natural</u> condition of the negro is the negroes enemy and desires his destruction, or he is totally ignorant of the nature and character of the african. I think the spirits that have been tampering with and endeavoring to impress you with such false unnatural principles must be Yankee spirits. They see you are preparing a pretty good article on slavery, and they wish to neutralize it.

You dont seem to know where you will be next; suppose you let the fates bring you around this way. Grapes are turning black, and if there are any plums, they will be good if it rains any more during the summer. It is now very dry here, and our garden crops are beginning to suffer and are rapidly drying up. It rained enough, however, to mature for me a fine crop of corn and sugar cane. The canes are tall and large, and will be ready for the mill in ten days; I feel easy always when I make a full crop of corn. There is no danger of scarcity of other substantial articles of food when we have plenty of corn.

The news from our armies is quite cheering. We are destroying the infernal yankees and their European abetters awfully. It would make me very happy to know that all mankind, male and female, except the <u>true</u> friends and sympathiser of the southern confederacy, had to come to Richmond and that Lee and his army had sufficient power and the inclinations to, and that they would set to work and utterly kill and destroy them from the face of the earth, damn them. Under a pretended neutrality the European governments are e[a]gerly looking on while they send men and means and prayers for our total anihilation, for which they can have no excuse except envy of our prosperity. They saw that we were an industrious, thrifty people, and they joined the lowest pitched race of people on earth, with the hope and intention to exterminate us.

And this by the deceptious poor devils is called strict neutrality, damn them.

If the fates can make any strong disposition of you let me hear from you.

Thine most truly.
Gideon Lincecum.

It is hard to reconcile these extreme and violent views with the well read, thoughtful, decent person Gideon showed himself to be in most other respects. He had a blindness on some subjects and perhaps even a touch of madness. Fortunately, his blind spots gave rise mostly to words, not action.

Gideon still sounded rather bloodthirsty when he wrote to his son-in-law at the end of the month.

Long Point. Texas. 31st July 1864

[No inside address or salutation]

Your letter, Durham, of 23rd inst., announcing the rather satisfactory news of the execution of the murderers of that worthy and very valuable young man Dick Powell, reached me the day after its date.[1] I consider it a good thing and am glad that the citizens of Austin have at last stumped up sufficient courage to deal out a little of their stored up justice. It is a great pity that they did not begin sooner. As this is the first instance, for several years, of a manifestation of justice in that unholy city, the presumption is that you are in possession of large stores of the divine articles and that you will, as you have ventured to commence the work, continue its distribution to every creature without the interference, either of mercy or favoritism.

I am so closely and so continually engaged, that I cannot enter in my letter upon any subject of interest. I must content myself by saying a few words in relation to my domestic operations. I am daily engaged boiling my sorgo sac, have been during the last two weeks, and shall not be able to get through in three weeks to come. We are producing very fine syrup and plenty of it. I do not wish to tantalize you or I would say that if there were any possible chance of conveyance, I would send you a barrel of it. I am the only male on the place, have to see to everything, even to standing over the steaming kettles a great portion of my time. Previous to grinding the cane, I had three weeks delightful and most interesting employment in making new, and coopering up old barrels and other vessels to be used in making and preserving the syrup after it is made.

We are all very healthy and as cheerful as we can be under the circumstances. We produce with our own hand everything that we really need. You mention that you have in your possession a box of caps for me. There, to that box of caps, hangs a nasty tale.[2]

Present me respectfully to your mother, to Cassandra and the boys, love, and for yourself.

As ever
Gideon Lincecum

[1] Richard Powell was one of the victims of the Willis Gang, which terrorized the Texas frontier during the Civil War. Three members of the Willis family were hanged by a mob in Austin in 1864 (Burkhalter, *Gideon Lincecum*, p. 137).

[2] The "nasty tale" may be the destruction of Gideon's bees by the birds, mentioned above. See also Gideon's letter to Durham, 15 November 1864, below.

As the summer wore on, Gideon's supply of paper was nearly exhausted, and his correspondence dropped off considerably. Also he was very busy. In late September, when he received a letter from a recent participant in the Louisiana campaign, he dashed off a reply almost immediately.

Long Point. Texas. 20th Sept. 1864

F. M. Gaston
Mound Prairie,[1] Tex.
My Dear young Friend.

Your very well written and highly interesting account of the Louisiana campaign of the present year, dated 4th instant, came to hand this evening, since dark. We had no company except "Jo," who is home on furlough—will leave for the army in La. next Friday. So I requested Sarah to read your communication, which she did, to the delight of the old Lady and myself, while Jo sat by, and said, as he was a participant in that fight of forty odd days, he had the right to hear your history of it, and to criticize it too. But as he listened, he confirmed all your statements, except the burning of the double bridges by the Yankees.[2] They were not burnt, according to his statement. The balance of your narative, he asserts to be very correct. We all listened, while Sarah read, with the deepest interest, and although we have seen several written accounts of that campaign, none were so full or so satisfactory. They all lacked system, and in their accounts they indulged in boasting of their successes without telling of their failures. In mild, good stile, you give both sides of the picture, satisfying the reader that it is true and authentic.

The old lady was mightily pleased with it, and was rather disposed, in her manner of speech about it, to brag a little. She was very highly interested with it. We are all well here, have a good corn crop, and that is a general thing throughout this portion of the state. Dock, Lysander, Lass, and Andy, all belong to Fords command on the Rio Grande.[3] Lysander is home now for a few days; he was sent in charge of some prisoners they had captured. They took them to Hempstead. He also brought home the body of John Morriss, who died near Brownsville of typhus fever.[4] His wife had him buried by the side of her mother, and she takes on so about him that her father thinks she will die. John was universally beliked by the Army of the Rio Grande, hence the expense they put themselves to in procuring a metalic coffin and sending him home. According to the newspapers, our army is holding its own everywhere pretty well, and it has done wonderful, but we are still hard pressed on all sides and we must continue to fight on, for subjugation would be a harder fate than for us to continue the war until every man, woman, and child in the South are dead.

In this vicinity there is no change worth naming since you were here. Hence there is nothing for me to say that would interest you. If you can get the time, while stationed at Mound Prairie, you must pay us a visit.

I am closely engaged getting in my crop, and as I am all the male on the place, I have to see it all done, which annoys me somewhat. It won't last always.

As ever, I am thine
Gideon Lincecum

[1] Mound Prairie is situated near Palestine in Anderson County. During the Civil War, iron products such as guns, iron singletrees, and plows were made in a foundry there (*New Handbook of Texas*, 4:860).

[2] Apparently Jo was wrong about the Double Bridges, which were fifteen miles southeast of Pleasant Hill. As Brig. Gen. Hamilton Bee's troops pursued the retreating Union army, they found the bridges burned and had to seek another route (*Official Records of the Rebellion*, series 1, 34:609–10).

[3] John Salmon (Rip) Ford (1815–97) served as a member of the secession convention, commanded an expedition to Brazos Santiago, and initiated a trade agreement between Mexico and the Confederacy. He was elected colonel of the 2d Texas Cavalry, with a command in the Rio Grande District, and between 1862 and 1865 he served as the commandant of conscripts as well as engaging in border operations protecting Confederate-Mexican trade (*New Handbook of Texas*, 2:1072–73). For more on Rip Ford's life, see Ford, *Rip Ford's Texas*.

[4] John Morriss is identified as a resident of Long Point in Burkhalter, *Gideon Lincecum*, p. 164n.

Writing about the same time to a bedridden friend who asked his opinion of the war, Gideon replied,

Long Point. Texas. 24th Septr. 1864

R. Keene[1]
Piedmont Springs

. . . You ask me for my views on the subject of "this Hellish war." Well, I view it as a fine, big, fat, Hell bending war, of the protracted type. I see no signs nor can I perceive any reason upon which to base a hope that it will cease in ten years. The boys are all to be sure, quite tired of it, but that don't mean that they will quit fighting so long as there is a yankee to be found this side of the Mason's and Dickson's line. To yield to Yankee dictation would be a damned sight worse fate than for us to continue the war until every man, woman, and child of the confederacy shall be slaughtered. Therefore let us all raise bristles and pitch in. To hoist the black flag suits my complaint, but I have advocated the propriety of the black flag from the start, and I am certain if we had done that we would not have had to fight all the world and the rest of the "niggers." Let us raise it now, and the foreigners will not take quite so much interest in our war as they have heretofore done. . . . All's well.—

As ever.
Gid.

[1] R. Keene has not been identified. Piedmont Springs was a popular health spa and resort as early as 1850. A grand four-story hotel was built there in 1860, and ads for it were still appearing in the *Houston Tri-Weekly Telegraph* early in the war (see, e.g., 7 July 1862, p. 1). Around 1865 the hotel became a hospital and the headquarters for Walker's Texas Division of the Confederate army, though by then the division was headed by Maj. Gen. John H. Forney (*New Handbook of Texas*, 5:192-93).

Nothing bothered Gideon more than reports of corruption on the part of Confederate officials, unless it was the prospect of falling under Yankee rule. To his friend Hannay, who was planning to leave Texas at last, via Mexico, to return to England, he wrote,

Long Point. Texas. 5th Oct. 1864

R. B. Hannay
Millican, Texas

Dear Friend—Your favor of 3rd instant reached me at 9 P.M. yesterday. All your predictions in regard to the action of the returning soldiers, seeking satisfaction, and the villainous cause of it are, I think, pretty well founded. I shall encourage the soldiers to take full satisfaction and to deal out vengeance in all cases where the evidence of fraud, in the action of the confederate officials and those who pretended to be C.S. officers, is satisfactorily made out. The soldiers and common people are too ignorant—too thoughtless—to know and maintain their individual rights. Over all this, the fear of death generally so strongly presided that submission to any condition with a prospect to save life is acceptable to them. I would prefer Anarchy to any form of government that has ever been instituted yet, and my reason for this preference is based upon the fact that the ignorance and dishonesty of the people are the only controlling forces put in action in what is called government, all forms of which are oppressive to the laboring people while it pretends to lighten their burden and protect their rights.

Give me anarchy. Everybody can understand that, and then they will all know what to do when a rascal lays a plan to filch away from them the profits of their labor. It would joy my old heart to see the soldiers and those that have been wronged turn upon the heartless scoundrels and wrack satisfactory vengeance upon them.

Sure enough then, you are about to make your departure. Your absence will produce a sullen void in my enjoyments. Our great hell bending war is knocking off from my fun, something or other every day. Well, let it go, with all I hold dear, for I had rather lose all, with life—yea, be ground to powder, and let every atom of that powder remain a thousand years possessing the most acute sensibility, than to be brought under Yankee rule. It would, in my feelings, be a degradation to which the fabled hall of theology would be a relief. But there is a law in my nature that will shield me from submitting to any such vile condition. I can prevent it. I know I can!

How or to what part of the Rio Grande are you going to, that will prevent you from passing by here? Shall I not see you?

Come what may I shall be resigned, for if your faith is true, and I hope it is, there is a future, of which this life is so small a part that we should not think so much of it, as to neglect the purification and culture of, but daub and soil our souls with filthy efforts to dress and show the external man—the animals in this incipient sphere. I am daily threatened with apoplexy, but I live so abstimeously that it must make a center shot to get me. Yet it won't be long before I go.

We are all well, and all send our best respects and best wishes for a successful voyage for you.

I remain as ever thine.
Gideon Lincecum

Apoplexy or no apoplexy, Gideon had ten years left to live, and it would not be long before he got a taste of "Yankee rule," for the military fortunes of the Confederacy were fading, as Sherman occupied Atlanta and Grant extended his lines around Richmond.

On 26 October, Gideon learned that Hannay had been unable to leave for Mexico. Gideon encouraged him to keep trying, since others had succeeded, and he added that he believed big changes were coming to Texas and to the divided nation, perhaps "holy anarchy."

Long Point. Texas. 27 Oct. 1864

R. B. Hannay
Millican, Texas
My Dear Sir.

Your communication of 20th inst. reached me at 9 p.m. yesterday. Although its contents are not very different from my expectations, it nevertheless excites my sympathies, and casts a darker shade upon the small hope I had been entertaining for your successful escape from the country for which you have so little love. I never believed it, but still I hoped that your last plan for making your escape would terminate favourably. . . .

If you could get out to Brownsville, you would soon meet with an oppertunity to ship for Europe. Some boys who would soon be old enough to enter the confederate service were sent off from this vicinity day before yesterday. They are on their way to Scotland via Matamoros. That countryman of yours, Thos Affleck, had a hand in sending them off under the pretext of educating them. It was said that Affleck was going to send his 13 year old son,[1] but I cannot say whether he did so or not; but if you had been here, doubtless, you might have got off as a kind of Mentor with them. I did not know that any such movement was in contemplation until they were on their way. I tell it now for your satisfaction!!

I have no doubt, if a man would station himself at Brownsville or Matamoros either, he would get employment to sustain him amply, and that he would not have to wait long before he would meet with a favorable chance to ship himself to any portion of Europe, on any terms and in any stile he might be able to afford the means to do.

. . . If you can get out to Brownsville, you will not have to tarry long before a chance to go further will present itself. On the subject of reconstruction, I have heard nothing in this country.[2] Some whisperings of that sort came down from far up the Yegua and from Fayette county, but they were low whispers—barely audible, and people talked of raising a company to hunt them up and kill them for that. But that is the talk that suits me, and also the condition of the north in their political affairs. If the yankees get to fighting about their election, and we on the subject of reconstruction, it will upset all the plans of the leaders of the present governments, and have a fine effect, on the reorganization of society, which would be one of the happy results that would naturally arise from the principles that must follow the universal and indiscriminate throat cutting supervening on the political splits & internal division amongst the people of a bloodthirsty nation. Hurra, for the prospect of sublime and holy anarchy. It will come, and I shall live to see it. Will it not be a glorious sight to see the motley masses assuming the right of attending to their own business, and when he is molested by any of the self constituted authorities, to see him split their d——d brains out. I have a long list of liberty hating rascals, which I shall show to our highly, and justly incensed warriors when they return; and I shall expect to see them purify society by hanging, killing, emasculation, &c &c &c. So mote it be.

If you go to the Rio Grande, you must be sure to call on us on your way. We should all like to see you before you go off forever. . . .

We are all well except the old Lady. She has been pretty bad sick ten or fifteen days. She was so unwell that we passed over the fiftieth anniversary of our union in the matrimonial tether without having any fuss. It took place on the 25th instant. She is a little better now. I hope she may get well, for I shouldn't like for her to set off to the good hunting ground before I get ready to go.

Thine Respectfully
Gideon Lincecum

[1] The 1860 Census listed the ages of the Affleck family members as follows: Thomas, forty-eight; Anne, forty-four; Dunbar, fifteen; John, eight. Dunbar was in the Confederate army, and in 1864 John was nearing the age when some other young men were fighting (Eighth Census, 1860, Washington County, Tex., p. 150).

[2] By "reconstruction" Gideon appears to have meant a radical change in Texas government, by bullet or by ballot. The election to which Gideon refers was, of course, the presidential contest between President Lincoln and his former commander, Gen. George Brinton McClellan, the Democratic candidate (McPherson, *Ordeal by Fire*, pp. 439–41, 456–58).

Gideon's Sarah got better, as he told his son-in-law three days later:

Long Point. Texas. 30 Octr. 1864

G. J. Durham
Austin, Texas
Dear Sir.

In a letter which I received yesterday from your city and which was written by one of the Representatives, it is stated that you have tendered your resignation of the office of State Collector. If so, what prospects have you to sustain yourself at Austin? The gentleman who wrote me the letter gave it as one of your reasons for resigning that the sallery of the office was useless, would not pay for provisions, <u>and that he thought</u> the prospect for you and family to suffer was the cause of the resignation.

In answer to this letter please state all the facts in the case, and what you have thought of doing? You must be pretty well run through already. Let me know all about it.

The old Lady has had a pretty severe spell; she has been sick about 15 days. She is now better, however; she rode out yesterday, and the prospect is that she will soon be well again. All the rest of the family are healthy.

I have just finished cribbing my corn, it is a bountiful quantity. Enough for you too, if you had your family near enough to use it.

Write soon. Respectfully

Gideon Lincecum

Gideon soon learned that Durham's situation was not bad, and he expressed his relief in a brief reply.

Long Point. Texas. 15 Nov 1864

G. J. Durham.

Dr Sr.

Your favor of 7th instant was received several days ago. We are glad to hear from you, that your prospects are not quite so shady as they had been represented to us.

I see no good reason why the Govn[t] should not feed and clothe her agents everywhere. Surely they have found out by this time that the shucks they issue and send out are neither food nor raiment.

Lysander used up the shot you left here killing partridges for the old Lady to eat during several spells of her ill health. I have on hand, however, 8 or 10 pounds of 4[s] which I will send to you the first favorable oppertunity.

We are all in good health now, and I think it likely that we can now remain so, until hog killing time at least. Of such provisions as we have on hand just now, we are not likely to overload the digestive apparatus, and as long as that is the case there is but little danger of sickness, but look out for swelled noses and sore throats when hog killing time comes.

Very Respectfully
Gideon Lincecum

There would be a lot of "hog killing" (and man killing) in Georgia during the next weeks, for on the same day that Gideon wrote to Durham, Gen. William Tecumseh Sherman began his devastating march from Atlanta to the sea.

Gideon wrote little about the war during this time. He was short of paper, and most of what paper he had was used for letters urging the adoption of his favorite remedy to curb rape and other antisocial ills: emasculation—by law if possible, by lynch mob if necessary. He was pleased when a Belton mob put his "cure" into use, and he used the incident to urge other communities to follow suit. He asked the press to promote the idea.[1]

Before the year ended, Gideon wrote another letter to the press, castigating the unpatriotic "draft-dodging" that was taking place as some parents sent their young sons to England or other areas to avoid their being conscripted. Uncharacteristically, Gideon signed this article with a pseudonym.

[undated]

Weekly News

In the "Weekly News" of the 21st inst. I notice a well written article, headed with the following question, "Is it loyal, or patriotic to send boys out of the Confederate States to escape the operation of the 'Conscript' laws?"[2]

I answer that it is neither loyal nor patriotic, but that it is treason to both. There are, however, a number of such characters amongst us; four such cases have recently occurred in this County (Washington), and it has made a very unfavourable impression on the minds of the german population as well as our own citizens. They are talking a good deal about it, particularly amongst the germans.[3] I heard one quite intelligent german, who exercises considerable influence with that class of our population, say, "Our sons are in the army, fighting for these men and their negroes, and we have other sons that will soon be of age to enter the field, but it is poor encouragement to our patriotism, to see these wealthy Americans sending their sons out of danger, some of them too, good looking, hardy young men, lacking only one month of the conscript age, and we have reasons to believe that if these people had the money for their gangs of negroes, that the parents would go with their traitor-branded sons."

The above is what the dutchman said to me, and since the time of that conversation, about a dozen germans, fathers, mothers, brothers, sisters, two of them lads about the conscript age, have left this vicinity and are now on their way to Mexico. The probability is that many more will follow the examples set for these people by the cowardly american property holders.—And so it is, Europe is ridding herself of her physically low pitched paupers by sending them to the U.S. where they get them killed off fighting for the thieving yankees, whilst a great many members of the Confederate States are ridding our government of almost an equal number of low pitched mental paupers, by traitorous parents who are constantly transporting their faint-hearted sons to Europe. What a damnable Commerce.

These men are already marked, and when the tight pull comes,[4] they will have cause to remember their flagrant acts of treason to the cause of freedom, and their dastardly sons will never be permitted to return to the land they have in the hour of peril so ignomeniously deserted. Let the Press hand these cases around freely.

Parrhesia[4]

[1] In reaction to the Belton incident, Gideon wrote, "I understand that a rape had occurred in your vicinity, which was perpetrated by a negro, who after a fair and impartial examination of the case by twelve good citizens, was found worthy to suffer the penalty of emasculation. The operation being performed, turned out to be a complete success, and that the negro is now well and returned to his duties as a slave" (Gideon Lincecum to Dr. John A. Ewing, Long Point, Tex., 25 October 1864, LP, Box 2E366). He enclosed a copy of his memorial advocating emasculation as a penalty for various crimes.

[2] Reluctantly, the South found it necessary to resort to conscription in April 1862, limiting it at first to white males age eighteen to thirty-five but later expanding the upper limit to fifty. Some exemptions were allowed, including the hiring of substitutes, but these loopholes were often abused and thus caused ill feeling (Current, ed., *Encyclopedia of the Confederacy*, 1:396–99). For a fuller treatment of the situation in Texas, see Marten, *Texas Divided*, pp. 50, 94–101.

[3] Texas Germans were divided on the questions of slavery, secession, and support for the Confederacy. The adoption of an antislavery resolution by a meeting of German liberals in San Antonio in 1852, although it represented a minority view, made all Texas Germans suspect in the eyes of Confederate supporters. After the Civil War began there were notable "damned Dutchmen" who flaunted their pro-Union sympathies, but many Texas Germans chose to send their sons to fight for the Confederacy. According to James Marten, it was "a large minority" of German Texans who tried to resist or at least ignore the Confederacy (Marten, *Texas Divided*, pp. 113–21). See also Current, ed., *Encyclopedia of the Confederacy*, 1:396–99.

[4] The "tight pull" probably refers to the tightening of a noose.

[5] Lois Wood Burkhalter notes that Parrhesius was a fifth-century Greek painter said to have painted grapes so perfectly that the birds tried to eat them (Burkhalter, *Gideon Lincecum*, p. 161).

About this time Gideon received a supply of paper and other materials that lifted his spirits and increased his correspondence. To his benefactor he wrote,

Long Point. Texas. 27th December 1864

Wm P. Doran[1]
Houston, Texas
Dear Sir.

. . . It was not intended that the entire Ptelea[2] article should be published. A scientific discription of the plant is of but little interest to the common reader, and it could have been omitted without injury to the aim and meaning of the article. It does well enough, however, as a commencing paper, as it will show where a full discription can be had, if any such botanic character of Texas medicinal plants should be desirable.

In the articles I may hereafter contribute on the subject of the botanic remedies found in Texas, I shall give only English discriptions.[3] Go to the white oak bayou bridge, and look again. The Ptelea is growing there in considerable clusters of brushy bushes, higher than your head, and there are several of them. Break the twigs and smell of them. Take the specimens which I send you herewith along when you go to the bridge and show them to the boys of that vicinity. They are more apt to recollect such things than the money jarred grown folks. I want you to find it and put it in action in your rotten Sodom.

I shall occasionally copy such articles from my moccasin tracks as I may think best calculated to meet the wants of the people. The next article I shall contribute will be a discription of the process of preserving the eye sight of people in advanced life to the end of existence.

I bored Cushing with a long, dull, private letter, which I mailed yesterday. Nothing in it for the paper. The object of that tedious letter was to inform him that I feared you had greatly overrated my acquirements and to post him in regard to my mental status and opinions on several subjects opened up in his letter to me, particularly on that of changing the penal laws of the state, which he is pleased to denominate my penitentiary hobby. Well, so long as I live I shall not cease to stir the minds of the people on the greatest of topics for the amelioration of the condition of humanity. Now is a favourable time to urge the movement forward, so far as to embrace the crime of rape. The mind of the masses just now on account of the frequent attempts to violate the white women by the negroes is labouring under considerable irritation; if the press would take this matter in hand, discussing its principles freely, it could be made to become a law at the next session of the legislature. . . .

I was proud to hear that you made your round trip so rapidly and that you had been able to collect and pack home such a pile of rocks.

When shall I hear from you again?

Thine in Righteousness,
Gideon Lincecum

[1] William P. "Sioux" Doran (1836–1901) was born in New York state but migrated to Texas before the Civil War. Known as "Sioux" because of a byline he used as a writer for Texas newspapers, he was with the *Houston Tri-Weekly Telegraph* at the beginning of the war. He became a war correspondent for the *Telegraph* and reported on the Battles of Shiloh, Vicksburg, and Galveston (Burkhalter, *Gideon Lincecum*, pp. 84–85).

[2] *Ptelea*, also known as Wahoo or Hoptree, is a genus of trees and shrubs containing alkaloids. They are a member of the Rutaceae (citrus or rue family). Gideon could be referring to *P. trifoliata*, a shrub or small tree that can be one to four meters tall with three leaves (George M. Diggs, Jr., Barney L. Lipscomb, and Robert J. O'Kennon, *Shinners' and Mahlers' Illustrated Flora of North Central Texas*, pp. 970–77).

[3] The shortage of drugs and medicine in the South during the war was a major problem that led many people to manufacture their

own medicines (Massey, *Ersatz in the Confederacy*, p. 117; Kerby, *Kirby Smith's Confederacy*, pp. 261–62). Gideon wrote numerous letters on herbal remedies to the editors of the *Houston Tri-Weekly Telegraph* and the *Galveston Tri-Weekly News*. In 1864 he directed his letters to Edward H. Cushing, publisher of the *Telegraph*, who not only encouraged him to send medical articles but proposed the publication of a collection of them under the title *Home Remedies for Home Diseases*. The article referred to here was apparently the first of a series. In Box 2E365 of the Lincecum Papers in the Center for American History at Austin is an unpublished manuscript of eighty-five remedies, which Gideon called "The Moccasin Tracks, or Home Remedies for Home Diseases."

The year ended with Sherman in Savannah. Gideon had his hands full as his slaves were "all frolicking about" (Gideon Lincecum to Sioux Doran, Long Point, Tex., 30 December 1864, LP, Box 2E366) enjoying their Christmas holiday. Before six more months were out, they would be experiencing their first taste of freedom as well.

CHAPTER 7

1865

The fortunes of the Confederacy were dimming rapidly as the new year began, but Gideon was not one to give up hope, nor was his wife Sarah, as he told the soldier, Joe Sniveley:

Long Point. Texas. 9 Jan. 1865

J. C. Sniveley
My Dear Sir.

Your favour of 20th ult. came today. . . . We are all . . . well as to health, and our prospects and provender gradually drawing to a sharper point as the wasteful influences of this infernal yanky war progresses. The damage they inflict by their low, mean, destructive enmity and the excuse it affords our own rascals for stealing our supplies will, if the war continues, make us all very poor. And the war must continue, for the Yankees won't quit, and we mustn't. The rule of his Satanic majesty would be far preferable, and it would be much less detrimental to the general interest of our people than any form of government that would be extended to us by the negro loving Yankee. I hope every man in the confederacy has made up his mind to submit to nothing but death from them. As Tom Gentry says, "that['s] my fix."[1]

I handed your letter of 20th ult. to Sarah; she seemed to be considerably excited in the regions of duty to our brave soldiers, and thinks she can do something by calling on some families she knows of who have no relatives in the army. As for ourselves, having six of our own family in the service, our resources are constantly kept down to the point of exhaustion. Sarah will be quite apt to make a draw on the non-soldier-clothing portions of our settlement when she goes out amongst them, and that will be as soon as the present bad weather subsides.

People here are all standing aghast at the recent bad news.[2] It wont be long until a reaction will take place, and then—as I hope, the bristles of the nation will all rise.

Very Respectfully
Gideon Lincecum

[1] Tom Gentry has not been identified.

[2] The "recent bad news" to which Gideon refers is no doubt General Sherman's capture of Savannah on 21 December, climaxing his devastating march through Georgia. Confederate forces suffered two more major defeats in short order. At Franklin, Tennessee, on 30 November Union troops led by Gen. John Scofield routed forces under Gen. John Bell Hood, who then lost a face-off to Gen. George "The Rock" Thomas at Nashville 15–16 December. With these disasters the fate of the Confederacy was virtually sealed, though Robert E. Lee still held Richmond and Petersburg (Current, ed., *Encyclopedia of the Confederacy*, 2:632–36; McPherson, *Ordeal by Fire*, pp. 463–66; Catton, *This Hallowed Ground*, pp. 356–69).

Besides hoping for the "bristles of the nation" to rise, Gideon was trying to raise bristles of another kind as well, for he was busy promoting and assembling the new carding machine invented by two resourceful Texans, Samuel Hayford and G. W. Johnson.[1] *A few days earlier he had sent an article to the* Galveston News *praising the invention and urging its widespread use.*

Long Point. Texas. 6 Jan$^{y.}$ 1865

Galveston News.

I have not as yet seen in the papers any notice of what, in my estimation, is the greatest and most useful invention of this warring age. One that is destined to revolutionize the cotton spinning business throughout the civilized portions of the globe. I have reference to a horse hair Carding machine, which was invented by Messrs. Hayford and Johnson of Austin County, Texas. These gentlemen, having obtained a pattent for their invention, are now engaged in putting up model machines, one of which they propose to furnish to each County that will purchase the right to manufacture them. Their terms are, as I think, quite moderate. Applications from a good many counties have been handed in, and they are coming in daily.

I visited their shop and saw the machine in action. It goes by hand, and a boy or girl of ten or twelve years of age can run it with sufficient speed to furnish rolls for fifteen spinners. Mrs. Johnson, the ingenious lady of one of the machinists, was kind enough to spin a few of the rolls on an ordinary spinning wheel, and presented the little broach of thread to me as a sample. It is far superior to anything that can be produced from rolls made by the hand cards.

I pronounce this machine to be, in all respects, a complete success. It takes the cotton from the seed; produces, with light labour, 30 good rolls to the minute; and the materials of which the machine is constructed are attainable in Texas. One of them will require, not exceeding 2½ sheets of tin, about six pounds of iron, a few wood screws, and the balance is pine wood and horse hair. To the purchaser the cost of it will not exceed $35–, and it is constructed on principles that place the question of its durability beyond doubt.

Carding rolls with the hand cards is the hardest and most annoying part of the labour in the cloth making process. This machine does away with that fatiguing work. Spinning is all that is to do now, and the thread is more even, smoother and much stronger. It will enable our patriotic ladies to clothe their friends in the army with about one fourth the labor.

The inventors of this labour saving machine are quite anxious, and are doing all they can, to introduce it into all the confederate states as speedily as possible; and as it will more than double the facilities for clothing our armies, it is to be hoped that the leading authorities of the states and military departments will see the propriety of taking this matter in hand,

and encourage the cloth making portion of our zealous and dedicated female population by giving impetus to its manufacture and distribution.

Gid—

[1] Samuel Hayford and G. W. Johnson, of Bellville, Texas, "invented a machine for carding cotton rolls" in 1864 and were commended by the Texas legislature for this labor-saving device, which would help the Confederate soldiers (Gammel, *Laws of Texas*, 5:848).

In a personal letter to the editor, Willard Richardson, that accompanied the article, Gideon pointed out that the inventors were not draft dodgers but former soldiers who were helping the cause in another way.

Long Point. Texas. 6 Jany. 1865

W. Richardson[1]
Dear Sir.

The gentlemen alluded to in the enclosed article were soldiers in the Army two years.[2] Hayford was discharged on account of a severe wound in the foot and ill health. Johnson was detailed for the purpose of manufacturing their Carding machine. They invented the plan of this machine during the tedium of their unemployed time while in the service.

The inventive powers of these gentlemen is only checked by want of means. Had they sufficient material aid to set their creative developments at full liberty, they possess the will and the patriotic ambition to, and they doubtless would, add to the already numerous resources of the South many valuable and useful inventions.

As these machines are much needed, it will oblige the struggling spinning and weaving portion of our female population to know where this great helper is to be had. On which account I hope the paper, herewith, may find favour with you, and that you may consider it (not this paper) worthy of a place in your weekly edition at least.

Very Respectfully
Gideon Lincecum

[1] Willard Richardson (1802–75) changed the *News* from an insignificant local paper to the wealthiest, most important newspaper of antebellum Texas, and it was one of only four newspapers founded during the Republic era that survived the Civil War (*New Handbook of Texas*, 5:572).

[2] Although the index to the *Compiled Service Records* lists Samuel Hayford as a first sergeant in Company F of the 16th Texas Infantry and indicates that his records are found on roll 382, there is a gap where his records should appear. George W. Johnson enlisted 20 May 1862 and was appointed regimental ordnance sergeant in Flournoy's Regiment of Texas Infantry. He also served in Company F of the 16th Texas Infantry. He was captured at Pleasant Hill on 9 April 1864. The final entry indicates that in April 1865 he was detailed to make carding machines at Bellville, Texas (National Archives, *Compiled Service Records*, roll 383).

Apparently Gideon had obtained the right to assemble a Hayford and Johnson machine at Long Point, and he wrote to the inventors for advice.

Long Point. Texas. 15 January 1865

Messrs. Hayford & Johnson
Bellville, Texas
Gentlemen.

I write to day for the sake of imparting some information that may suit your business, and also to ask a few questions in regard to my own. The weather has been too bad for me to get the rotten stone; it is in the bank of a creek, which is now full of mud & water. If sand paper is a dissideratum with you, there is a ream or two of it here. I have made enquiry about it, but as there is little demand I suppose it may be had on fair terms. There are no wood screws except the large ones I told you of when I was in your shop.

I trusted altogether to my old dutch friend that day, and he did not get the relative velosity of the revolving brushes. Is that confined to a rule? There is but one direction for the saws to revolve, the first brush to take the cotton from the saws must not run in opposition; the last or roll brush must revolve in the same direction as the first brush does. The middle brush revolves, not in opposition, but feeds the roll by its greater speed, and the middle brush is supplied with cotton from the saws by the first brush, not by its opposition but by its still greater velocity. Is that right?

We have no lathe here upon which small irons can be turned, upon which account I shall not be able to make the bearings very true, I fear.

There is one thing I have forgot, and that is where the band comes from that runs the middle and last brushes? I have put nothing up yet, and this may all come right when that happens. If I should accidentally gear it some other way that runs as light, it will make no odds with the machines.

I wrote and sent to the "News" a little article on the uses and duribility of this labour saving machine. They may give it a place in the paper.

Very Respectfully.
Gideon Lincecum

Gideon urged others to follow his lead and obtain the right to make copies of this new machine. He explained the licensing system in a letter to an inquiring friend.

Long Point. Texas. 30 Jan. 1865

A. W. Moore[1]
Bastrop, Texas

Your letter of 28th. inst. reached me this morning and as it discourses on a subject in which I feel the deepest interest, I hasten to reply.

To your questions I answer that Hayford and Johnson of Bellville, Austin County, are the inventors, and there is no humbug in it. They are selling the right to manufacter them to the counties at fifty cents a head for the number of votes cast in the year 1860. Our county cast 1400 votes that year and she has purchased the right for the county at $700—paid in cotton, which was raised by subscription in a day or two. Now the county will encourage by contract the setting up of one or more shops in the county, who will pay over the first machines they make to those patriotic gentlemen who subscribed the cotton. And so the matter will all be settled without taxing the people to pay for the pattent. After the $700— is paid, the shop or shops of this county will be entitled to the pay for all the machines they may put up thereafter.

Hayford and Johnson are selling model machines to the counties that purchase the right at $35—and they are of opinion that they can be produced cheaper when the shops get properly under way. You say you have a good mechanic and can procure more if necessary. Why cant you influence your county commissioners so far as to get them to authorize you to purchase a county right and set up a shop yourself to supply machines to your citizens. There is money in it, if properly managed; anyhow, there is no danger of losing and it will supply the soldier families with a labour saving power that is much needed just at this time. The hardest and most dreaded portion of the labour in the thread making process is to card the rolls on hand cards. This little horse hair <u>carder</u> does away almost entirely with that painful work. The cotton is thrown up in the seed and comes out rolls of the best possible character. The durability of this machine rests on indisputable principles. When well put up, [it] will last a lifetime. Coming at the time it has, it will, if the counties are active in getting it in motion, give great relief to our patriotic ladies who are struggling so bravely to clothe our suffering soldiers.

Go soon to Bellville, regester your name, and as soon as it comes your turn, they will make a model machine for the county, which you can take home, and copy as often as you please, if your county procures the right, or if they will authorize you to secure the right for the county. . . .

Very Respectfully
Gideon Lincecum

[1] A. W. Moore is listed as residing in Bastrop in the 1860 Census (Eighth Census, 1860, Bastrop County, Tex., p. 274). He was an active business leader in that town, a trustee of Bastrop Academy, and an incorporator of the Bastrop Iron Manufacturing Company in 1863 (Gammel, *Laws of Texas*, 3:1414–15, 5:741–42).

Gideon continued to promote the machine for some time, as indicated by a letter some three weeks later:

Long Point. Texas. 19th Feb 1865

Judge Garrett[1]
Dear Sir.

The day was so far spent Saturday when I got through with the examination of the carding machine, & the crowd was so hard to satisfy that I was forced to leave the place without speaking to you or expressing my views on the machine and its uses to any member of the Court. That, however, would have been but little use, as I could only have expressed what seemed to be with but one or two exceptions the general opinion of those that examined it. All I heard speak on the subject except one man, who was laying upon his belly upon the table, were well pleased and wanted them made and thrown into market as fast as possible.

The demand for the carders will, I think, be considerable if they can get them in a reasonable time. Three or four shops in the County would not probably be too many. This, however, is only a suggestion, for I am not posted in regard to the facilities for procuring the necessary material for their construction. If the machine can be made as good and sold on the terms they are furnished at by Hayford and Johnson, the inventors, there will be quite a number of them required to satisfy our struggling community, whose cloth making processes would most certainly be greatly facilitated by the aid of a plentiful supply of this, to my mind, great labour saving invention.

Very Respectfully
Gideon Lincecum

[1] The 1860 Census of the area listed a man named O. H. P. Garrett (Eighth Census, 1860, Washington County, Tex., p. 229). According to Wilfred O. Dietrich, Garrett was the Washington County judge in 1866. The records for the Civil War years are incomplete, and it is likely that he served in this capacity during that period as well (Dietrich, *The Blazing Story of Washington County*, rev. ed., p. 167).

In the meantime, Gideon felt that the war was going somewhat better, while his hatred of the Yankees was becoming more intense than ever, as he told his friend Hannay:

Long Point. Texas. 27 January 1865

R. B. Hannay
Brownsville, Texas
My Dear Sir.

. . . The war continues finely, and we have nothing to complain at so far. We are, to be sure, becoming daily poorer—our comforts dimineshing—but this is the natural results of war, and we were looking for it, and consequently, are not taken by surprise.

We are all however, healthy, and ready and willing to put up with anything that can befall us, except subjugation to Yankee rule. Death, in any form, Satan or any imp of the infurnal regions to rule over us in preference to any Yankee arrangement. Earthquakes, devastation, Showers of fire and brimstone, would be cradle rocking, pleasant entertainment, sweet smelling refreshments to the Soul of my feelings when compared to Yankee dictation, damn them. . . .

Gideon Lincecum

Writing four days later to Dick Keene, his invalid friend in Jefferson, Gideon called the conflict "a hell, thundering, big war" and predicted "it will continue as long as the priests and speculators can keep the boys fighting. . . . [T]hey got it up, and they will keep it going as long as it will pay."[1]

Gideon continued to be very busy, almost too busy to write, as he told "Sioux" Doran.

Long Point. Texas. 7th Feb. 1865

"Sioux"
Houston, Tex.
My Dear Sir.

Your interesting and quite flattering communication of 31st ult. came to hand yesterday. It was long en route.

I acknowledge myself indebted one little letter, but you are not to complain at me, for it is not from neglect. It is from too much outside preasure. My boys are all gone to the war, and I am forced to be overseer and everything else about the place, trying to keep things together, and by cultivating my farm, to produce, if possible, sufficient grain and other articles of food for man and horse to enable me to accomodate, as I have from the beginning of the war, all the traveling soldiers that may call at my place, free of charge. That keeps me pretty busy, leaving me but little time to write letters. . . .

I am, every time the weather will permit me, at work on a carding machine, which I am putting up to aid the cloth making processes that is going on in my family. We have made considerable quantities of cloth with the hand cards, and if I can make the carding machine do what I now think it will, the owner of the traditional history of the origin and progress of the Chahta [Choctaw] people[2] will be able to get along more bravely with her spinning and weaving operations, and a greater number of soldiers will get coats, overshirts and pants, than formerly.

I shall be obliged to you for any of the Yankee papers of a recent date, but dont put yourself to trouble to get them for me. You placed me under lasting obligations for the favours already done me in that way, and as I have no possible way or chance to reciprocate, I cannot urge you to repeat them with any plausible claim.

As to the character of the money loving people of Texas west, it is as natural as the Cactus and other thorny growth of that region. I visited San Antonio last summer, and I looked upon the place as the last stand on the road to perdition. I got a peep at perhaps a thousand heads. They were all organized on the same plane. Flat top heads, twinkling eyes, nasal organ large, and hooking, ample jaw, and heavy back brain. The natural language of such developments is, look out for No. 1. The longest stick gets the persimions. &c I have no desire to visit that town anymore. There was nothing lovely to be seen in the place, or on the road that goes there. . . .

I shall conclude my letter without feeling that I have said anything that can interest such a mind as you possess. A mind that roams over creation, picking and culling the pretty flowers and sweet fruits can find nothing in this epistle that is worth storing away, I am sure.

Thine in holyness.
Gideon Lincecum

[1] Gideon Lincecum to Dick Keene, Long Point, Tex., 31 January 1865, LP, Box 2E366.

[2] Gideon had decided to give his daughter Sarah his potentially valuable manuscript of Choctaw traditional history. While he lived among the Choctaws in Mississippi, Gideon made repeated visits to one of their sages, Chahta-Immataha, in order to write down (in the Choctaw language) an oral history dictated by the old man. During the Civil War Gideon found the original manuscript and, after spending some time relearning the Choctaw language (which he had not used since moving to Texas), translated it in hopes of earning money through its publication (Lincecum and Phillips, *Adventures of a Frontier Naturalist*, pp. xxii–xxiii, 95–101; see also Wolfe, "The Traditional History of the Chahta People").

Gideon wrote to his son Lysander later in the month, expressing concern over demoralization that was surfacing, even in the army:

Long Point. [mid February 1865]

Lysander Lincecum
Army of the Rio Grande, Texas
Dear Lysander.

. . . You say that many of the men of the army of the Rio Grande have deserted, and that not exceeding half the original number remains.[1] This is very bad & must lead to some severity in the military discipline. The war will continue, for Lincoln and his abolition friends wills it, and we are compelled to keep our army up. It is an easy matter to see, that with the present insubordination of our troops, that it can not be done. The demoralization and insubordination of the army must be arested. To effect this all important object in the army discipline you will soon hear of a good many executions. The Gene[r]al in Chief of the confederate army [Robert E. Lee] is a strict disciplinarian and more, he intends to have an Army which must be organized from the men found within our limits. All the efficient men that can be found, without exceptions, will be enrolled. It is known where they are to be found, and if they dont run away soon, they will be enrolled to a certainty. If they fly their country to get clear of defending it, they are not entitled to, nor will they ever be entitled to, anything within our boundary, and it will benefit [illegible due to page tear] for them.

I understand from your letter that Las and Andy are dissatisfied and talk of coming home.[2] I had a better opinion of them. I thought they had the firmness to hang on to what they had entered into to the last. At any rate, not to give up untill the field should be abandoned by every body else. They have a great name with the people here, and I do hope that they may think that good name worth preserving.

I suppose Norton is tired of swapping the confederacy for Mexico.[3] I think there are many more who are equally sick of it. I hope they will not try to get back. We have no use for such men. They only serve to clog the action and excite the spirit of insubordination amongst our soldiery at best.

You did not mention having seen Illingworth. Do you know where he is? I wrote to Hannay some time ago requesting him to tell Illingworth to send me a ream of good writing paper by some trusty wagoner. If you see him tell him if he can do so without inconvenienece he will oblige me very much by sending the paper to me.

. . . We send by the mail that takes this some late papers. You will see that they contain the principle movements in the important changes that have been recently made in our military arrangements.

Nothing worth your attention has transpired in this vicinity since you left. Everything moving on about as usual and all in health.

If any more news reaches us of interest, I will forward the papers.

Your Father
Gid

[1] Desertions had already proved a considerable problem among Texas troops at times, especially in northeast Texas and Louisiana in 1863 and 1864 (Kerby, *Kirby Smith's Confederacy*, pp. 91, 279–81; Joseph Howard Parks, *General Edmund Kirby Smith, C.S.A.*, pp. 263, 429–30, 478; *Official Records of the Rebellion*, series 1, 26:278–80, 469–71; 48, pt. 2:17, 398–403.

[2] "Las and Andy" are Lascassas and Leander Lincecum, grandsons of Gideon.

[3] "Norton" has not been identified.

Gideon, certainly, was not abandoning hope or the cause, and he continued to find grounds for encouragement. To an army officer he wrote:

Long Point. Texas. 5 March 1865

Lt. W. H. Hensley[1]
Hempstead, Texas
Dear Sir.

Your communication of 27th ult. took me altogether by surprise. I was not long since wondering what had become of you, as I had not heard anything of you in a long time. Your letter explained, and I shall now try to keep posted in future. I had not heard that you had been a prisoner, and that is the reason I had lost you. I hope you may not get <u>trapped</u> again.

I think, from present appearances, that we may expect a favorable change in our affairs soon. The new appointments and changes that have recently taken place in the military department of our Government is significant, and in my opinion augars success.[2] It has excited in the minds of the people, who were wavering and talking about reconstruction, a great recoil. They are bolder now and are every where speaking of our power to fight on and to sacrifice everything; not only our homes, negroes and all other property, Aye, and our wives and little ones on the altar of freedom, sooner than consent to reconstruction, or any other connexion with the Cursed Yankees. Death in any form would be a fate far perferable to any kind of connexion with that hell deserving, God dishonoring, truth hating race of Creatures. Let us all stand to our posts and there is no danger of our having to join them in any thing.

As to stragglers or loose men in this vicinity, they are rarely met with. But should I see any one who looks suspicious, I will communicate to him the great good chance for comfortable quarters and little danger there will be incurred by going into service at Millican.

Very Respectfully,
Gideon Lincecum

[1] W. H. Hensley enrolled 1 March 1862 and was mustered into Capt. R. S. Poole's Company of the 2d Regiment, Carter's Brigade. On a prisoner of war roll dated 11 January 1863, he was listed as a second lieutenant, Company A, 24th Regiment, Texas. He was taken prisoner at Arkansas Post, Arkansas, and received at Camp Chase, Ohio, 30 January 1863, departing for Fort Delaware, Delaware, on 10 April 1863 (National Archives, *Compiled Service Records*, roll 460).

[2] In February, President Davis had appointed Robert E. Lee "General-in-Chief of the Confederate Armies," replaced his secretary of war, and, on Lee's insistence, returned Gen. Joseph Eggleston Johnston to command the Army of Tennessee, in hopes of stopping

Sherman from linking with Grant's troops in Virginia (Current, ed., *Encyclopedia of the Confederacy*, 1:205; Douglas S. Freeman, *Lee's Lieutenants: A Study in Command*, 3:634–35, 642).

Although the military scene in Texas remained quiet save for the blockade and the presence of Federal troops in Brownsville, it was far from quiet elsewhere. As the month of March progressed, so too did the march of General Sherman's troops as they advanced through North Carolina, just as they had through Georgia and South Carolina earlier, pillaging and burning their way toward a union with Grant's main force near Richmond. Not even such dire news could shake Gideon's confidence and spirit, and he continued to lead cheers for the Confederacy and call for damnation of the Yankees, as well as continuing to provide hospitality to any soldiers passing his way, as he reported to the Boone Moores:

Long Point. Texas. 9th March 1865

D. B. and Emily Moore
Hondo Vally, Texas
Dear Brother and Sister.

Your kind and quite interesting communication by the hands of Mr. Davis came to hand on the 7th inst., 41 days on route. Mr. Davis & his friend Mr. McCombs[1] staid with us two nights and left in good health and high spirits for the army, which is not far off at this time. Nearly all of the Texas troops are now stationed in the state, at various places east of the Brazos. It is not thought, however, that they will remain idle long, as 'tis generally believed now they they will soon get [illegible] the Mississippi. We had news last evening that our troops had evacuated both Richmond and Charleston.[2] This is the result of having a man at the head of affairs who had [illegible] pets or favorites to take care of.[3] Genl. R. E. Lee, who is now chief in the military department, has made a great change in the phisiognomy of our Armies within the last 30 days. Organization and Consolidation seems to be the order of the day since he took the lead, and the people everywhere are inspired with renewed Spirits, and confidence in the Supremacy of our great leader.[4] I have never witnessed so great a change in the minds and actions of the people, on any subject, as has taken place with them everywhere since that fact was made public, that Lee had been made Chief in Command. I think that the grand movements that are now being made throughout the Armies of the Confederacy, augars big things, ultimates at which the world will stand aghast and wonder. I have never felt any uneasiness in respect to the finale of this revolution. Success, in my estimation, is certain sooner or later, and now I feel doubly assured. It is the same from every quarter I can hear from. They are unanimous in the declaration, that all they have is in for the war. Negroes and all must go now. . . .

This Country is spoilt, the grass all plowed up, the roads turned into the ravines and other impassable places, & every man you meet is your enemy! Well, he will tell you a lie for two bits advantage in any little trade & thats no friendship. I am not complaining at them, for I knew what sort of thing man is long ago, and might have left the Country before they got so thick around me. But you, in your letter, complain at the few scattering rogues which infects your Country, who are occasionally appropriating to themselves a beef or a poney. That is a mere trifle when Compared with our Country. Here, the rogues come prepared with written authority to take your truck. These papers are made out and signed by some Commanding general, quarter Master, or the president, Secretary of the treasury, or the lord, or devil—some high authority; and they go to peoples houses with these papers, and after some strutting and bombastic parade, the people become frighten[ed] and the rascals apropriate whatever they take a fancy to, particularly if there is no man at the house. All of this goes to show that yours is the preferable Country to dwell in, for while you encounter an occasional rascal, and they wide scattered, we dwell in the midst of thousands, all cut and dried and ready to apropriate any thing from the fruit of a henroo[s]t to a good saddle horse. Your rogues do business on their own hook; ours on governmental authority, and they are more greedy. Yours steal and run off. Ours steal, provoke you to prosecute, gain the property, and make the owner pay the cost of suit. . . .

Our family now consists of the old lady, Sarah and myself. Lysander is in the army. During his absence, his wife stays with Leonora. If it was not for the great number of soldiers that stop with us on their way to and from the army, we shuld have a lonesome time of it. It is a very rare thing for us to be without company of nights. I have fed away nearly four good crops of corn and bacon to the soldiers and have not as yet made any of them pay a Cent. My house is becoming more popular every day, and I use all the industry and economy I am master of to keep it up. I should grieviously hate to be compelled to turn a soldier off for want of ability to feed him and his horse. Yet I see that such a thing can happen, for the soldiers tell us they are directed to stop here for 2 miles on each side of us. Well, as long as I have any thing that a Soldier or his horse can eat, he shall be welcome to it, whether other people does so or not. I do not hold them responsible for anything I do, nor do I feel accountable for their derelictions. They be damned. . . .

Eight of my children and grand children are in the army. All that are old enough are in the field except three; Lon, Leander and Cul [Lucullus], and they are detailed for service at home. I think sometimes of going into the army myself, a thing I should most certainly do if our damned quarter masters and commissaries would stop theiving and do their duty. With full rations and other army Conveniences which have been abundantly furnished by the tax payers, I could stand a camp life very well; but without a tent, proper blankets and full rations, I could not do well, but fully as well as many delicately formed young men. All these things, if we had an honest set of officers, could be furnished to our camps in the greatest profusion. Such is the nature of War.

Nothing of an exciting character, either good or bad, have taken place in this Vicinity in a long time; so we have no tales of woe or joy to narrate about home concerns. . . . All of our family who have been tried, have the character of being brave soldiers, and they are all alive at last accounts. . . .

Your Brother
Gid

[1] Mr. Davis and Mr. McCombs have not been identified.

[2] The news of the evacuation of Richmond and Charleston was, on the one hand, premature, and on the other hand, quite tardy. Richmond would not be evacuated by Lee's troops until 2 April, and Charleston had fallen on 18 February (McPherson, *Ordeal by Fire*, pp. 480–81, 471–74; Catton, *This Hallowed Ground*, pp. 384, 375).

[3] A year earlier, on 24 February 1864, President Davis had appointed Gen. Braxton Bragg as his chief of staff, "charged with the conduct of the military affairs of the Confederacy," but had retained his own constitutional power as commander-in-chief. Lee, now general-in-chief, replaced Bragg and had greater authority (Freeman, *Lee's Lieutenants*, 3:315–16, 634–35, 641). It is unclear if Gideon's criticism of the "head of affairs" was directed against Davis or Bragg, but it was probably the former.

[4] On 24 March 1865 a notice appeared in the *Galveston News* as follows: "A general meeting of the citizens of Washington County will be held at Brenham on Friday the 24th, for the purpose of reviving patriotic ardor and encouraging our soldiers, our Generals, and our President in this mortal struggle for national life and for lib-

erty." In the *News* of 3 April 1865 a lengthy report on a mass meeting held in Washington County, signed "Reporter," began as follows: "It would have gratified any patriot and revived the drooping spirits of any good citizen . . . to have been present at this meeting."

Although Gideon could report "nothing of an exciting character" taking place at Long Point, he had some bad news to report to his friend Hannay, who had finally reached Mexico.

Long Point. Texas. 26 March 1865

R B. Hannay
Matamoras, Mexico
Dear Sir.

Your kind letter bearing two dates, 11th and 15th Feb., reached me a week ago, and afforded considerable satsfaction. . . .

[O]n the Brazos a few days ago, a very great and shameful outrage . . . was perpetrated by a . . . two-fisted du[t]chman; and although he was captured and is about to be severely dealt with, the spirit of resentment that nestles in my bosom will not soon be satisfied.

The cause was successful rape on the person of a helpless widow woman; he belonged to General Walker's division,[1] and when they first got hold of this William, the excitement ran so high that the General ordered that he be shot without trial. The civil authority, however, claimed him; he was surrendered and is now in prison awaiting trial.[2] It is very painful to me to be the messenger of bad news. It would perhaps be wrong for me to withhold from you the disagreeable intelligence. The unfortunate lady alluded to above is your brothers widow.

Thine as ever,
Gideon Lincecum

[1] John George Walker (1822–93) was a U.S. Army officer from 1846 to 1861 and a Confederate officer from 1861 to 1865. In 1862 he was promoted to major general and assigned to the Trans-Mississippi theater. In 1863 he took command of a new division that subsequently became known as Walker's Texas Division or Walker's Greyhounds. He led the division with distinction in the Red River Campaign and was wounded at Pleasant Hill on 9 April 1864 (*New Handbook of Texas*, 6:795–96). By the time of the reported crime, Walker's old division was commanded by Maj. Gen. John H. Forney (Warner, *Generals in Gray*, pp. 90–91, 319–20).

[2] Although no published report of this rape was found, a letter published in the *Galveston News* (27 March 1865) commented on the general problem of rowdy behavior by soldiers in the area at this time:

> "Hempstead, Texas, 22 March 1865.
>
> Ed. News:—Within the last three days two soldiers have been shot, by citizens, in this place. One, a member of the 2d Texas Infantry, was seriously wounded and the other, belonging to Wharton's Cavalry Corps, instantly killed. . . .
>
> Personal difficulties have become almost a daily passtime and shooting is of such frequent occurrence that it has become dangerous for a person, however law-abiding he may be, to visit the place. In almost every instance, drunkenness is the cause of the difficulty. To remedy this evil, would it not be well to suggest through the medium of your paper, that Maj. Gen. Walker either close the numerous whisky shops in the place, or send up a company of infantry to control and guard the town.
>
> [signed] X"

This unfortunate incident was perhaps another sign of the demoralization that was spreading in Texas, in the armed forces, and throughout the South, as March gave way to April, and before long, Appomattox. Gideon had surprisingly little to say about the war in its closing days. The channels of communication were closing down and the mails had slowed to a crawl. A week after Lee's surrender at Appomattox, Gideon had not heard of it and was still urging a fight to the end. On that date he wrote to Joe Sniveley and commented on a recent murder in Houston that was the main topic of conversation, news of Lincoln's death not having yet reached the town.

Long Point. Texas. 16 April 1865

Jos. C. Sniveley
Wood's Regt., C.S.A.
My Dear sir.

Yours of 9th inst. was received yesterday. . . .

Everyone that I have heard speak of the killing that was enacted a few days since at Houston seemed to express more satisfaction than sorrow on the subject.[1] All, however, that I have heard speak were Soldiers belonging to various companies of his command—perhaps 100 in all—had a good many charges against them. They all mention the Yellow bayou affair;[2] and besides several other things of less moment, thay unanimously charge him with partiality and a preference in bestowing his promotions for his kinfolks. Well, Soldiers will complain you know. But I never heard any of them talk that way about Genl. T. Green.

You think some important move is about to transpire, so do I. I suppose, without any authority for such supposition, that preperations are now being made, for an attempt to reenforce Gen. Lee by crossing the Mi[ss]. river, and by running the blockade. This last experiment would be a daring exploit—attends with much peril. We must try any possible thing and not stop for conjectured dangers. If it was left to me to say whether the confederate states should submit to a reunion and yanky rule, or every man, woman and child in them be swallowed up in one grand crash, I should prefer and unhesitatingly decide on the latter as being the least of the two evils. . . .

Truly thine
Gideon Lincecum

[1] Under the heading "Death of Maj. Gen. John A. Wharton," the *Galveston News* (7 April 1865, p. 2) reported as follows: "We have to report one among the heaviest national calamities with which our country has been visited during the war, in the death of General Wharton. He was shot through the heart in this city [Houston] at the hour of 10 o'clock yesterday morning, by Col. George Baylor, and death ensued immediately." Elsewhere in the same edition the full transcript of "Testimony before the jury of inquest on the body of Major-General Wharton" was published. According to another source, "Wharton was killed by fellow officer George W. Baylor in a personal quarrel that grew out of 'an unpleasant misunderstanding over military matters.'" Even though Wharton was found to have been unarmed, Baylor was acquitted of murder charges in 1868. John Austin Wharton had distinguished himself at Shiloh, Murfreesboro, and Chickamauga. For a good summary of the affair, see Kerby, *Kirby Smith's Confederacy*, p. 402. For Wharton's career, see Warner, *Generals in Gray*, pp. 331–32. For Baylor, see *New Handbook of Texas*, 1:422–23.

[2] Gideon apparently believed that the quarrel between Wharton and Baylor grew out of the Battle of Yellow Bayou, which was the site of the last skirmish of the Red River Campaign, 17–18 May 1864 (*New Handbook of Texas*, 5:494–95). Many complained about Wharton's management of the battle, according to Anne J. Bailey (*Between the Enemy and Texas*, p. 189).

On 20 April Gideon received payment of four hundred dollars "from the Confederate States for services rendered" from 1 July to 31 October the previous year,[1] but one hun-

dred dollars per month for four months was far from compensating him for his contribution to the war effort. He was prepared to give still more, indeed, everything, *if necessary. He wrote his friend the newspaper editor, Cushing, about his situation and feelings.*

Long Point. Texas. 25 April 1865

E. H. Cushing
Houston, Texas
My Dear Sir.

. . . Since the war commenced, I have sold nothing, not even to the amount of fifty dollars worth. But I gave away to the volunteers all my horses, blankets, a considerable amount of clothing, and to the passing soldiers fed away three good crops, and now nearly through the fourth without making any charge whatever. I have also paid my taxes and tithes up to date. I am now, however, at the end of my row and can pay no more taxes but by selling property. I have no objection to that, for I would willingly sacrifice all I own, and my own old time cracked carcase into the bargain, if by that means I could add any appreciable strength to our bleeding armies. But if I write the book,[2] it will be done in view of raising funds to pay my share of the taxation, so that I may not be compelled to sell anything that a soldier or his horse can eat. . . .

I dwell at the cross roads where the soldiers pass daily, and they must have food for themselves and horses as long as I can produce a crop of corn on my place, if every other consideration is left neglected. . . .

Our great, grand war is entering the last stage, I think now. Prospect good for a long, glorious paroxysm of guerilla purification. O, if they had sense enough to supply the emasculators knife philosophically!

Thine truly —Gideon Lincecum

[1] One page of Gideon's letterpress volume was used to make a copy of a receipt addressed to "Wm. Cooke, Capt. and Post Qr. Master, 2nd District, Texas," for four hundred dollars' payment to Gideon Lincecum of "Your certified account."

[2] The proposed book of herbal remedies, which Gideon was calling "Moccasin Tracks," was discussed in chapter 5 above.

Two days later Gideon received confirmation of Lincoln's assassination and rejoiced at the news:

Long Point. Texas. 27 Apl. 1865

My Dear Sioux.

. . . I see by the papers that came today, that the story of this killing of the cold hearted tyrant Lincoln is no joke. I hope the man who performed that great piece of public service to the nations may make good his escape, and that he may live to burst the sculls of a few more of the despots. Wouldn't it be a glorious thing for the next news to be that some just avenging spirit has sent Andy Johnson to keep company with old Abe.[1] The slaying of the two above named tyrants, however, will make but little difference in reference to the affairs of the southern cause, if Seward is suffered to remain alive.[2] But the killing has commenced, and there is no telling how many haters of free government may be blotted out before the avengers are satisfied. Oh! May they slide safely through the ranks of humanity, plucking out the opposers of liberty until there are no tyrants left.

As to the fate of Lees army, we may, to be sure, look upon it as one amongst our disasters, but we must mend it by renewed energy, and at last, if we cannot force the invading robbers from our soil, we can all die in the effort and thereby emblazon the name of our nation higher up on the escutcheon of fame than by any thing else we can do. Let us all vow to do that. What say you?

What would be the value of existence under the control of yankee fashion of government? I wouldn't give a damn for such a life, nor do I intend to be the owner of such a life.

. . . And now receive my blessing, which I pour out on you, as it costs nothing, as free as water.

Thine in Christ.
Gideon Lincecum

All's well.

[1] Andrew Johnson was on the Booth conspirators' list of targets and was to have been shot at the same time as Lincoln, but his designated assassin lost his nerve and did not follow through with his deed (David H. Donald, *Lincoln*, pp. 587, 596, 599).

[2] Secretary of State William H. Seward was stabbed at his home by one of the Booth conspirators but survived his wounds. The would-be assassin, Lewis Paine (who went by various names), was soon captured and later hanged (Donald, *Lincoln*, pp. 587–88, 596–99).

If Gideon's "Thine in Christ" seems at odds with his bloodthirsty glee over Abraham Lincoln's death, he was far from being alone in such an anomaly. The long, bitter struggle had hardened the edges of many a soul, Northern as well as Southern.

There were no hard edges, however, in Gideon's compassion for the returning soldiers. Not only did he feed them and doctor them, but he also played his violin to lift their spirits—so much so, apparently, that he wore out the strings of his old black box and was grateful when given some new ones. To his benefactor he wrote:

Long Point. Texas. 29 April 1865

M. A. Healy[1]
Brownsville, Texas
My Dear Sir.

Please accept of my most sincere thanks for the kindness you have conferred on my family, myself, and many weary soldiers, whose drooping spirits are to be cheered up at my house by the sound of those very superior Violin strings you forwarded to me by Mr. J. Johnson.[2]

Johnson got home sick, but he sent the strings to day by his little son, and they are now safe and sound in my possession. They are first class strings, and upon them I intend to make many soul stirring sounds. I take good care of them, and I here venture the prediction that you will be back before they are plaid out, and I will have a chance to regale your musical developments with sweet chords from them. . . .

And now receive my blessing, and believe me, as ever, thine in Christ.

Gideon Lincecum

[1] Healy is identified as a Brazoria hardware merchant in Burkhalter, *Gideon Lincecum*, p. 291.

[2] A possible match for "Mr. J. Johnson" is John Johnston of Brenham, who had four young children in 1860 (Eighth Census, 1860, Washington County, Tex., p. 155).

Hosting and doctoring the soldiers took so much of Gideon's time and resources that his correspondence suffered:

Long Point. Texas. 5 May 1865

Sioux Doran

. . . As another excuse for a short stale letter my place abounds with sick soldiers and their nurses, and if you and I should be deprived of all sources of fun by it, they must and shall have full and satisfactory attention. This duty I am performing not to go into the public prints, or to be seen or heard of by man, but because I am behind hand in my dues to the dear, self sacrificing soldiers, and am striving to pay up as fast as possible.

[Gideon Lincecum]

By 6 May the fighting had ended east of the Mississippi River,[1] but it was still going on in Texas, primarily at the southern tip near Brownsville. There were fears that the Union army might mount a major invasion of Texas, now that the Union had so many troops and ships available from the eastern theater, and restlessness, if not anticipation, was stirring in the slave quarters. One of the Lincecum slaves took off with a horse, and Gideon alerted his soldier son, Lysander, who was with Commander John S. (Rip) Ford on the Rio Grande,[2] to be on the lookout for him if he tried to get to Mexico.

Long Point. Texas. 8 May 1865

L. R. Lincecum
Onin's Co., Giddings Btn.
Dear Son.

Old Billy has got himself into difficulty on account of taking up and making way with a stray horse, which was made known by the confession of Cul's Gus and Lon's Tom, who were being punished for offenses of a similar character;[3] and Billy getting news of the developements that had been made by the two boys above named and the threatening talk among the neighbors, became frightened and jumped off. Your mother says that Dick told her that his daddy said that he was going to hunt Master San. He has been gone only one day, and I think it quite likely that he will try to make a final escape in some direction as towards the Rio Grande, on account of the great amount of train travel and negro teamster[s] on the road promises most; he might think it safest to attempt it in that direction. It will be well enough for you to look out for him and also to make it known to those men stationed about the crossing places in the river and in the towns. If you should find him, relieve him of the cause of his dishonest proclivities, by castration. Do you hear?

There is no local news worth telling in this beat. Captain McNelly is camped on Mill creek near Pheares' place, and has stirred up the lag behinds and the disloyal rascals fearfully.[4] Has arrested quite a number of them and sent them off to Gen. Walker at Houston. Amongst the number is Cordy Frances.[5] [As for] Whitener,[6] I just this moment heard that they did not capture Whitener and two other young men who had been concerned in robbing a Mexican train, but they got Wm. Ledbetter of Fayette county,[7] who is accused of treason, and it is thought that him and Frances will be shot.

People are not very healthy, but very few down sick. All well here.

Your Father.

[1] Following Lee's surrender of the Army of Northern Virginia at Appomattox on 9 April, Joseph E. Johnston surrendered his forces to Sherman on 26 April, and Richard Taylor surrendered the remaining forces east of the Mississippi River on 4 May. The forces west of the Mississippi, including Texas, were surrendered by Edmund Kirby Smith's deputies in New Orleans on 26 May. Smith, finding himself a "commander without an army," signed the surrender on the Federal ship *Fort Jackson* off Galveston on 2 June (McPherson, *Ordeal by Fire*, pp. 484–85; Parks, *General Edmund Kirby Smith*, pp. 475–78; Kerby, *Kirby Smith's Confederacy*, pp. 424–26).

[2] On 13 May 1865, John Salmon (Rip) Ford led Confederate forces in the last land battle of the war at Palmito Ranch, near Brownsville. His men knew that the war had ended, for on 1 May 1865 they had obtained a copy of the *New Orleans Times* that contained the news of Lee's surrender, Lincoln's death, and the surrender negotiations between Johnston and Sherman. In the next ten days, several hun-

dred Confederate soldiers left the Army of the Rio Grande and went home, but those who remained did not hesitate to follow Ford's command into a battle that cost the Federals more than a hundred men, while the Confederates suffered only a few dozen wounded (*New Handbook of Texas*, 5:25). Members of Gideon's family who served in Ford's last command were two sons, Lucullus and Lysander, and two grandsons, Lascassas and Leander. See Gideon Lincecum to Dr. A. Weir, 20 May 1865, below.

[3] Gus and Tom were slaves of Gideon's sons, Lucullus and Leonidas. Billy and Dick were also Lincecum slaves.

[4] Leander H. McNelly (1844–77) was born in Virginia and moved to Washington County, Texas, in 1860. On 5 September 1861 he was enrolled as a private in Capt. G. W. Campbell's Company F of Col. Thomas Green's 5th Texas Cavalry. After being involved in numerous battles and distinguishing himself, he was promoted to captain in February 1864 and assigned to company scouts in the 2d Regiment of Sibley's Brigade. In 1865 he was transferred to General Walker's cavalry corps and ordered to Washington County to arrest deserters (*New Handbook of Texas*, 4:445–46; National Archives, *Compiled Service Records*, roll 34 [listed as "L. H. McNallie" and "Leander McAnally"]). Mill Creek rises in two branches in Washington County. The East Fork rises three miles northeast of Burton and the West Fork rises four miles southwest of Burton. The two branches unite in central Austin County (*New Handbook of Texas*, 4:734–35). Two families named Phears are listed as residing in Brenham in the 1860 Census (Eighth Census, 1860, Washington County, Tex., p. 224).

[5] "Cordy Frances" is identified as Cordman Frances of Burton, Washington County, in Burkhalter, *Gideon Lincecum*, p. 166n.

[6] There was an A. S. Whitener residing in Union Hill in 1860 (Eighth Census, 1860, Washington County, Tex., p. 199).

[7] Identified as William Hamilton Ledbetter, Jr., of Fayette County, in Burkhalter, *Gideon Lincecum*, p. 166n.

How Billy fared we do not know. Gideon had other problems about which to worry, including the possible Union invasion. His friend Cushing in Houston was particularly alarmed and had written to Gideon for help in hiding his valuables.

Long Point. Texas. 9 May 1865

E. H. Cushing
My Dear Sir.

Yours of 1st inst. came as usual on the ninth day. To which I reply, Yes. All that I can do that will aid you or any other true friend to the confederate cause will be done as freely as the wind blows or the water flows. But is mine a safe place, think you, to make deposits? My residence is at a very public cross roads. It is, however, 125 miles from the sea coast. Houston, 80 miles, is the nearest point navigable. If anything should happen to make it necessary, I can store 2 or 3 wagon loads. If you can think of no better and safer place, you shall be welcome to the use of mine. I have a quantity of what I think to be valuable manuscript, and I had been trying to think of some plan to preserve them in case of an invasion;[1] and you seem to think this place is safe enough. Well, do you just use it as seemeth good in your own eyes.

Thine most Respectfully
Gideon Lincecum.

[1] Gideon refers here to his "Traditional History of the Chahta People." Near the end of the Civil War, Gideon buried this manuscript and a number of his letterpresses in sealed metal containers, one of which proved leaky, resulting in the eventual loss of nine hundred letterpress pages due to dampness (Burkhalter, *Gideon Lincecum*, p. vii).

The feared invasion did not materialize for more than a month, when it took the form of an army of occupation, resistance having ceased with Gen. Kirby Smith's surrender of the remaining Confederate forces (except for Gen. Stand Watie's Indians in Oklahoma Territory). A short time before Smith's surrender, Gideon wrote a long letter to his old friend Dr. Weir, giving an account of his family's participation in the war and his own feelings about the outcome.

Long Point. Texas. 20th May 1865

Dr. A. Weir
Harmony Hill, Texas.
My Dear Friend.

Devastating war may roll over the land, governments may rise and fall, and politicians may face to the rear and merit and receive damnation, but friendship established upon the basis that ours was will not cease, nor even decline, while the life lasts. . . .

Your kind favor came up from Brenham, that filthy scab on the inguinal region of Washington County, yesterday morning. I was proud of it, not only on account of its having been so long since I received a letter from you, but on account of the calm, reasonable manner in which I find you, at this advanced stage of our troubles, capable of discussing the various important subjects which it contained. I supposed that you are apprised that there are some men who went into our great war, or rather plunged into it in grand stile, who are now greatly and sordidly changed, and this change took place with them as soon as they discovered that their plans for securing place and making money had failed. The thought of losing what little property they have on hand has run them frantic, and they talk about their poor, suffering wives and children, as if they were all idiots and cripples, showing very clearly that they feel that "life is sweet" under any circumstances, and that if they can only keep what little they have got about them they can submit to any kind of degradation.

Well, that picture does not fit my case, and I am glad to find that it misses you fully as far. My feelings and sentiments stand unchanged upon the same platform they did at the commencing, except perhaps that the Yankees have lowered themselves a few degrees in my estimation. You "would like to have my views upon the general policy and tendencies of our legislations." I have no confidence in any of it. In my present frame of mind, I would prefer anarchy to any of it.

In reference to my children, I may say, and I will begin with them as they came into the world. Leonidas is war tax collector for this county and has been from the commencing. Leander resides 15 miles from here on the Austin road, has his fourth wife, and what is more uncommon still, has become a sober respectable man, not having been intoxicated since some time previous to the war. He was detailed at the start to remain where he is and take care of the soldiers' families as far as medical attention may be required, he being with very few exceptions the only man left in that district, [as] there was a general turnout with those [from] Nails Creek and [illegible] such hunters. Lucullus was also detailed for the same purpose, & his district included all that country lying between Long Point and the Yegua and for 10 miles beyond the creek, including that lovely country where you and I camped one night and you had the ague. . . . Lachaon (Dock) is first Lieut. in [illegible] company on the Rio Grande. Lysander belongs to the same company. Lysander got married four days before his company marched. On being asked by his mother, why he acted so foolish in these perilous time[s], his reply was that he wanted somebody to write letters to, that would have no excuse that could prevent them from responding to his letters.

Mary is healthy, and her children have their natural shapes . . . ; Leonora has 7 children, they are well enough looking, tipped off with a little too much of the Campbell. Lee was left as she had lived, very poor, and she is struggling to keep up. Cassandra stays at Austin; she has not visited us since the war. Sarah is not married. Perhaps she never will. She has peculiar notions on that topic. She makes music for the soldiers that stop with us, and that's every night, (I help her) and keeps up a very extensive army correspondence. (I don't help her in that). The old lady is still pretty healthy, attends the milking of mornings, and knits and sews a great deal. I am here, just about as when you saw me, except that I am gradually becoming more nervous. I cannot continue to write long until I become quite shaky. But that's nothing; the great wonder is that I have stood it so well so long. Our brood at present numbers 55 live ones—10 dead. I am not boasting of them, for the world is crammed with that sort, and there is no sense, nor is there any use, in forcing into existence another big litter. So now you have a pretty full account of my family of children, as they stand at present. I had forgotten to mention Lycurgus' four boys; they are all in the army, and are said to be brave soldiers. Cash and Jo, the two oldest, were with Tom Green and participated in <u>all</u> his battles, and on down to yellow bayou, and came clear without even a scratch. At Fort Butler, Jo got knocked down with a brick bat but it left no mark. The other two boys, Las and Andy, are in the army on the Rio Grande.

About the how the war is going to terminate, or the plan upon which it has been conducted, I can say nothing sensible, for if I have heard any truthful reports on the subject I didn't know it. To pick out of the great mass of what has been published about it, from first to last, what looks most like the truth is that the two great parties in Congress made a bet on the fighting qualities of the northern and southern people. They then put things in order for it, set them to fighting and kept them at it until their partners in the game had plundered the fighters homes of all that was worth having. [They] shipped it off, and are now abandoning the army to follow their gains, while a new set are preparing to take command of the impoverished hosts, with the intention to make slaves of them. May the devil take all governments; give me anarchy. Governments of all forms, have been instituted for no other purpose, but to filch away from the laboring classes the profits of their productions. The machinery fixed up by the legislation of all countries are very numerous and successful. They consist of churches, courthouses, jails, penitentiaries, incorporations, internal improvements, banks, gambling houses, incorporated whore houses, assignation houses, law, war, &c. &c. And all this, when in full action, is what is called government. The writers on governments are nothing more than blind makers, employed by the government workers to hang up their blinds before the honest laborers. All the lying historians are writing under pay for the same purpose, that is, to make blinds for the people. To any man possessing a particle of sympathy for the human species, anarchy would look far preferable.

But these are things about which I know but little. I was not formed by nature for any kind of government; circumstances over which I had no control fixed my destiny. If I had had the choosing, I would not have preferred an agricultural community. Nature intended me for the forests, but dropped me in a locality that was soon overrun and cut down by a race of world spoilers. Well, it went pretty hard with me, though I think I can bear it now to the end, which cannot be very far distant. Come when it may, I am ready. . . .

As ever, thine.
Gid

Gideon had been ready for war in 1861 and now he was ready for peace—or anarchy—with surprising equanimity.

Chapter 8

After the War

On 19 June 1865 Maj. Gen. Gordon Granger,[1] who had just arrived in Galveston with the Federal occupation force, issued an order declaring an end to slavery in Texas, the last of the Confederate states in which Lincoln's Emancipation Proclamation of 22 September 1862 was put into effect. Although theoretically the proclamation had applied to all areas of rebellion, including Texas, since 1 January 1863, only now had the "Day of Jubilee" come for African-American Texans. For Gideon and other Texas slaveholders, it meant a substantial loss of capital and, to a considerable extent, the loss of their labor force. Gideon later observed, "When the war broke up, and I had time to look around, I found I had lost everything but the homestead. It is the truth that I did not have a blanket, nor horse nor mule nor jackass left to my name, nor one single dollar."[2]

He may have overstated his case a bit, but there can be no questioning of his next four words in that letter: "I went to work."

For Gideon "work" meant giving up, for a time at least, his pursuit of the natural sciences and returning to his practice of botanical medicine. It also meant his taking hold of the plow again, in the absence of his slaves, who had left the plantation with or without his encouragement.[3] While many of Gideon's neighbors gave up in despair, he wasted little time bemoaning his fate and chose, instead, to tackle the challenge as if it were a new frontier. He had met the challenge of other frontiers in Georgia, Alabama, Mississippi, and pre-war Texas. He was no stranger in the "Land of Beginning Again."

[1] Maj. Gen. Gordon Granger (1822–76) was a graduate of West Point, a veteran of the U.S.-Mexican War, and a Union stalwart at the Battle of Chickamauga. Before coming to Galveston he led the Union occupation of Mobile (Warner, *Generals in Gray*, p. 181; *New Handbook of Texas*, 3:280). For Granger's order, see Campbell, *An Empire for Slavery*, p. 249.

[2] Gideon Lincecum to S. B. Buckley, Long Point, Tex., 24 December 1865, LP, Box 2E364.

[3] In another letter to Buckley, Gideon boasted of his grace with the plow (at the age of seventy-two): "They say I guide the plow cleverly, and that my attitude and movements, while doing so, are quite graceful. While these remarks were being made, however, I heard no allusions in comparison to the great Cincinnatus!" (Gideon Lincecum to S. B. Buckley, Long Point, Tex., 21 January 1866, LP, Box 2E364). As to the departure of Lincecum's slaves, see Gideon's letter to J. C. Sniveley, 17 July 1865, below.

Ten weeks into this new start, he gave a report to his friend "Sioux" Doran:

Long Point. Texas. 1st Sept. 1865

W. P. Doran
Houston, Texas
Dear Sir.

. . . We are jogging on here without any perceptible change in our home affairs, but that is a small matter. Yet with many it goes hard, and they are getting along with it badly. To judge from their actions and sayings, one is forced to the conclusion that their greatest trouble is the fear that somebody will think them no smarter than a nigger. And it seems to hang so heavy on their minds, that they can't say a soft word for poor [illegible].

I am promising myself, and I have the health, the will and the knowledge of the subject that I have chosen, sufficient to enable me to do a great deal; but the confused and unsettled condition of the minds of the people is such that there is no promise in that—Community, at this time, really does not seem to have any settled point in view. All are anxious to make money, and if they had it, nine tenths of them would leave the country. They don't seem to have any other country in their minds; it is to leave here—to get away from their ruined homes—to any place, to be out of sight of their once thriving and happy situations. No one is willing to hazzard an opinion as to what will be the result of this dreadful suspense, and many of them have no heart to try anything. Some again, and I am one of them, have made up their minds to make the best of the bad condition, fully believing that it won't always be so.

We are all well and trying to fight down all obstructions. Really there is nothing to fight, except the battle for existence, and my whole family could always fight successfully on that battle field. . . .

As ever, truly thine.
Gideon Lincecum

Writing again to Doran later that month, Gideon reflected further on his situation and attitude:

Long Point. Texas. 5 September 1865

W. P. Doran
My Dear sir.

. . . having lost all my means in a late, magnificent game, which was played by a set of inefficient Generals, I have been forced to go to work. I am not complaining at the work, for I do it willingly, but it consumes time and many times leaves me without a subject to write. I shall write only when I have something to say that I think will interest or benefit the person I am about to address. At my age, with such an organism as I possess, such useful though[t] does not often occur. Happen what may, I know that I shall sustain myself whilst I live, but the effort will consume time and thereby shorten my opportunities for writing. But that's nothing. . . .

You say you hope necessity has not caused me to go out into the woods to scrape up something to sustain life. What else could it be? And what other condition could a man be in, who had staked all he had on the great national game, and kept and fed great numbers of the players and their horses four years, and it is not done yet, I am still feeding and rendering comfortable, as I am able, numbers of the poor homeless, good fellows, who have lost their all, like I did, in betting on the big game without knowing the integrity of the leaders of the play.

There is nothing strange in this matter: we gambled with experienced "black legs," and we have lost. Now all we have to do is act like men of sense; if we can, go to work, mending our condition as fast as possible, and when we all get rich again, let us not make the bets and deposit the stakes until we are sure that we know all about the powers and <u>honesty</u> of the gamesters. There is a good deal in that prudent precaution, I tell you, in all kinds of gambling, and it is more essentially necessary when we risk our stakes on the political arena.

I am not communicating this as to one who does not know these facts, but to let you see that I know it too. I do not look upon all this as a grieviance—but a blunder, a circumstance which by energetic industry, and proper mental culture, can all be mended up, and made even better than before, in a few years. Any how, let us not complain. . . .

Most Respectfully Thine,
Gideon Lincecum

In the face of near impoverishment, Gideon sought to obtain some income from his botanical medicine practice, but he recognized the hard times his patients—or customers—faced. To one he wrote:

Long Point, Texas. 6 Sept. 1865.

S. H. Parsons[1]
Liberty, Texas.
Dear Sir:

. . . The war has made me poor and I have resumed practice again, old as I am. It is easier for me than any other business I can think of, though I am unusually stout and healthy, and always sober!

I do not intend to visit cases, but will prescribe and furnish medicine, in any chronic form of disease.

I am not furnishing you any medicine and shall charge for prescription only. But if you are, like myself, an impoverished rebel, don't send the fee.

If it is convenient, send me ten dollars.

Very Respectfully
Gideon Lincecum (Gid)

[1] S. H. Parsons has not been identified.

Five months after the beginning of Federal occupation, Gideon was still hard at work but was optimistic that his own day of emancipation from such drudgery was not far off. He longed to return to research and writing, as he told Doran:

Long Point. Texas. 19th Nov. 1865

W. P. Doran
Houston, Texas
Dear Sir.

Your very flattering communication, <u>without a seal</u>, came to hand this evening. In regard to your request for me to write for the paper, it is true, as you remark in your letter, that my poverty stricken condition demands all the time and energy that I can stump up, to keep up appearances to a very ordinary pitch. I am not discouraged nor out of heart any way, but there is no use in trying to disguise the fact that it is about all I can do, with my present appliances and surroundings, to find sufficient time to perform all the labor and duties that are of necessity incumbent on me. That's nothing to talk about. It won't be so long. I shall soon rise, with the ears, fingers, and noses of all difficulties and antagonisms bit off in my mouth; that done, as soon as I can pick my teeth and clean my mouth of the filth of the contest, I may be in a condition to make observation and find something worthy of your paper to write about. . . .

As to the danger of an insurrection of the negroes in this county, I have heard nothing of it. But such a thing could be going on and our citizens know nothing about it. We have no police, nor does any one seem to care what the negroes may do now or hereafter. . . .

Very Respectfully
Gideon Lincecum

No insurrection of the former slaves took place, but labor conditions were very unsettled. Gideon's freed slaves had left; in fact, he had encouraged them to depart. Some wanted to come back, but he discouraged that. He expressed his position in several letters to young Joseph Sniveley:

Long Point. Texas. 17 July 1865

J. C. Snively
New Albany [Ind.]
Dear Friend.

. . . I told my negroes that if they remained with me they would not feel free, and I also aided them in procuring good places; they have made pretty good crops. They are not satisfied however, they say they work harder and see less satisfaction. They have all made application for the privilege to coming home next year. I can't take on that responsibility again. . . .

In righteousness, Thine.
Gideon Lincecum

In a second letter to Sniveley on this subject, more than a year later, Gideon explained his situation further and contrasted it with that of his son-in-law, J. V. Matson, who lived nearby.

Long Point. Texas. 9 Sept. 1866

J. C. Snively
New Albany, Ind.
My dear young friend.

. . . Your kinspeople here consists now of only our family [and] J. V. Matson's. They are healthy and doing well of course. I suppose Matson will crib a larger crop of both corn and cotton than he ever did. He is a managing, money making man under any circumstances. He hired negros enough to tend all three of his farms, and one way and another, managed to get pretty fair work out of them. They are, however, a very poor dependence, and but few men will employ them next year. I hear almost everybody say that they have tried the experiment and find a great deal of disappointment and vexation and no profit. They are thoroughly satisfied that <u>free negro</u> labor will not pay, and most of them have abandoned the idea of using it. I turned mine loose at the start and have done very well without them. They all want to come back next year, but except I find that they are about to starve, I cannot think of pestering myself with the responsibility of directing their action any more. Formerly I made them keep plenty of everything both to eat and wear for themselves and my family too. Now they are exempt from the labor of furnishing my family, and if they can't sustain themselves, I don't think I can go farther than to advise them what course to pursue. I can see, though, that if there is no favorable change in the action of the negro bureau's agents towards them, that their condition will soon be an awful affair.[1] . . .

In righteousness I am thine
Gideon Lincecum

[1] Gideon is referring to the federal Freedmen's Bureau, which had been created by Congress to assist the former slaves in making the adjustment to freedom and to monitor their treatment by the white population. See Barry A. Crouch, *The Freedmen's Bureau and Black Texas*.

Earlier Gideon had observed that the labor situation was improving, as most of the freedmen had had enough of their "jubilee" and returned to work, but not on his farm:

Long Point. Texas. 4th March 1866

W. P. Doran
Galveston, Texas
My Dear Sir.

. . . Our fields are in fine order now, and people, and negroes and all, are working in good style. A great change seems to have taken place in the action of the negro within the last 6 weeks. Having disposed of what money they had on hand, he has quieted down to his acknowledged, natural sphere, and has gone freely to work. Those who are working for part of the crop are performing better, as a general thing, than those who are working for money. However, I hear of but little complaint recently, from either condition, and farmers are beginning to put up a little and are talking about future prospects for improvements. We have the negro here with us, and to prevent him from becoming a damaging incumbrance and nuisance, we must take pains and teach him the philosophy and use of existance. There is no use in curling up our noses in disgust at inevitableness. If the late political fracas at Washington don't interfere with the negroes, we shall, in a very short time do well with them and for them.[1] But I think I see in that Washington difficulty a greater and better chance for thunder and brimstone burning than that which we have just passed over. That, when it comes, will be no onesided affair. It will grind and crush and grate over the surface of all North America, establishing for itself a character of a war worth talking about. . . .

With great respect and esteem.
Gideon Lincecum.

[1] "The late political fracas at Washington" is probably the storm created in late February 1866 by President Johnson's veto of the renewal of the Freedmen's Bureau and his subsequent violent verbal attack on the Radical Republican leaders in Congress, two of the steps leading to his eventual impeachment (McPherson, *Ordeal by Fire*, pp. 511–12).

Posterity has already decided that the war Gideon and his generation had "just passed over" was not only "a war worth talking about" but also worth the writing and publishing of many books (justifying, we trust, this book as well). Just what Gideon saw ahead is not clear, but it is unlikely that he expected the Confederacy to rise again. A news report dated 12 March 1866 on the Texas state convention may be instructive: "The ordinance of secession is disposed of by the Convention. Mr. Slaughter's substitute was adopted and ordered to be engrossed; it reads as follows; 'Be it ordained by the people of Texas, in convention assembled, That we acknowledge the supremacy of the Constitution of the United States and the laws passed in pursuance thereof, and that an ordinance adopted by a former convention of the people of Texas, on February 1, 1861, entitled an ordinance to dissolve the Union between the State of Texas and the other States, united under compact styled the Constitution of the United States of America, be and the same is hereby declared null and void, and the right heretofore claimed by the State of Texas to secede from the Union is hereby distinctly renounced.'"[1]

[1] *Texas Observer* (Rusk, Tex.), 24 March 1866, reprinted in *Texas Extra: A Newspaper History of the Lone Star State, 1835–1935*, p. 98.

For Gideon and many of his Texas neighbors, the worst of Reconstruction seemed over, a year after it had begun. Many ordeals and challenges lay ahead, and full recovery would take another century—or more. But the darkest days were over—for most—and Gideon could write with more than his usual optimism just one year and six days after General Granger had issued his historic order.

Long Point. Texas. 25 June 1866.

R. B. Hannay.
Matamoros, Mexico
My Dear Sir.

Your interesting communication of 23rd ult. came to hand on the 10th inst., and having no news at the time that would interest you, I delayed my reply until today. . . .

I do not understand it, but it is true that the people are improving their homes and all the little towns are being built up more rapidly than has been the case since I came to Texas.

The main street at Navasota is a solid wall of houses continuing all the way to Gen. Blackshears farm[1] and they have a south Navasota rapidly going up. Old Camp[2] is at the head of that enterprise. They have 12 sawmills in the pinery over there and they can't do half the work called for. Our crops are pretty good. Corn is all safe and if the worms don't eat the cotton up, it promises to be a pretty good half crop in this county.

Long Point has caught the spirit of progress and is improving smartly. Inhabitants 150.

Alls well—[3] Thine as ever.

Gideon Lincecum

[1] A former member of the Georgia militia and veteran of the Creek Campaign of 1836, Gen. Thomas E. Blackshear (1809–67) moved to Texas and settled near Hollendale in Grimes County. According to the 1860 Census, he was a wealthy farmer, with real and personal property valued in six figures (Eighth Census, 1860, Grimes County, Tex., p. 236). He died of yellow fever in 1867 (*History of Grimes County*, ed. Grimes County Historical Committee, pp. 224, 236).

[2] Ira Malcolm Camp (1811–95) moved to Texas from Georgia in 1846 and settled in Grimes County. On the stage line from Huntsville to Austin, he built a two-and-a-half-story rock house known as "Camp Inn" (*History of Grimes County*, pp. 247–48). On the front page of its 20 October 1863 edition, the *Galveston News* commended Mr. Camp for a contribution to the war effort: "Mr. Camp, of Navasota, has presented us with a bottle of castor oil of his own manufacture. We have not yet tested its quality but those who have say it is a good article. We know of no article . . . so much needed and Mr. Camp is certainly supplying a great desideratum both to the country and to the army. His enterprise will doubtless be well rewarded." An ad in the same newspaper indicated that "the cold pressed oil" was available at "reasonable rates" (unspecified) and that "soldier's wives who are poor can have it at half price." The scarcity and the unreasonably high price of castor oil imported through the blockade was

a widespread problem in the South, and many families manufacured it on a small scale (Massey, *Ersatz in the Confederacy*, p. 122). In 1864 Gideon wrote Mr. Camp a letter telling him that Sarah had made use of a bottle of "Camp's pure, clarified, transparent Castor oil." Gideon praised the product, saying, "I consider it a great thing for the sick and afflicted of our portion of the state that you took that branch of the manufactoring business in hand" (Gideon Lincecum to Ira M. Camp, Long Point, Tex., 20 October 1864, LP, Box 2E366).

[3] Of course all was not well throughout the former Confederate States. The long ordeal of Reconstruction was barely begun. For a good examination of this vital phase of American history, see Eric Foner, *Reconstruction: America's Unfinished Revolution, 1863–1877*, and for its Texas phase, see Carl H. Moneyhon, *Republicanism in Reconstruction Texas*.

All did seem well in Long Point (a town that today no longer exists), and for Gideon, the time was arriving for him to return, in part at least, to his passionate pursuit of natural history, where many observations and discoveries awaited his sharp eye. The first letter he wrote to his old friend Élie Durand in Philadelphia after the war reflects some ambivalence on this topic.

Long Point, Texas, 24th Dec. 1865

E. Durand
Acad[y.] Nat. Sciences
Phil[a.]
My Dear Sir.

. . . You express much regret at the breaking up of our agreable, as you are pleased to call it, correspondence. No one could regret the abrupt manner in which our, as I think, quite profitable correspondence was cut short than myself. I tried, as you requested me to do, to get a letter through to you several times,[1] but as I heard no more of you, I suppose they did not reach you, and now I am not sure that you will ever see this. If, however, you do get it, I claim an immediate answer.

I shall not be able to interest you any at this writing. Every thing is ruined here, so badly that it will require three or four years to repare and fix up our homes so we can spare time to investigate any of the science, except perhaps those branches which are concerned in procuring the actual material for sustaining existance. What I could do was of but small importance in a scientific point of view and that little has been ruthlessly suspended by the gross animal action of a half civilized race of speculator. I hope your time and spirit of investigation has not been so badly interrupted. I have clearly lost four full years of my already greatly extended period of existance. I had finished up my duties to my numerous brood of children, having procured good homes for them, on which they were all doing well. And being satisfied with my success, I had appropriated the evening of my life to the examination of natural things. . . .

Fraternally thine,
Gideon Lincecum

[1] Elsewhere in this letter Gideon indicates that the last letter he received from Durand during the war had been dated 10 November 1861 and had reached him on 11 March 1862.

Despite Gideon's professed fear that he had nothing of scientific interest to relay to Durand, the letter renewing their correspondence was lengthy and the topics discussed included Texas grapes, fossils, ants, and medicinal plants. It is clear that despite his stern pronouncements about having nothing to do with "Yankees" after the war, Gideon was ready to resume communication with Northern scientists. A letter to "Sioux" Doran on 4 March 1866 mentioned preparations for the first of several new ventures in exploring Texas botany and collecting specimens: ". . . I have employed Mr. Epperson,[1] *a first rate mechanic, to make me a substantial ambulance [wagon with springs], and shall be ready by the 5th of April to set out on an extensive botanic excursion. I shall strike the San Jacinto at tide water, and go up it, exploring its branches thoroughly to its source."*

[1] "Mr. Epperson" is identified as R. S. Epperson, who purchased some of Gideon's land (Deed Records, Washington County, Tex., vol. T, p. 439).

Gideon's "extensive botanic excursion" of 1866 was cut short. On the fifth day, when he had proceeded only as far as Lake Creek in Montgomery County, it became obvious that a recent severe hailstorm had devastated the flora, making the collecting of specimens impossible. After the death of his wife Sarah on 2 February 1867, Gideon became restless and used the wagon built by Mr. Epperson for three separate expeditions that year. In March he set out with two grandsons on a three-month tour westward that encompassed nineteen counties and resulted in a lengthy report to the governor on potential agricultural resources and mineral wealth; in August he ventured deep into east Texas with his daughter Sally and her new husband, Gideon's old friend Sioux Doran, and after two weeks came home ill with fever; and in December, accompanied by a grandson and another boy from Long Point, he traveled to the Gulf Coast, one of his favorite haunts. He became so active in collecting for the Smithsonian Institution after the Civil War that in their correspondence files there are about two hundred pages of letters exchanged between Gideon and Spencer Baird or Joseph Henry.[1]

[1] For detailed descriptions of Gideon's many collecting excursions, see Lincecum, Phillips, and Redshaw, *Science on the Texas Frontier*.

In a letter to an old friend he had not heard from for a long time, Dr. Alva Curtis, Gideon reflected on the past five years.

Long Point. Texas. 19 July 1866

A. Curtis. A.M., M.D.[1]
Cincinnati, Ohio
My Dear Friend.

. . . Previous to the war I was in as good condition as any old man need desire. My children all close around me on good homes I had provided for them, all of them self sustaining and doing well. I had ceased to attend to any business that had money for its object and was spending the evening of my long life very pleasantly in the investigation of some of the natural sciences, but the war came and blotted out four years of my precious time, besides robbing me of all my material aids, leaving me so poor that I was compelled to go to work to secure subsistence for my old lady and myself. I am succeeding very well but it very much retards the progress of my investigations and experimentations. I have nevertheless just commenced the study of entomology. That branch of natural history has been shamefully neglected by me, and so I am at this time eagerly persuing the bugs, and butterflies, hoping, late in the day as it is, to be able to familiarize myself with the most of them before sun down. . . .

As ever
Most Respectfully thine
Gideon Lincecum

[1] Alva Curtis (1797–1881) was born in New Hampshire. He became an agent of Samuel Thomson, who had patented his botanical medical system and published *New Guide to Health; or Botanic Family Physician* (1825). In 1835 Curtis became the editor of the *Thomsonian Recorder*, and in 1836 he began instructing medical students at his home in Columbus, Ohio, under the banner "Botanico-Medical School." While Gideon was practicing botanical medicine in Mississippi, he began corresponding with Curtis in 1839 and published several articles in the *Botanico-Medical Recorder*, edited by Curtis (Haller, *Medical Protestants*, pp. 37, 53–55; Jerry Bryan Lincecum, "Medical Controversy in the Nineteenth-Century South: Botanics vs. Allopaths," *Caduceus* 10 [1994]: 135–40).

In June 1868, Gideon, infuriated by the heavy-handed policies of Radical Reconstruction, declared his personal independence from Texas and the United States and emigrated to Tuxpan, Mexico, where he joined a colony of former Confederates and established himself in a new "Land of Beginning Again." For five years he flourished there as a farmer and a scientist, familiarizing himself with the flora and fauna of Mexico, as recorded in Adventures of a Frontier Naturalist *and* Science on the Texas Frontier.

In 1873 Gideon returned to Texas for what he expected to be a brief visit, only to be overtaken by illness. On 28 November 1874 the pen he had wielded like a mighty sword was laid to rest for eternity.

Appendix

Index of Lincecum Family Members

Leonora Lincecum Campbell (1830–?) and George W. Campbell (1831–62?). Leonora was the ninth child of Gideon. She married George W. Campbell in Washington County on 5 July 1851. Campbell was captain of Company F, 5th Regiment, Texas Mounted Volunteers (Cavalry) under Col. Thomas Jefferson Green of Gen. Henry Hopkins Sibley's New Mexican Brigade. It was mustered 5 September 1861 and included two of Gideon's grandsons, Cassianus and Joseph, as well as many other Washington County boys. Campbell survived the battles in New Mexico and the exhausting retreat to Texas but was too ill to continue with Green's regiment. He returned home and drank himself to death, according to Gideon, leaving his wife and seven children in dire straits (Burkhalter, *Gideon Lincecum*, p. 81; Hall, *Sibley's New Mexico Campaign* p. 272; National Archives, *Compiled Service Records*, roll 32).

Sarah Matilda (Sallie) Lincecum Doran (1833–1919) and William P. (Sioux) Doran (1836–1901). Sallie was the eleventh of Gideon's children and his favorite. It was she who collected his letters and papers, and her sons donated them to the University of Texas. In December 1865 she married William P. "Sioux" Doran (1836–1901), who was born in New York state but migrated to Texas and supported the Confederacy in the Civil War, serving both as a soldier and as a war correspondent. Known as "Sioux" because of a byline he used for forty-one years as a writer for Texas newspapers, he was with the *Houston Tri-Weekly Telegraph* at the beginning of the war. In April 1862 he enlisted as a private in John P. Austin's 2d Texas Infantry, Company A, but was honorably discharged 15 June

1862 (because of defective hearing). He became a war correspondent for the *Telegraph*, and with the rank of major he reported on the Battles of Shiloh, Vicksburg, and Galveston. One of his published accounts is of the Battle of Sabine Pass (Burkhalter, *Gideon Lincecum*, pp. 84–85; National Archives, *Compiled Service Records*, roll 265).

Cassandra Lincecum Durham (1832–77) and George J. Durham (1820–68). Cassandra was Gideon's tenth child, born in Columbus, Mississippi. In 1852 she married George John Durham, who held a political job during the administration of every president and governor of Texas until after the Civil War. He was one of the signers of the petition for a people's secession convention. When Capt. B. F. Carter organized the Austin City Light Infantry on 24 April 1861, Durham enrolled as orderly sergeant and with its seventy-five members left for San Antonio. However, he was called back to Austin as state war tax collector for the Confederacy. The Durhams lost two young daughters (Sarah and Mary Leonora) to diphtheria in April 1862 (Burkhalter, *Gideon Lincecum*, pp. 82–83; *New Handbook of Texas*, 2:736; National Archives, *Compiled Service Records*, roll 437).

Brazos Lincecum (1842–?). Gideon's nephew, the son of his late brother Garland, lived in Caldwell County, Texas, where he enlisted 25 July 1861 as a private under the command of Capt. John J. Myers, Lone Star Mounted Rifles, 25th Brigade. In March 1864 Brazos was among a group of thirty-five soldiers charged with desertion after they became disgusted with their leader and went home on 2 February 1864. Since they gave themselves up voluntarily, all but two of the men, including Brazos, were simply returned to the regiment without punishment. After the war he became a successful trail boss in the cattle business (National Archives, *Compiled Service Records*, roll 174; Burkhalter, *Gideon Lincecum*, p. 163; J. Marvin Hunter, *The Trail Drivers of Texas*, p. 120).

Cassianus (Cass or Cash) Lincecum (b. 1839) and Joseph (Jo) Lincecum (b. 1842). Grandsons of Gideon, sons of Lycurgus, older brothers of Lascassas and Leander. Members of Capt. G. W. Campbell's Company F, 5th Regiment, Texas Mounted Volunteers (Cavalry) under Col. Thomas Jefferson Green of Gen. Henry Hopkins Sibley's New Mexican Brigade. It was mustered 5 September 1861 (Burkhalter, *Gideon Lincecum*, p. 81; Hall, *Sibley's New Mexico Campaign*, p. 274; National Archives, *Compiled Service Records*, roll 34 [under "C. Linzzigum" and "J. C. Lincecum"]).

Emaline (or Emmaline) Jones Lincecum (1815–89). The widow of Gideon's brother Garland (1799–1853) and mother of his nephew, Brazos (see above), who fought in the Civil War. She is listed as residing in Lockhart in the 1860 Census (Eighth Census, 1860, Caldwell County, Tex., p. 201; Patricia Fogle Crisler, "Lincecum-Roberts History," *Plum Creek Almanac* 12, no. 2 [fall 1994]: 96).

John Peachland Lincecum (1820–1907). The son of Gideon's brother Grant (1798–1862), who settled in Catahoula Parish, Louisiana, with his father, was often addressed as "Nephew John." Gideon corresponded with him frequently as a means of keeping in touch with the family of Grant, to whom he refused to write because Grant was an ardent "religionist" (Burkhalter, *Gideon Lincecum*, pp. 113–14).

Lachaon Joseph (Dock) Lincecum (1827–1909). The seventh child of Gideon, he married Elizabeth Cleveland in 1852. A beef contractor during the Civil War, he bought beef cattle and drove them to the Confederate army, at one time swimming 956 head across the Mississippi River at Natchez. Later he enlisted at Camp Randle under Capt. Thomas L. Scott and served under Col. John S. Ford on the Rio Grande (Burkhalter, *Gideon Lincecum*, pp. 87–88).

Lascassas (Lass) Lincecum (b. 1845) and Leander (Andy) Lincecum (b. 1845). Grandsons of Gideon, twin sons of Lycurgus, younger brothers of Cassianus and Joseph, they were born in 1845 in Columbus, Mississippi. During the Civil War they served under Col. John S. Ford on the Rio Grande and took part in his routing of Federal troops from Brownsville in 1864. Their uncle, Lysander, wrote to Gideon that "both make very good soldiers, they don't care for anything but to eat, sleep and ride a horse." Both of their names appear on a list of prisoners of war from J. M. Onin's company of Colonel Giddings's battalion, surrendered at New Orleans by Gen. Edmund Kirby Smith, 26 May 1865 (National Archives, *Compiled Service Records*, roll 193; Burkhalter, *Gideon Lincecum*, pp. 87–88).

Leander W. C. Lincecum (1823–83). The fourth son of Gideon. During the early Civil War period he was detailed as a physician to remain in Washington County and care for the sick in the families of absent soldiers, but in 1863, at the age of forty-one, he enlisted as a private under Capt. James R. Hines (Burkhalter, *Gideon Lincecum*, p. 79).

Leonidas L. (Lon) Lincecum (1821–76). The fourth child of Gideon, during the Civil War he was war tax collector for Washington County but in the last months of the war joined his brothers and nephews in the Confederate army of the Rio Grande, under the command of Col. John S. Ford (Burkhalter, *Gideon Lincecum*, p. 86).

Lewis Shellhouse (Lincecum). A slave owned by Gideon's mother, Sally Hickman Lincecum (1778–1848), Lewis accompanied her when she went to live with Gideon's brother Grant in Catahoula Parish, Louisiana. Since he and Gideon were about the same age and had been childhood playmates, he is frequently referred to (as Lewis or Lewis Shellhouse) in Gideon's letters to Grant's son, John P. Lincecum, his chief correspondent among the Louisiana branch of the family. After the Civil War, Lewis took the surname of Lincecum and moved to Dallas, Texas, corresponding with Gideon from that location (Burkhalter, *Gideon Lincecum*, p. 72).

Lucullus Garland (Cul) Lincecum (1818–?). The eighth child of Gideon, he married Kate Lauderdale in 1853. A practicing physician all his life, during the Civil War he was at first detailed to remain in Washington County to care for families of soldiers. On 5 January 1863 he enlisted at Brenham and became a second corporal under Capt. L. N. Halbert, Company G, 23d Brigade, commanded by Brig. Gen. John Sayles (Burkhalter, *Gideon Lincecum*, p. 86).

Lycurgus Lincecum (1815–49). The first born of Gideon and Sarah's children, he was sent to Texas by Gideon ahead of the rest of the family and arrived in 1847, in time to volunteer for service in the U.S.-Mexican War. During his service in Mexico he contracted an illness that resulted in his early death, 3 February 1849. Among his children were four sons who served in the Civil War: Cassianus (Cass), Joseph (Jo), and the twins Lascassas (Lass) and Leander (Andy) (Burkhalter, *Gideon Lincecum*, pp. 80–81).

Lysander Rezin (San) Lincecum (1836–?). The twelfth child of Gideon, he married Mollie (Maggie) Wood in 1864, just a few days before entering military service. He attempted several times to enlist in the Confederate army but was turned down because of his asthma. Finally accepted for duty in 1864, he joined John S. Ford's command on the Rio Grande as a corporal. His nephews Lascassas and Leander, the twin sons of Lycurgus, served with him, and like them, he is listed as a prisoner of war from J. M. Onin's company of Colonel Giddings's battalion, surrendered at New Orleans by Gen. Edmund Kirby Smith, 26 May 1865 (National Archives, *Compiled Service Records*, roll 193; Burkhalter, *Gideon Lincecum*, pp. 87–88).

William (Billy Lon) Lincecum (b. 1847). Listed as the oldest son of Leonidas Lincecum in the 1860 Census for Washington County, Billy was thirteen years old at that time. Thus he was no more than fifteen years of age when he was accepted in the Confederate army at Fort Hébert on 3 January 1862 as a private in Nelson's Regiment of Texas Cavalry. He was listed as "sick in hospital" from 28 February through 30 June 1862, and on 20 November 1862 he was again listed as sick. This time his father brought him home to recuperate. However, he returned to the army and in April 1864 was serving as a corporal in the Texas 10th Infantry, Company C, of the Trans-Mississippi Department (National Archives, *Compiled Service Records*, roll 267 [as "Linthecum, Wm." and "Linthicomb, Wm. T."]; Burkhalter, *Gideon Lincecum*, p. 145).

Mary Catherine Lincecum Matson (1825–?) and James V. Matson. Born in Mississippi, Mary was the sixth of Gideon's children. She and James Matson married in Washington County, Texas, in 1848, soon after Gideon's family arrived in Texas. Matson was a farmer and a large slaveholder. In 1862 he formed a cavalry company and offered it for service, but apparently it was never accepted. After the Civil War he made work contracts with his former slaves in order to continue farming on a large scale (Burkhalter, *Gideon Lincecum*, pp. 79–80, 168).

Sarah Bryan Lincecum (1797–1867). Gideon and Sarah Bryan were married on 25 October 1813 in Eatonton, Georgia. They had thirteen children, ten of whom lived to adulthood. In 1860 their surviving children and grandchildren numbered fifty. Of their five sons and five grandsons who served in the Confederate ranks, none was seriously injured (Burkhalter, *Gideon Lincecum*, pp. 56, 68, 88).

Daniel Boone Moore (1805–89) and Emily Lincecum Moore (1813–84). Gideon's sister Emily married Daniel Boone Moore in Mississippi when Gideon and Sarah lived there, and the two couples were especially close. The Moores moved from Washington County to the western Texas frontier, first settling near Uvalde and then moving to a location near Castroville, in Medina County (Burkhalter, Gideon Lincecum, pp. 118, 154).

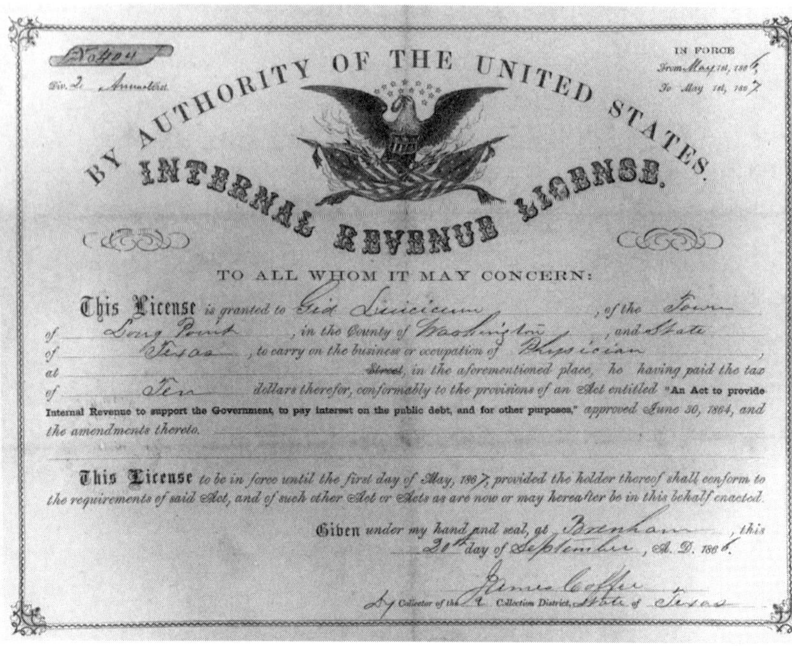

No. 404

Div. 2 Annual

IN FORCE From May 1st, 1866, To May 1st, 1867

BY AUTHORITY OF THE UNITED STATES.

INTERNAL REVENUE LICENSE.

TO ALL WHOM IT MAY CONCERN:

This License is granted to Gid Lincecum, of the Town of Long Point, in the County of Washington, and State of Texas, to carry on the business or occupation of Physician, at Street, in the aforementioned place, he having paid the tax of Ten dollars therefor, conformably to the provisions of an Act entitled "An Act to provide Internal Revenue to support the Government, to pay interest on the public debt, and for other purposes," approved June 30, 1864, and the amendments thereto.

This License to be in force until the first day of May, 1867, provided the holder thereof shall conform to the requirements of said Act, and of such other Act or Acts as are now or may hereafter be in this behalf enacted.

Given under my hand and seal, at Brenham, this 20th day of September, A. D. 1866.

by Collector of the 2 Collection District, State of Texas

Federal license to practice medicine issued to Gideon Lincecum in 1866 (courtesy The Center for American History, University of Texas at Austin)

Selected References

Records and Documents

Congressional Globe. 37th Cong., 3d sess. Washington, D.C.

Deed Records. Washington County, Tex. Mss. in County Clerk's Office, Courthouse, Brenham, Tex.

Lincecum, Gideon. Papers. Center for American History, University of Texas at Austin, Austin, Tex.

National Archives and Records Administration. *Compiled Service Records of Confederate Soldiers Who Served in Organizations from the State of Texas*. 445 rolls. Microfilm.

U.S. Bureau of the Census. Eighth Census. 1860.

———. Ninth Census. 1870.

———. Seventh Census. 1850.

Books

Adams, James Truslow, ed. *Dictionary of American History*. 8 vols., Rev. ed. New York: Charles Scribners Sons, 1976–78.

Alberts, Don E. *The Battle of Glorieta: Union Victory in the West*. College Station: Texas A&M University Press, 1998.

———. *Rebels on the Rio Grande: The Civil War Journal of A. B. Peticolas*. Albuquerque: University of New Mexico Press, 1984.

Allaby, Michael, ed. *A Dictionary of Plant Sciences*. 2d ed. New York: Oxford University Press, 1998.

Bailey, Anne J. *Between the Enemy and Texas: Parsons's Texas Cavalry in the Civil War*. Fort Worth: Texas Christian University Press, 1989.

Ball, Douglas B. *Financial Failure and Confederate Defeat*. Urbana: University of Illinois Press, 1991.

Basler, Roy P., ed. *The Collected Works of Abraham Lincoln*. 9 vols. New Brunswick, N.J.: Rutgers University Press, 1953–55.

Boatner, Mark M., III. *The Civil War Dictionary*. New York: David McKay Co., 1959.

Brown, Norman D., ed. *Journey to Pleasant Hill: The Civil War Letters of Captain Elijah P. Petty, Walker's Texas Division, CSA*. San Antonio: Institute of Texan Cultures, 1982.

Buenger, Walter L. *Secession and the Union in Texas*. Austin: University of Texas Press, 1984.

Burkhalter, Lois Wood. *Gideon Lincecum, 1793–1874: A Biography*. Austin: University of Texas Press, 1965.

Campbell, Randolph B. *An Empire for Slavery: The Peculiar Institution in Texas, 1821–1865*. Baton Rouge: Louisiana State University Press, 1989.

———. *A Southern Community in Crisis: Harrison County, Texas, 1850–1880*. Austin: Texas State Historical Association, 1983.

Caren, Eric C., comp. *Texas Extra: A Newspaper History of the Lone Star State, 1835–1935*. Edison, N.J.: Castle Books, 1999.

Carroll, Bret E. *Spiritualism in Antebellum America*. Bloomington: Indiana University Press, 1997.

Catton, Bruce. *A Stillness at Appomattox*. New York: Doubleday, 1953.

———. *Terrible Swift Sword*. New York: Doubleday, 1963.

———. *This Hallowed Ground: The Story of the Union Side of the Civil War*. New York: Doubleday, 1956.

———. *U. S. Grant and the American Military Tradition*. Boston: Little, Brown, 1954.

Channing, Steven A. *Crisis of Fear: Secession in South Carolina*. New York: Norton, 1974.

Compiled Index to Elected and Appointed Officials of the Republic of Texas. Austin: State Archives Division of Texas State Library, 1981.

Correll, Donovan S., and Marshall C. Johnston. *Manual of the Vascular Plants of Texas*. Renner, Tex.: Texas Research Foundation, 1970.

Cotham, Edward T., Jr. *Battle on the Bay: The Civil War Struggle for Galveston*. Austin: University of Texas Press, 1998.

Coulter, E. Merton. *The Confederate States of America*. Vol. 7 of *A History of the South*. Baton Rouge: Louisiana State University Press, 1950.

Craigie, William A., ed. *A Dictionary of American English on Historical Principles*. 4 vols. Chicago: University of Chicago Press, 1938.

Crist, Lynda L., and Mary S. Dix, eds. *The Papers of Jefferson Davis*. Vol. 6. Baton Rouge: Louisiana State University Press, 1989.

Crouch, Barry A. *The Freedmen's Bureau and Black Texas*. Austin: University of Texas Press, 1992.

Current, Richard Nelson. *Lincoln's Loyalists: Union Soldiers from the Confederacy*. Boston: Northeastern University Press, 1992.

———, ed. *Encyclopedia of the Confederacy*. 4 vols. New York: Simon and Schuster, 1993.

Curtis, Lewis P. *Anglo-Saxons and Celts: A Study of Anti-Irish Prejudice in Victorian England*. Bridgeport, Conn.: Conference on British Studies, University of Bridgeport, 1968.

Day, James M. *The Texas Almanack, 1857–1873*. Waco: Texian Press, 1967.

Dewey, Davis Rich. *Financial History of the United States*. 12th ed. New York: Longmans Green, 1934.

Dietrich, Wilfred O. *The Blazing Story of Washington County*. Rev. ed. Wichita Falls, Tex.: Nortex Offset Publications, 1973.

Diggs, George M., Jr., Barney L. Lipscomb, and Robert J. O'Kennon. *Shinners' and Mahlers' Illustrated Flora of North Central Texas*. Fort Worth: Botanical Research Institute of Texas, 1999.

Donald, David H. *Lincoln*. New York: Simon and Schuster, 1995.

Dudley, William S., ed. *The Naval War of 1812: A Documentary History*. 3 vols. Washington, D.C.: Naval Historical Center, 1985.

Eaton, Clement. *A History of the Old South*. 2d ed. New York: Macmillan, 1966.

———. *Jefferson Davis*. New York: Free Press, 1977.

Ericson, Carolyn R., and Frances T. Ingmire, eds. *First Settlers of the Republic of Texas*. St. Louis: Ingmire Publishers, 1982.

Evans, Eli N. *Judah P. Benjamin, the Jewish Confederate*. New York: Free Press, 1988.

Faulk, Odie B. *General Tom Green, Fightin' Texan*. Waco, Tex.: Texian Press, 1963.

Faust, Drew Gilpin. *Mothers of Invention: Women of the Slaveholding South in the American Civil War*. New York: Vintage Books, 1997.

Fehrenbacher, Don E., ed. *Abraham Lincoln: Speeches and Writings, 1859-1865*. 2 vols. New York: Library of America, 1989.

Ferris, Norman B. *The Trent Affair: A Diplomatic Crisis*. Knoxville: University of Tennessee Press, 1977.

Foner, Eric. *Reconstruction: America's Unfinished Revolution, 1863–1877*. New York: Harper and Row, 1988.

Foote, Shelby. *The Civil War: A Narrative*. 3 vols. New York: Random House, 1958–74.

Ford, John Salmon. *Rip Ford's Texas*. Edited by Stephen B. Oates. Austin: University of Texas Press, 1963.

Fornell, Earl W. *The Galveston Era: The Texas Crescent on the Eve of Secession*. Austin: University of Texas Press, 1961.

Frazier, Donald S. *Blood and Treasure: Confederate Empire in the Southwest*. College Station: Texas A&M University Press, 1995.

Freeman, Douglas S. *Lee's Lieutenants: A Study in Command*. 3 vols. New York: Charles Scribner's Sons, 1942–44.

Gallaway, B. P., ed. *Texas, the Dark Corner of the Confederacy: Contemporary Accounts of the Lone Star State in the Civil War.* 3d ed. Lincoln: University of Nebraska Press, 1994.

Gammel, Hans P. N. *The Laws of Texas, 1822–1897*. 10 vols. Austin: Gammel, 1898.

Grimes County Historical Commission. *History of Grimes County: Land of Heritage and Progress*. Navasota, Tex.: Grimes County Historical Commission, 1982.

Hall, Martin Hardwick. *Sibley's New Mexico Campaign*. Austin: University of Texas Press, 1960.

Haller, John S., Jr. *Medical Protestants: The Eclectics in American Medicine, 1825–1939*. Carbondale: Southern Illinois University Press, 1994.

Harlow, Jerry A., et al. *A History of Monroe County, Mississippi*. Aberdeen, Miss.: Monroe County Book Committee, n.d.

Hewett, Janet B., ed. *Texas Confederate Soldiers, 1861–65*. 2 vols. Wilmington, N.C.: Broadfoot Publishing, 1997.

Hewitt, Lawrence Lee. *Port Hudson, Confederate Bastion on the Mississippi*. Baton Rouge: Louisiana State University Press, 1987.

Hunter, J. Marvin. *The Trail Drivers of Texas*. Bandera, Tex.: Frontier Times Press, 1920.

James, Edward T., ed. *Notable American Women, 1607–1950: A Biographical Dictionary*. 3 vols. Cambridge, Mass.: Belknap Press of Harvard University Press, 1971.

Johannsen, Robert W. *Stephen A. Douglas*. New York: Oxford University Press, 1973.

Johnson, Ludwell H. *Red River Campaign: Politics and Cotton in the Civil War*. Baltimore: Johns Hopkins Press, 1958.

Johnson, Robert W., and Clarence C. Buel, eds. *Battles and Leaders of the Civil War*. 4 vols. New York: Century, 1884–87.

Kerby, Robert L. *Kirby Smith's Confederacy: The Trans-Mississippi South, 1863–1865*. 1972. Reprint, Tuscaloosa: University of Alabama Press, 1991.

Landolt, George L. *Search for the Summit: Austin College through Twelve Decades*. Sherman, Tex.: Austin College Alumni Association, 1970.

Lincecum, Jerry Bryan, and Edward Hake Phillips. *Adventures of a Frontier Naturalist: The Life and Times of Dr. Gideon Lincecum*. College Station: Texas A&M University Press, 1994.

Lincecum, Jerry Bryan, Edward Hake Phillips, and Peggy A. Redshaw. *Science on the Texas Frontier: Observations of Dr. Gideon Lincecum*. College Station: Texas A&M University Press, 1997.

Long, E. B., with Barbara Long. *The Civil War Day by Day: An Almanac, 1861–1865*. Garden City, New York: Doubleday, 1971. Reprint, New York: DaCapo Press, 1985.

Lonn, Ella. *Desertion during the Civil War*. London: Century, 1928.

Lubbock, Francis R. *Six Decades in Texas: Memoirs of Francis Richard Lubbock*. Edited by C. W. Raines. Austin: Ben C. Jones, 1900.

Luraghi, Raimondo. *A History of the Confederate Navy*. Translated by Paolo E. Coletta. Annapolis, Md.: Naval Institute Press, 1996.

Marten, James. *Texas Divided: Loyalty and Dissent in the Lone Star State, 1856–1874*. Lexington: University Press of Kentucky, 1990.

Massey, Mary Elizabeth. *Ersatz in the Confederacy*. Columbia: University of South Carolina Press, 1952.

McComb, David G. *Galveston: A History*. Austin: University of Texas Press, 1986.

———. *Houston: A History*. Austin: University of Texas Press, 1981.

McPherson, James M. *Battle Cry of Freedom: The Civil War Era*. New York: Oxford University Press, 1988.

———. *Ordeal by Fire: The Civil War and Reconstruction*. 2d ed. New York: McGraw-Hill, 1992.

Melton, J. Gordon. *Encyclopedia of American Religions*. 6th ed. Detroit: Gale, 1999.

Moneyhon, Carl H. *Republicanism in Reconstruction Texas*. Austin: University of Texas Press, 1980.

Mott, Frank Luther. *A History of American Magazines*. 5 vols. Cambridge, Mass.: Harvard University Press, 1930-68.

Oakes, James. *The Ruling Race: A History of American Slaveholders*. New York: Vintage Books, 1983.

Oates, Stephen B. *Confederate Cavalry West of the River*. Austin: University of Texas Press, 1961.

Official Records of Union and Confederate Navies in the War of Rebellion. 30 vols. Washington, D.C.: Government Printing Office, 1894–1922.

Owsley, Frank Lawrence. *King Cotton Diplomacy: Foreign Relations of the Confederate States of America*. 2d ed., revised by Harriet Chappell Owsley. Chicago: University of Chicago Press, 1959.

Paludan, Phillip Shaw. *A People's Contest: The Union and Civil War, 1861–1865*. 2d ed. Lawrence: University Press of Kansas, 1996.

Parks, Joseph Howard. *General Edmund Kirby Smith, C.S.A.* Baton Rouge: Louisiana State University Press, 1954.

———. *John Bell of Tennessee*. Baton Rouge: Louisiana State University Press, 1950.

Potter, David M. *The Impending Crisis, 1848–1861*. New York: Harper and Row, 1976.

Rable, George C. *The Confederate Republic: A Revolution against Politics*. Chapel Hill: University of North Carolina Press, 1994.

Randall, James G. *The Civil War and Reconstruction*. Boston: D. C. Heath, 1937.

Remini, Robert V. *Andrew Jackson and the Course of American Empire, 1767–1821*. Vol. 1. New York: Harper and Row, 1977.

Reynolds, Donald E. *Editors Make War: Southern Newspapers in the Secession Crisis*. Nashville, Tenn.: Vanderbilt University Press, 1970.

Schmidt, Charles F. *History of Washington County, Texas*. San Antonio: Naylor, 1949.

Sears, Stephen W. *To the Gates of Richmond: The Peninsula Campaign*. New York: Ticknor and Fields, 1992.

Shea, William L., and Earl J. Hess. *Pea Ridge: Civil War Campaign in the West*. Chapel Hill: University of North Carolina Press, 1992.

Sibley, Marilyn McAdams. *Lone Stars and State Gazettes: Texas Newspapers before the Civil War*. College Station: Texas A&M University Press, 1983.

Sowell, A. J. *Early Settlers and Indian Fighters of Southwest Texas*. Austin: B. C. Jones, 1900. Reprint, Austin: State House Press, 1986.

Steiner, Paul E. *Disease in the Civil War: Natural Biological Warfare in 1861–1865*. Springfield, Ill.: Charles C. Thomas, 1968.

Sword, Wiley. *Embrace an Angry Wind: The Confederacy's Last Hurrah—Spring Hill, Franklin, and Nashville*. New York: HarperCollins, 1992.

Taylor, John M. *Bloody Valverde: A Civil War Battle on the Rio Grande, February 21, 1862*. Albuquerque: University of New Mexico Press, 1995.

Taylor, Richard. *Destruction and Reconstruction: Personal Experiences of the Late War*. New York: D. Appleton & Co., 1879.

Thomas, Emory M. *The Confederate Nation, 1861–1865*. New York: Harper and Row, 1979.

Tyler, Alice Felt. *Freedom's Ferment: Phases of American Social History to 1860*. 1944. Reprint, New York: Harper and Row, 1962.

Tyler, Ron, ed. *The New Handbook of Texas*. 6 vols. Austin: Texas State Historical Association, 1996.

Vandiver, Frank E. *Ploughshares into Swords: Josiah Gorgas and Confederate Ordnance*. Austin: University of Texas Press, 1952.

United States War Department. *War of the Rebellion: A Compilation of Official Records of the Union and Confederate Armies*. 128 vols. Washington, D.C.: Government Printing Office, 1880–1901.

Warner, Ezra J. *Generals in Blue: Lives of the Union Commanders*. Baton Rouge: Louisiana State University Press, 1964.

———. *Generals in Gray: Lives of the Confederate Commanders*. Baton Rouge: Louisiana State University Press, 1959.

Wilbarger, J. W. *Indian Depredations in Texas*. 1889. Reprint, Austin: Eakin Press, 1985.

Williams, Kenneth P. *Lincoln Finds a General: A Military Study of the Civil War*. 5 vols. New York: Macmillan, 1949–59.

Willis, J. C. *A Dictionary of the Flowering Plants and Ferns*. 8th ed. Revised by H. K. Airy Shaw. London: Cambridge University Press, 1973.

Winfield, Nath, and Judy Winfield. *All Our Yesterdays: A Brief History of Chappell Hill*. Waco, Tex.: Texian Press, 1969.

Winters, John D. *The Civil War in Louisiana*. Baton Rouge: Louisiana State University Press, 1963.

Wooster, Ralph A., ed. *Lone Star Blue and Gray: Essays on Texas in the Civil War*. Austin: Texas State Historical Association, 1995.

Wright, Marcus J., comp., and Harold B. Simpson, ed. *Texas in the War, 1861–1865*. Hillsboro, Tex.: Hill Junior College Press, 1965.

Articles, Periodicals, and Manuscripts

Addington, Wendell G. "Slave Insurrections in Texas." *Journal of Negro History* 35 (1950): 408–34.

Ammen, Daniel. "DuPont and the Port Royal Expedition." Pp. 761–91 in Vol. 1 of *Battles and Leaders of the Civil War*, edited by Robert W. Johnson and Clarence C. Buel. 4 vols. New York: Century, 1884–87.

Barr, Alwyn. "Texas Coastal Defense, 1861–65." *Southwestern Historical Quarterly* 65 (July 1961): 1–31.

Boston Investigator.

Bradford, A. L., and T. N. Campbell. "Journal of Lincecum's Travels in Texas, 1835." *Southwestern Historical Quarterly* 53 (October 1949): 180–201.

Crisler, Patricia Fogler. "Lincecum-Roberts History." *Plum Creek Almanac* 12, no. 2 (fall 1994): 96.

Cumberland, Charles C. "The Confederate Loss and Recapture of Galveston, 1862–1863." *Southwestern Historical Quarterly* 51 (October 1947): 109–30.

Daily True Delta (New Orleans).

Frazier, Donald S. "Sibley's Texans and the Battle of Galveston." *Southwestern Historical Quarterly* 99 (October 1995): 175–98.

Galveston News.

Goertzen, Chris. "Gideon Lincecum, 'Killie Krankie,' and Fiddling in Early Texas." Pp. 11–31 in *Between the Cracks of History: Essays on Teaching and Illustrating Folklore*, ed. Francis E. Abernethy. Denton: University of North Texas Press, 1997.

Houston Tri-Weekly Telegraph.

Lincecum, G. "A Collection of Plants from Texas." *Proceedings of the Academy of Natural Sciences* 13 (1861): 98.

Lincecum, Jerry Bryan. "Medical Controversy in the Nineteenth-Century South: Botanics vs. Allopaths." *Caduceus* 10 (1994): 135–40.

New York Times.

Phillips, Michael. "White Violence, Hegemony, and Slave Rebellion in Dallas, Texas, before the Civil War." *East Texas Historical Journal* 37, no. 2 (1999): 25–35.

Spiritual Telegraph.

Thomas, Emory M. "Rebel Nationalism: E. H. Cushing and the Confederate Experience." *Southwestern Historical Quarterly* 73 (January 1970): 343–55.

White, William W. "The Texas Slave Insurrection of 1860." *Southwestern Historical Quarterly* 52, no. 3 (January 1949): 259–85.

Wolfe, Cheri Lynne. "The Traditional History of the Chahta People: An Analysis of Gideon Lincecum's 19th Century Narrative." Doctoral diss., University of Texas at Austin, 1993.

Wooster, Ralph. "Life in Civil War East Texas." *East Texas Historical Journal* 3 (1965): 93–102.

———. "Texas." Pp. 195–215 in *The Confederate Governors*, ed. W. Buck Yearns. Athens: University of Georgia Press, 1985.

Electronic Databases

Library of Congress Online Catalog. <http://lcweb.loc.gov/catalog/ >. 18 October 1999.

Index

M